Creativity, Wisdom, and Trusteeship

Anna Craft | Howard Gardner | Guy Claxton
Editors

Creativity, Wisdom, and Trusteeship

Exploring the Role of Education

CORWIN PRESS
A SAGE Company
Thousand Oaks, CA 91320

For information:

Corwin Press
A SAGE Company
2455 Teller Road
Thousand Oaks, California 91320
www.corwinpress.com

SAGE Ltd.
1 Oliver's Yard
55 City Road
London EC1Y 1SP
United Kingdom

SAGE India Pvt. Ltd.
B 1/I 1 Mohan Cooperative Industrial Area
Mathura Road, New Delhi 110 044
India

SAGE Asia-Pacific Pte. Ltd.
33 Pekin Street #02-01
Far East Square
Singapore 048763

Printed in the United States of America.

Library of Congress Cataloging-in-Publication Data

Creativity, wisdom, and trusteeship: exploring the role of education/[edited] by Anna Craft, Howard Gardner, and Guy Claxton.
      p. cm.
Includes bibliographical references and index.
ISBN 978-1-4129-4939-2 (cloth)
ISBN 978-1-4129-4940-8 (pbk.)
   1. Creative thinking. 2. Wisdom. 3. Education—Aims and objectives. I. Craft, Anna.
II. Gardner, Howard. III. Claxton, Guy. IV. Title.

LB1062.C744 2008
370.15'7—dc22   2007023893

This book is printed on acid-free paper.

07   08   09   10   11   10   9   8   7   6   5   4   3   2   1

Acquisitions Editor:	Faye Zucker
Managing Editor:	Carol Chambers Collins
Editorial Assistants:	Gem Rabanera, Brett Ory
Production Editor:	Cassandra Margaret Seibel
Copy Editor:	Sarah J. Duffy
Typesetter:	C&M Digitals (P) Ltd.
Proofreader:	Victoria Reed-Castro
Indexer:	Terri Corry
Cover Designer:	Michael Dubowe
Graphic Designer:	Monique Hahn

Contents

Acknowledgments

Many people have contributed to the production of this book and the ideas represented in it. Our thanks are due to the members of the Creativity in Education Special Interest Group, which is part of the British Educational Research Association, who organized the seminar which inspired the book; and also to the Economic and Social Research Council, which sponsored the event. Two hundred or so colleagues participated in that event, making what turned out to be pivotal contributions. The valuable ideas shared on that day helped to frame our early thinking about a book with three stimulus chapters and a range of responses, concerned with three issues vital to education in the twenty-first century: wisdom, creativity, and trusteeship. To the contributors with whom we have debated the ideas since, and whose work is produced here, we extend our heartfelt appreciation. Our thanks are due to the many educators and students with whom we come into contact through our varied work in different parts of the world, whose efforts keep us mindful of the challenges and the opportunities involved in fostering young learners' engagement in an uncertain and rapidly changing world. We are grateful, too, to our editors at Corwin Press—in particular Faye Zucker, who saw the potential in our proposals and saw our manuscript through the first few months of development; to Gem Rabanera, Carol Collins, Cassandra Seibel, and Sarah Duffy, who took the project through its final stages; and to the reviewers who commented fully on an earlier draft. Finally our thanks are due to those closest to us who have witnessed the gestation of this project, whose support and encouragement is greatly appreciated.

Anna Craft, Howard Gardner,
and Guy Claxton
April 2007

PUBLISHER'S ACKNOWLEDGMENTS

Corwin Press acknowledges the contributions of the following reviewers:

Tom Bentley
Executive Director of
  Policy and Strategy
Department of Premier
  and Cabinet
Victoria, Australia

Geoffrey Caine
Educational Consultant
Caine LLC
Idyllwild, CA

Robert Di Giulio
Professor
Johnson State College
Johnson, VT

Lynn Erickson
Independent Consultant
Everett, WA

Maria Kaylor
Assistant Professor
University of Texas
  at San Antonio
San Antonio, TX

Jack Miller
Professor
Department of Curriculum,
  Teaching, and Learning
Ontario Institute for Studies in
  Education (OISE)
University of Toronto
Toronto, ON

David Perkins
Professor
Harvard University
Cambridge, MA

Tim Smit
Chief Executive
The Eden Project
Bodelva, Cornwall, United Kingdom

Marilee Sprenger
Independent Consultant
Peoria, IL

Ruth Thomas
Professor
University of Minnesota
Minneapolis, MN

About the Editors

**Anna Craft** is Professor of Education at the University of Exeter, in England, where she established and leads the CREATE research cluster. She is also Professor of Education at The Open University, in England, and founder-director of The Open Creativity Centre. She is founding coeditor of Thinking Skills and Creativity (Elsevier) and founding coconvener of the British Educational Research Association Special Interest Group, Creativity in Education. At the time of writing she had held a visiting appointment at Harvard University for four years. She has held visiting appointments at the Hong Kong Institute of Education. Her most recent books include *Creative Learning 3–11 and How We Document It* (Trentham Books 2007), *Reflective Practice in Early Years Education* (Open University Press 2007), *Creativity in Schools: Tensions and Dilemmas* (Routledge 2005), *Creativity and Early Years Education* (Continuum 2002), and *Creativity Across the Primary Curriculum* (RoutledgeFalmer 2000). Her empirical work, informed by constructivist and sociocultural views of learning, seeks to impact practice, policy, and theory in education.

**Howard Gardner** is the Hobbs Professor of Cognition and Education at the Harvard Graduate School of Education. He is a leading thinker about education and human development; he has studied and written extensively about intelligence, creativity, leadership, and professional ethics. His most recent books include *Good Work* (Harvard Business School Press 2004), *Changing Minds* (Harvard Business School Press 2004), *The Development and Education of the Mind* (Psychology Press 2005), *and Multiple Intelligences: New Horizons* (Basic Books 2006). His latest book, *Five Minds for the Future* (Harvard Business School Press), was published in April 2007.

 **Guy Claxton** is Professor of the Learning Sciences at the University of Bristol Graduate School of Education, where he directs the research initiative on Culture, Learning, Identity, and Organisations (CLIO). His books include *The Wayward Mind: An Intimate History of the Unconscious* (Little Brown 2005), *Learning for Life in the 21st Century: Sociocultural Perspectives on the Future of Education* (Blackwell Publishing 2002, coedited with Gordon Wells), *Wise Up: Learning to Live the Learning Life* (Bloomsbury/ Network Press 1999), and the best-selling *Hare Brain, Tortoise Mind: Why Intelligence Increases When You Think Less* (Fourth Estate 1997). His current work focuses on the development of infused approaches to the cultivation of positive lifelong learning dispositions in schools. The resulting Building Learning Power approach has influenced practice in schools throughout the United Kingdom, Australia, and New Zealand.

About the Contributors

Christopher Bannerman is Professor of Dance and head of ResCen, the Centre for Research into Creation in the Performing Arts, at Middlesex University. He has worked in the dance profession as a dancer, choreographer, and arts education worker, and has served as a panel member for two Higher Education Research Assessment Exercises and a specialist assessor for the Quality Assurance Agency. He has also served as chair of the Arts Council of England's Advisory Panel for Dance and has recently been appointed chair of London North Creative Partnerships and as a member of the Dance Forum of the Department for Culture, Media and Sport (DCMS) UK. His work with ResCen reflects a deep interest in the creative powers of artists and the ways in which these activities link and intersect the art forms. In 2006 he contributed to and edited the book *Navigating the Unknown* (Middlesex University Press) with his ResCen colleagues.

Patrick Dillon has degrees in biological science, economic history, and education. He works at the University of Exeter, in England, where he is an Emeritus Professor, and the Universities of Joensuu and Helsinki, in Finland, where he is a docent and visiting professor. He has worked in higher education for 25 years, before which he worked in industry and taught in primary and secondary schools. He has cross-disciplinary interests in education, culture, and technology that encompass cultural heritage education, creativity, design education, and e-learning. He also researches and writes on landscape and environmental education, out of which has emerged a belief in the value of integrating ecological perspectives into theories of education. He has recently proposed a pedagogy of connection for facilitating work across and between disciplines.

David Henry Feldman is a Professor in the Eliot-Pearson Department of Child Development at Tufts University, in the United States. Trained at the universities of Rochester, Harvard, and Stanford, he has also served on the faculties of the University of Minnesota, Yale University, and (as a visiting professor) at Tel Aviv University and the University of California at San Diego. His disciplinary identification is primarily with the field of cognitive development, to which he has contributed nearly two hundred books, articles, reviews, and edited volumes, including several on creativity. He participated in the recent publication of *Creativity and Development* (Oxford University Press 2003) as an editor and author. That work and others have pursued the possibility that there may be a set of deep commonalities between major creative ideas and the kinds of cognitive developmental advances that all children experience.

Helen Haste is Professor of Psychology at the University of Bath and Visiting Professor at the Harvard Graduate School of Education. She has a long record of research and publication in moral, social, and political values, and on the interface of science and culture, including issues in gender and science. Her work includes research on culture and metaphor, on the public image of science (particularly in the media), and on ethics and citizenship education. She was a consultant for the Organisation for Economic Co-operation and Development on a project looking at future competencies and their educational implications. She is a fellow of the British Psychological Society and of the Royal Society of Arts, and an academician of the Academy of Social Sciences. She was president of the International Society for Political Psychology in 2002. In 2005, she received the Nevitt Sanford Award for lifetime contribution to political psychology from the International Society of Political Psychology.

Hans Henrik Knoop is Associate Professor of Psychology at the Danish University of Education, in Copenhagen, and has published widely in the areas of learning, creativity, play, and morality. He is a frequently invited speaker in Denmark and has presented his work in many countries, including China, Finland, Germany, Norway, the Philippines, the United Kingdom, and the United States. As an academic expert he has been appointed to important Danish committees on educational issues regarding general pedagogy, cross-curricula competencies, the use of computers in education, and the ethics of assessment in education. Internationally he has been engaged in a major educational developmental project in Eastern Europe and served as an academic expert for the European Union. His work has been supported by public and private grants, and his research projects involve collaborations with colleagues at Harvard University, Stanford University, and Claremont Graduate University, as well as private enterprises such as the LEGO Learning Institute and Danfoss Universe.

Jonathan Rowson holds a first-class degree from Oxford University in philosophy, politics, and economics, and an MEd from Harvard University in mind, brain, and education. His current Economic and Social Research Council–funded doctoral work is supervised by Guy Claxton at the Bristol Graduate School of Education. His research examines what "acting wisely" involves how wisdom-related dispositions can be cultivated. In another life he plays chess semiprofessionally and has been the British Chess Champion (2004, 2005, 2006). His academic research is often informed by his practical experience as a chess grandmaster, and in his chess writing he frequently draws upon his knowledge of cognitive science. His most recent books, *The Seven Deadly Chess Sins* (Gambit Publications 2001) and *Chess for Zebras* (Gambit Publications 2005), have been translated into several foreign languages.

Dean Keith Simonton has a PhD in social psychology from Harvard University and is Distinguished Professor of Psychology at the University of California, Davis. His research program has produced over 320 publications, including *Genius, Creativity, and Leadership* (Harvard University Press 1984); *Why Presidents Succeed* (Yale University Press 1987); *Scientific Genius* (Cambridge University Press 1988); *Psychology, Science, and History* (Yale University Press 1990); *Genius and Creativity* (Ablex 1997); *Origins of Genius* (Oxford University Press 1999); *Great Psychologists and Their Times* (APA Books 2002); and *Creativity in Science* (Cambridge University Press 2004). He has received the William James Book Award, the George A. Miller Outstanding Article Award, the Rudolf Arnheim Award for Outstanding Contributions to Psychology and the Arts, the Theoretical Innovation Prize in Personality and Social Psychology, the Sir Francis Galton Award for Outstanding Contributions to the Study of Creativity, the Award for Excellence in Research from the Mensa Education and Research Foundation, and the Robert S. Daniel Award for Four Year College/University Teaching.

Robert J. Sternberg is Dean of the School of Arts and Sciences and Professor of Psychology at Tufts University. Formerly, he was the IBM Professor of Psychology and Education and Professor of Management at Yale University. His PhD is from Stanford University, and he has eight honorary doctorates. He has been president of the American Psychological Association as well as four of its divisions, and is currently president of the Eastern Psychological Association. He has also edited two journals, *Psychological Bulletin* and the *APA Review of Books: Contemporary Psychology*. He is the author of over 1,100 books and articles, and the winner of roughly two dozen awards. His main interests are in intelligence, creativity, wisdom, and leadership.

Dave Trotman is principal lecturer in education and professional studies at Newman College of Higher Education, in Birmingham, England. A former teacher in secondary and primary schools, with a curriculum specialization in arts education, his research interests include creativity and imagination, management of change processes, and collaborative professional learning cultures. He works extensively with primary phase practitioners on initial teacher education and inservice programs, where he teaches aspects of educational policy, curriculum design, and organizational change processes. His doctoral research examined teacher interpretations of pupil imaginative experiences in primary phase education (work which has since been extended to secondary phase education), the outcomes of which have been published in national and international journals covering curriculum, teacher education, philosophy of education, and qualitative research methodology. His current research focuses on the development of approaches to practitioner research as part of whole-school qualitative evaluation and the representation of qualitative research in the areas of creativity, imagination, and affect.

1

Nurturing Creativity, Wisdom, and Trusteeship in Education

A Collective Debate

Anna Craft, Howard Gardner, and Guy Claxton

As the title of this book indicates, this volume has three points of departure: the concept of creativity, the concept of wisdom, and the notion of trusteeship, all three set in the educational milieu of our time. The three editors came to believe that, at this historical moment, a blend of creativity and wisdom combined with revisiting the notion of trusteeship in education would be highly desirable, and perhaps even necessary, for the survival of the world as we know it and as we would like it to be.

INVITING COLLEAGUES TO PARTICIPATE IN PRINTED DEBATE

Accordingly, we prepared a series of reflections—which we term the three target chapters—on the often uneasy connections among creativity, wisdom, trusteeship, and education. We then circulated these target chapters to a set of contributors representing several scholarly disciplines and varieties of educational practice. In the essays that constitute this volume, the contributors offer their critiques of our essays as well as their own thoughts about the nature of, and the relationship between, creativity and wisdom. In this introductory essay we summarize some of the major lines of work in the psychological study of creativity, wisdom, and trusteeship; comment on the educational milieu of our time; and say a few initial words about the contributions that follow and the structure of this volume as a whole.

CREATIVITY

The concept of *creativity* has been explored by scholars over the centuries. Creativity was initially seen as divine inspiration in Greek, Judaic, Christian, and Islamic traditions (Rhyammar and Brolin 1999), but since the Enlightenment, and particularly after the Romantic era, it has been increasingly seen as the human capacity for insight, originality, and subjectivity of feeling. Toward the end of the nineteenth century, psychological exploration began to be undertaken—for example, through the pioneering work of Galton (1869). Over the course of the twentieth century, a number of distinct traditions addressed issues of creativity. The psychoanalytic approach (Freud 1908/1959, 1910/1957, 1916/1971; Jung 1973; Winnicott 1971) emphasized unconscious motivations and processes. The behaviorist approach brought attention to the conditions that rewarded original responses and products (Skinner 1953, 1968, 1971, 1974). Researchers in the personality tradition highlighted the personal and temperament traits of creative individuals (Barron 1969; Eysenck 1952; MacKinnon 1962). And a humanist tradition considered the crucial role of expression and invention in the lives of individuals (Maslow 1954/1987, 1971; Rogers 1970).

Researchers and practitioners interested in creativity in the classroom have drawn on several other traditions, more avowedly cognitive in thrust (cf. Wallas 1926). Influential first were efforts to measure the trait of creativity through quantifying aspects of divergent thinking (Guilford 1950, 1967; Mednick 1962; Torrance 1962, 1974; Wallach 1971), which led to the development of practical techniques to foster creativity such as brainstorming and question asking (De Bono 1995). A second cognitive strand focused on the mental models—often computational in flavor—characteristic of creative thought (Bruner 1962; Johnson-Laird 1988; Simon 1988). A third strand consisted of case studies of top-flight creators (Csikszentmihalyi 1996; Gardner 1993; Gruber 1974/1981; John-Steiner 1997). Finally, these individual-centered efforts have been complemented by scholars who view creativity in a broader context. Authorities have focused on organizational climate/culture and on various forms of collaboration (Amabile 1988; Csikszentmihalyi 1988; Feldman, Csikszentmihalyi, and Gardner 1994; John-Steiner 2000; Sternberg and Lubart 1991, 1995). Overall, there has been a gradual shift toward facilitating everyday creativity at home and at work, and less of a focus on measurement and prediction (Craft 2005).

The diverse approaches all reflect the *value-neutrality* of creativity; the ends to which creativity is put are not seen as significant—and indeed the apparent *universalization* of creativity (Jeffrey and Craft 2001) in educational policymaking across the world underlines this position. Our book calls into question that unproblematized, value-neutral position on creativity as it applies to education in particular. The book raises the possibility that creativity ought to be conceived of in relation to other human virtues—in particular to wisdom (cf. Sternberg 2003).

WISDOM

Despite twenty-five years of social scientific studies exploring the notion of wisdom, there is as yet no consensual definition of this trait or even a robust tradition of studying it. Accounts of wisdom are located in multiple domains and perspectives, from the sociocultural (Takahashi and Overton 2005) and the philosophical (Osbeck and Robinson 2005) to the psychological (Kunzmann and Baltes 2005), and this enormous diversity may in part account for the lack of a consensual foundation.

Within the psychological literature, as was the case with creativity, the dominant approaches are cognitive (Bassett 2005). Both the Berlin School (led by Baltes) and the Sternberg approaches emphasize a metacognitive stance toward the practicalities and pragmatics of life. A third approach construes wisdom in relation to Piagetian stage theory of development (Piaget 1932; Piaget and Inhelder 1969). Here, wisdom is deemed an aspect of postformal development—indeed as exceptional self-development—enabled through a decentering of the ego and the capacity to think dialectically and to acknowledge alternative truths and inherent contradictions (see, e.g., Cook-Greuter 2000; Kitchener and Brenner 1990).

Perhaps the richest view of wisdom to date, and the one with greatest potential for use in the classrooms, has been developed by the aforementioned researchers at the Max Planck Institute. These investigators conceptualize wisdom as bringing together characteristics of knowledge, mental capacities, and virtue (Baltes and Kunzmann 2004; Baltes and Staudinger 2000). Wisdom is seen as "an expert knowledge system about fundamental problems related to the meaning and conduct of life" (Baltes and Stange 2005, 196), which enables appropriate courses of action that take account of multiple perspectives.

The Berlin School identifies five criteria for labeling any action *wise* (Baltes and Staudinger 2000), two of which are *basic*:

- rich factual knowledge of human nature and human life course
- rich procedural knowledge of possibilities for engaging with life problems

The remaining three are seen as *metacriteria* and are considered by the group to be "unique to wisdom" (Baltes and Stange 2005, 196):

- life-span contextualism (i.e., understanding of multiple contexts of life and their interrelationships in concurrent temporality as well as over the life span)
- value tolerance and relativism (i.e., understanding of differences between individuals, group, and wider social/cultural values and priorities)
- knowledge about handling uncertainty (including limits in knowledge—both one's own and collective, regarding the world at large; Baltes and Stange 2005)

For reflective educators who seek to foster the development of wisdom among students in schools, this perspective is particularly significant. Yet one must be wary of attempts to reduce wisdom to a purely *cognitivist* account. Any full account of wisdom should take into account as well the motivational and contextual factors that are likely to engender or thwart wise thoughts and wise actions.

TRUSTEESHIP

Every culture depends upon individuals who are considered wise. Typically, in traditional societies, it is the elders who are the repository of wisdom; in more recent times, religious leaders and experts with a wide perspective have assumed that role. We sense that in modern secular societies religious leaders do not automatically command respect, and experts are typically valued more for their technical flair than for their breadth of knowledge. Accordingly, there is a dearth of individuals who naturally come to occupy the status of *wise person*.

At a premium, therefore, are individuals whom we dub as *trustees*. Those who occupy that role are well known, widely respected, and seen as being nonpartisan, disinterested. Most trustees work within a particular domain; the most impressive are valued across large sectors of the society. Nearly any person who is mentioned as a trustee would generate a measure of controversy, but in the recent history of the United States, we would mention such persons as the scientist Jonas Salk, the journalist Walter Cronkite, and the civic leader John Gardner; in Britain, individuals like the historian of ideas Isaiah Berlin, the BBC executive Lord Reith, or the entrepreneur Anita Roddick might be cited. Such individuals serve as role models whom younger persons can look up to and hope to emulate.

In the absence of such trustees, young persons either direct their admiration to celebrities or display cynicism about the possibility of good work.

THE TENSION BETWEEN CREATIVITY AND WISDOM

With the common construal of creativity outlined above comes a set of assumptions which encourage, emphasize, and venerate individual engagement and success, in a way that may run counter to wise action. As Sternberg (2003) argues,

> wisdom is not just about maximizing one's own or someone else's self-interest, but about balancing various self-interests (intrapersonal) with the interests of others (interpersonal) and of other aspects of the context in which one lives (extrapersonal), such as one's city or country or environment or even God. Wisdom also involves creativity, in that the wise solution to a problem may be far from obvious. (p. 152)

Sternberg's *balance theory* of wisdom thus characterizes wisdom in terms of successfully balancing interests. It also recognizes that "wise solutions are often creative ones" and proposes that wisdom is related to "creatively insightful thinking" (p. 158).

Sternberg (2003) makes the point, however, that "although wise thinking must be, to some extent, creative, creative thinking . . . need not be wise" (p. 158). Since the policy perspective on the generation of creativity in classrooms by teachers and schools appears to be value neutral, lacking a moral and ethical framework, the very encouragement of creativity in education raises fundamental questions and dilemmas. It could certainly be argued that creativity developed without wisdom may not serve children, their families and communities, and the wider social and cultural groupings to which they belong—and thus its uncritical encouragement may be seen as a questionable endeavor.

THE EDUCATIONAL MILIEU TODAY AND TOMORROW

Traditionally, education around the world has pursued three goals: a mastery of the basic literacies; learning the fundamentals of major disciplines (mathematics, logic, and music in an earlier era; history, biology, and psychology today); and inculcating the fundamentals of citizenship and morality, often from a religious perspective. These goals remain today, despite the secularization of education in many parts of the world, but the task of educators becomes ever more demanding and complex (Gardner 1991, 1999, 2007).

How are educators to respond, for example, to the forces of globalization: the rapid circulation around the world of currency, ideas, cultural models, and human beings, who migrate in large numbers from one culture to another and perhaps back again to the original site (Suarez-Orozco and Qin-Hilliard 2004)? A second problematic issue concerns the powerful new forms of communication technology—not just radio and television but, above all, the new digital media, including computers for work, computer games, friendship networks, virtual realities, and the like. These media can be put to positive educational uses, but they have equal potential for taking students away from their studies and even involving them in antisocial acts (Jenkins 2006). More generally, computers can carry out an increasing number of human functions, thus putting an educational premium on those capacities that have not yet been automated—such as, as far as we know, wisdom. A third issue relates to the way in which teachers should acknowledge the pressing planetary problems—global warming, other kinds of ecological disasters, hostility between nations and religions, severe diseases like AIDS and malaria, and, perhaps above all, the unprecedented capacity of humans to decimate the world's population with nuclear weapons or some kind of biological or chemical toxic agents.

Even educators who are sharply focused on the three traditional goals cannot simply ignore these larger forces—they are brought to school by students, they cast a shadow on the curriculum, and they may even dominate over the goals of parents, teachers, and the wider citizenry. Young people, though sometimes naïve, are often highly concerned and even idealistic about these issues. Thus, it is vital to rethink both the goals and the means of education in the twenty-first century. The development of human characteristics such as creativity and wisdom looms large in these debates.

As we discussed in our brief review of the literature, creativity preceded wisdom as a concern in the classroom—perhaps to the detriment of the pressing human priorities noted above. Of course, creativity may also be construed as playing a vital role in surviving and thriving in a very uncertain immediate and wider context. But much of the debate about how creativity may contribute within education to the preparation of generative citizens is underpinned, internationally, by a particular model of engagement—Western individualism, fed by the market economy—which colors ambient values to a strong degree. Accordingly, creativity as played out in education and in work is vulnerable to a variety of forms of "blindness," including a disregard for diversity in culture and values, a lack of engagement with the question of how we might foster wisdom, increasing barriers to doing good work through decreasing trust, and a hesitation to assume responsibility for improving society.

A discussion about what we might call *wise creativity* or *good creativity,* and how we might develop trusteeship in fostering this, is long overdue. In these pages, we seek to harness *possibility thinking* (Burnard et al. 2006; Craft 2001; Cremin, Burnard, and Craft 2006), to contemplate how we might conceptualize good creativity and how creativity within education in particular might respond to this rapidly shifting world. As editors we seek to nurture a debate among practitioners, researchers, and policymakers about the ways in which we might refresh our approach to the education of children and young people. The authors pose questions about how to frame creativity in a way that pays attention to outcomes as well as processes, and that sees responsibility as sitting equally with self-realization. Concretely, does creativity, as nurtured within education, need to be wiser? If so, what does this mean, and what practical implications follow?

What does it mean, for example, to view classroom practice as a reflective, intellectually demanding endeavor? In this book, we seek to catalyze a debate about the role and meaning of reflective practice among those working with students in classrooms, in developing curriculum, pedagogy, and assessment practices, so as to foster learning that encompasses both creativity and wisdom. The pressing need for such a stance is documented by the finding, from Harvard's GoodWork Project, of a decreasing tendency among ambitious young people to prioritize the *common good* (Fischman et al. 2004). The young persons who were studied frequently bent rules and cut corners for self-aggrandizement. All too rarely did they see themselves as part of a community in which peers and others, including respected elders, provide a set of reference points which inform their actions. Such findings underscore the challenge for education and for educators in fostering the emergence of wisdom (i.e., appropriate action taking account of multiple forms of understanding and knowledge, as well as possibly incommensurate needs and perspectives).

FORMAT OF AND CONTRIBUTIONS TO THIS VOLUME

In a collective and collaborative effort to encourage such reflection, we open in Part 1 of our volume with three target chapters on the subject of creativity, wisdom, and trusteeship. In Part 2, a series of nine responses from colleagues are given, and in Part 3, the editors (authors of the three target chapters) offer a synthesis-response to the nine intervening chapters given in Part 2.

The target chapters in Part 1 were originally papers given at a symposium held at the University of Cambridge in April 2005 and attended by some two hundred researchers, practitioners, and policymakers. This book is derived from debates begun during the Cambridge symposium, and continued since, with colleagues who were present at the symposium as well as those who were not, but whose work we anticipated would shed valuable light on the implications of creativity, wisdom, and trusteeship for education.

At the Cambridge symposium, the three editors of this book each approached the subject of creativity and wisdom in education from a different angle, but we sought to extend thinking and practices around several themes: terminological, conceptual, and empirical differences between creativity and wisdom; the immediate and the wider (even global) contexts in which creativity occurs; the motivations for creativity; the means for developing wise forms of creativity; the implications of these considerations for teachers and schools; and, finally, the ways in which the broader society nurtures and honors trustees—wise figures whose concerns encompass global survival.

In Chapter 2, Anna Craft discusses the cultural saturation of policy and practice regarding creativity in education and problematizes the universalized calls for creativity which can be seen emerging globally. She discusses the purposes to which creativity is put in relation to values implied by a creativity agenda in education driven by globalized economic imperatives. Dilemmas and constraints facing schools are highlighted together with areas for consideration by educators, one of which is the problem of how creative student aspiration is encouraged within this challenging values context in such a way that values the role of the trustee in fostering creativity with wisdom.

In Chapter 3, Guy Claxton tackles the concept of wisdom head-on. He argues that rather than trying to define *wisdom* as an abstract, unitary quality, we seek to identify a collection of dispositions that might be at play in agreed instances of wise action. In analyzing a series of putative instances of wise action, Claxton draws out a candidate list of such dispositions, which includes perspicacity, disinterestedness, and empathy—as well as creativity. Thus he concludes that wisdom often requires creativity, but that creativity may equally often lack (some of) the essential qualities of wisdom. Claxton also offers some suggestions as to how the contributory dispositions for wisdom might be cultivated in educational settings.

In Chapter 4, Howard Gardner asks whether, and under what conditions, individuals who are creative can turn their talents toward socially constructive ends. His approach is built on a large-scale empirical study of highly regarded professionals working in various domains. Gardner argues that *good work* or *humane creativity* consists of work that is excellent, engaging, and carried out in an ethical manner. Such high-quality work is difficult to achieve and sustain at times when market forces are powerful and attractive role models (which he calls *trustees*) are on the wane. Nonetheless, when working with younger individuals, it should be possible to meld aspects of creativity and wisdom in future workers and leaders.

The authors of the remaining chapters were invited to respond to the issues raised by the three lead authors and thus to engage in a debate with us. In Chapter 5, Dean Keith Simonton addresses the themes of perception and context, considers what it means to apply creativity wisely, and asks how and why educators in schools may respond. He highlights some of the similarities and differences between creativity and wisdom, exploring ways in which these two exceptional human assets, as he refers to them, may be integrated and applied particularly in education. Simonton suggests the need for wise creativity to function in an adaptive way, so as to incorporate social and ethical ramifications of ideas and creative outcomes. He suggests that, in balancing originality against functionality, the creator may in fact be prone to living a more mentally balanced life as well as acting in relationship to more broad-based values.

In Chapter 6, David Henry Feldman considers motivation—what we use our creativity for and what it means to apply creativity wisely. He takes up the relationship between creativity and wisdom in a more skeptical fashion, asking whether creativity and wisdom may actually be fundamentally incompatible. Feldman's answer is that this determination depends on how we conceive of both creativity and wisdom. He suggests that in creative efforts which are focused in the social, political, religious, or spiritual domains, creativity and wisdom go hand in hand, in that creativity without wisdom is meaningless in such contexts. This observation leads him to consider the extent to which we may be describing creativity at all, given its distinct manifestation within contrasting domains. In particular, he acknowledges that creativity may involve breaking with the norm rather than respecting it, to differing degrees depending on context. He proposes a means by which we may understand both creativity and wisdom in terms of a transformational impulse.

In Chapter 7, Jonathan Rowson focuses on what it means to apply creativity wisely. He ponders what the disposition toward creativity and wisdom might entail; he warns of the dangers, when holding education in mind, of commodifying creativity and wisdom such that they become products to, as he puts it, "squeeze in to a bloated timetable." He argues for an understanding of creativity and wisdom which accounts for motivation and disposition, and which captures the complexity of relationships among motivation, values, habit, and freedom. His argument leads into a consideration of how educators in schools can respond, and he anticipates tensions and dilemmas thereto. Accordingly, he considers approaches to pedagogy and implications for the practitioner—placing emphasis on the cultivation of dispositions toward both creativity and wisdom in fostering learning through experience and by example. Meaning-making is all important in the process of learning to act wisely in relation to creative engagement.

In Chapter 8, Helen Haste's initial focus is on three areas: perceptions of the context in which creativity is manifested, motivational issues in relation to what creativity is used for, and queries about what it means to apply creativity wisely. She questions to what extent we may reconcile the perspectives on creativity, wisdom, and ethics explored by the three lead authors. Her response seeks to integrate them by recognizing a tension in our collective and individual lives between managing continuity and generating and coping with change at the same time. Addressing how educators can respond to this tension, she proposes five "key competencies" as foci for education, as the basis of fostering the capacity in children for creative transformation. Each, she argues, has cognitively creative and ethically creative dimensions. These pose challenges to educators: in tackling the unwitting culture of anxiety propagated so often within school, in fostering the use of dialogue in developing and recognizing multiple perspectives, and in encouraging a view of rationality which recognizes the influence of subjectivity.

In Chapter 9, Patrick Dillon develops the themes of context to creativity, what it means to apply creativity wisely, and how educators in schools may develop wise creativity. He argues that creativity, wisdom, and trusteeship are cultural patterns emerging from engagement between individuals and their contexts, with culturally situated implications for how we foster these patterns. Education, he suggests, in favoring certain kinds of cultural patterns, or niches, can be seen as an intervention in behaviors and ideas, one that involves a rich engagement between environment and culture. The location-specificity, as well as the context- and temporal-dependence of creativity, wisdom, and trusteeship, are vital to Dillon's perspective. He emphasizes the situatedness of each and thus highlights the tension between generality and specificity in understanding any of these terms, while also recognizing the interconnectedness of local and wider systems.

In Chapter 10, Hans Henrik Knoop analyzes what it means to apply creativity wisely, set in the broader social, political, and economic context of what creativity is used for. He stresses the contribution of the collective in exploring the "wisdom of the crowd" and arguing that creativity and wisdom may be seen as two sides of the same coin. His analysis of accelerating growth in economy and shifting political values, with joint consequences of degradation (environmental and other), explores the mirroring, in culture, of biology. He discusses, therefore, the intricate and intimate relationships between individuals and their surroundings.

The question of how creativity and wisdom may be understood in performance arts is raised by Christopher Bannerman in Chapter 11. He examines the context in which creativity is manifest, and he puts forth an embodied approach to what it means to apply creativity wisely. He argues for a view of creativity that emphasizes interconnectedness between creators and the live balance between the individual and the collective, together with the integration of "knowledge and skills coupled with spontaneous insight." Bannerman's reconciliation of creativity with wisdom, like Knoop's and Dillon's, and to a degree Haste's, involves recognizing that the group can involve both collective and individual creative processes, serving as a vehicle for building "situated wisdom."

The final two chapters are concerned in different ways with leadership, specifically with reference to the role of the educator. In Chapter 12, exploring what it means to apply creativity wisely, Robert J. Sternberg explores the Wisdom, Intelligence, and Creativity, Synthesized (WICS) model of leadership. He outlines each of these components and suggests ways in which they can be productively synthesized. The main goal of schools should be to produce leaders who embody these traits rather than automatons who merely reproduce inert knowledge on demand.

In Chapter 13, Dave Trotman focuses on the teacher. He explores questions related to the context in which creativity is manifested, with particular reference to its wise deployment by professional educators. The target chapters stimulated him to contemplate "the mystery and emotional heart of what it is to learn, teach, educate, and be truly creative." Professional judgment emerges as pivotal in fostering creativity, wisdom, and trusteeship among learners. Trotman explores aspects of professional educational judgment which are significant in developing creativity with wisdom in education. He also identifies a body of teachers who could be considered trustees of creative education in that they are skilled practitioners technically as well as inspirational shape-shifters. The restoration of professional judgment could liberate other educators to approach their work in similarly informed ways.

The aim of the book is, naturally, to foster debate; the writing of it has involved the sharing of perspectives between the editors and the response authors. As a conclusion, in Chapter 14 the three lead authors offer responses to some of the key themes and issues arising from the debate, further deconstructing and then reconstructing creativity, wisdom, and trusteeship in relation to the endeavor of education.

REBALANCING TIPPING POINTS?

As a whole, this book reflects a perspective on the educator as a reflective practitioner—one who considers actions and intentions by reflecting both *in* and *on* practice (Schon 1987). Despite the current global focus on accountability (Ball 2003), manifest in the pressure on teachers and institutions to demonstrate certain kinds of performance, to raise standards, and to work from what often appear to be rigid curricula, standards, and templates, the culture of reflection on practice survives. This insistence on retaining professional artistry and integrity effectively provides a counterbalance to the reduction of the classroom practitioner to technician and resurfaces the essential debate around values in education. We seek to contribute to the debate which explores means and ends in reinvigorating both cognition and education at a time in global history when we may be approaching alarming tipping points in ecological, political, or cultural matters. We hope then to problematize creativity, to integrate it synergistically with wisdom, and to propose ways in which trusteeship may be meaningfully developed or resurrected in the twenty-first century.

REFERENCES

Amabile, T. 1988. A model of creativity and innovation in organizations. In *Research in organizational behavior,* Vol. 10, ed. B. M. Staw and L. L. Cunnings, 123–67. Greenwich, CT: JAL.

Ball, S. J. 2003. The teacher's soul and the terrors of performativity. *Journal of Education Policy* 18:215–28.

Baltes, P. B., and U. Kunzmann. 2004. Two faces of wisdom: Wisdom as a general theory of knowledge and judgement about excellence in mind and virtue vs. wisdom as everyday realization in people and products. *Human Development* 47:290–99.

Baltes, P. B., and A. Stange. 2005. *Research project 6. Wisdom: The integration of mind and virtue.* Center for Lifespan Psychology. http://www.mpib-berlin.mpg.de/en/forschung/lip/pdfs/research_project_6.pdf.

Baltes, P. B., and U. M. Staudinger. 2000. Wisdom: A metaheuristic (pragmatic) to orchestrate mind and virtue toward excellence. *American Psychologist* 55:122–36.

Barron, F. X. 1969. *Creative person and creative process.* New York: Holt, Rinehart, and Winston.

Bassett, C. L. (2005). Laughing at gilded butterflies: Integrating wisdom, development, and learning. In *Handbook of adult development and learning,* ed. C. Hoare, 281–306. New York: Oxford University Press.

Bruner, J. S. 1962. *On knowing: Essays for the left hand.* Cambridge, MA: Harvard University Press.

Burnard, P., A. Craft, T. Cremin, with B. Duffy, R. Hanson, J. Keene, L. Haynes, and D. Burns. 2006. Documenting "possibility thinking": A journey of collaborative enquiry. *International Journal of Early Years Education* 14:243–62.

Cook-Greuter, S. R. 2000. Mature ego development: A gateway to ego transcendence? *Journal of Adult Development* 7:227–40.

Craft, A. 2001. Little c creativity. In *Creativity in education,* ed. A. Craft, B. Jeffrey, and M. Leibling, 45–61. London: Continuum.

———. 2005. *Creativity in schools: Tensions and dilemmas.* Abingdon, England: Routledge.

Cremin, T., P. Burnard, and A. Craft. 2006. Pedagogy and possibility thinking in the early years. *Thinking Skills and Creativity* 1:108–19.

Csikszentmihalyi, M. 1988. Society, culture and person: A systems view of creativity. In *The nature of creativity,* ed. R. J. Sternberg, 325–39. Cambridge, UK: Cambridge University Press.

———. 1996. *Creativity: Flow and the psychology of discovery and invention.* New York: HarperCollins.

De Bono, E. 1995. *Serious creativity.* New York: HarperCollins.

Eysenck, H. J. 1952. *The scientific study of personality.* London: Routledge and Kegan Paul.

Feldman, D. H., M. Csikszentmihalyi, and H. Gardner. 1994. *Changing the world: A framework for the study of creativity* Westport, CT: Praeger.

Fischman, W., B. Solomon, D. Greenspan, and H. Gardner. 2004. *Making good: How young people cope with moral dilemmas at work.* Cambridge, MA: Harvard University Press.

Freud, S. 1908/1959. Creative writers and day-dreaming. In *The standard edition of the complete psychological works of Sigmund Freud*, Vol. 9, ed. J. Strachey, 141–54. London: Hogarth Press.

———. 1910/1957. Leonardo da Vinci and a memory of his childhood. In *The standard edition of the complete psychological works of Sigmund Freud,* Vol. 11, ed. J. Strachey, 59–137. London: Hogarth Press.

———. 1916/1971. *The complete introductory lectures on psychoanalysis.* London: Macmillan.

Galton, F. 1869. *Hereditary genius: An enquiry into its laws and consequences.* London: Macmillan.

Gardner, H. 1991. *The unschooled mind.* New York: Basic Books.

———. 1993. *Creating minds.* New York: Basic Books.

———. 1999. *The disciplined mind: What all students should understand.* New York: Simon & Schuster.

———. 2007. *Five minds for the future.* Boston: Harvard Business School Press.

Gruber, H. 1974/1981. *Darwin on man: A psychological study of scientific creativity.* 2nd. ed. Chicago: University of Chicago Press.

Guilford, J. P. 1950. Creativity. *American Psychologist* 5:444–54.

———. 1967. *The nature of human intelligence.* New York: McGraw-Hill.

Jeffrey, B., and A. Craft. 2001. The universalization of creativity. In *Creativity in education,* ed. A. Craft, B. Jeffrey, and M. Leibling, 1–13. London: Continuum.

Jenkins, H. 2006. *Confronting the challenge of participatory culture in media education for the 21st century.* Occasional paper on digital media and learning. http://www.digital learning.macfound.org/atf/cf/%7B7E45C7E0-A3E0-4B89-AC9C-E807E1B0AE 4E%7D/JENKINS_WHITE_PAPER.PDF.

John-Steiner, V. 1997. *Notebooks of the mind: Explorations of thinking.* 2nd ed. New York: Oxford University Press.

———. 2000. *Creative collaboration.* New York: Oxford University Press.

Johnson-Laird, P. N. 1988. Freedom and constraint in creativity. In *The nature of creativity,* ed. R. J. Sternberg, 202–19. New York: Cambridge University Press.

Jung, C. 1973. *Memories, dreams, and reflections.* New York: Pantheon.

Kitchener, K. S., and H. G. Brenner. 1990. Wisdom and reflective judgment: Knowing in the face of uncertainty. In *Wisdom: Its nature, origins and development,* ed. R. J. Sternberg, 212–29. New York: Cambridge University Press.

Kunzmann, U., and P. Baltes. 2005. The psychology of wisdom: Theoretical and empirical challenges. In *A handbook of wisdom: Psychological perspectives,* ed. R. J. Sternberg and J. Jordan, 110–35. New York: Cambridge University Press.

MacKinnon, D. 1962. The nature and nurture of creative talent. *American Psychologist* 20:484–95.

Maslow, A. H. 1954/1987. *Motivation and personality.* New York: Harper & Row.

———. 1971. *The farther reaches of human nature.* Harmondsworth, England: Penguin.

Mednick, S. A. 1962. The associative basis of the creative process. *Psychological Review* 60:220–32.

Osbeck, L. M., and D. M. Robinson. 2005. Philosophical theories of wisdom. In *The mind's best work,* ed. D. N. Perkins, 61–83. Cambridge, MA: Harvard University Press.

Piaget, J. 1932. *The moral judgment of the child.* London: Routledge & Kegan Paul.

Piaget, J., and B. Inhelder. 1969. *The psychology of the child.* London: Routledge & Kegan Paul.

Rhyammar, L., and C. Brolin. 1999. Creativity research: Historical considerations and main lines of development. *Scandinavian Journal of Educational Research* 43:259–73.

Rogers, C. R. 1970. Towards a theory of creativity. In *Creativity,* ed. P. E. Vernon, 137–51. Harmondsworth, England: Penguin.

Schon, D. 1987. *Educating the reflective practitioner.* San Francisco: Jossey-Bass.

Simon, H. A. 1988. Creativity and motivation: A response to Csikszentmihalyi. *New Ideas in Psychology* 6:177–81.

Skinner, B. F. 1953. *The science of behavior.* New York: Macmillan.

———. 1968. *The technology of teaching.* New York: Meredith.

———. 1971. *Beyond freedom and dignity.* London: Jonathan Cape.

———. 1974. *About behaviourism.* London: Jonathan Cape.

Sternberg, R. J. 2003. *Wisdom, intelligence, and creativity synthesized.* Cambridge, UK: Cambridge University Press.

Sternberg, R. J., and T. I. Lubart. 1991. An investment theory of creativity and its development. *Human Development* 34:1–31.

———. 1995. *Defying the crowd: Cultivating creativity in a culture of conformity.* New York: Free Press.

Suarez-Orozco, M., and D. Qin-Hilliard. 2004. *Globalization: Culture and education in the new millennium.* Berkeley: University of California Press.

Takahashi, M., and W. F. Overton. 2005. Cultural foundations of wisdom: An integrated developmental approach. In *A handbook of wisdom: Psychological perspectives,* ed. R. J. Sternberg and J. Jordan, 32–60. New York: Cambridge University Press.

Torrance, H. 1962. *Guiding creative talent.* Englewood Cliffs, NJ: Prentice Hall.

———. 1974. *Torrance tests of creative thinking.* Lexington, MA: Ginn and Company (Xerox Corporation).

Wallach, M. A. 1971. *The intelligence-creativity distinction.* Morristown, NJ: General Learning Press.

Wallas, G. 1926. *The art of thought.* New York: Harcourt Brace.

Winnicott, D. W. 1971. *Playing and reality.* New York: Routledge.

PART ONE

Stimulus Chapters on Creativity, Wisdom, and Trusteeship

2

Tensions in Creativity and Education

Enter Wisdom and Trusteeship?

Anna Craft

T he case for fostering creativity in education can be seen as a response to the conditions and pace of life and the global market economy. The political call for creativity is one which often couches creativity as if it were a universal attribute. This argument states that people need to be more creative to survive and thrive in the twenty-first century (A. Craft 2004; Seltzer and Bentley 1999). This case is made explicitly in policy documents in various parts of the world. In England, the white paper *Excellence in Schools* (Department for Education and Employment 1997) talks of preparing young people for the twenty-first century by recognizing the different talents of all people. This was built on by the National Advisory Committee on Creative and Cultural Education (NACCCE; 1999) report advocating the skills and approaches which are required by employers and which education should equip young people with. The report acknowledges that, rather than purely seeking high standards of academic achievement, employers now require "people who can adapt, see connections, innovate, communicate and work with others" (NACCCE 1999, 13). Many would argue that such views provide a foundation for other, more recent policy statements in England.

It is a similar story in many other countries. The Scottish Executive (2004) Web site contains the following statement by Frank McAveety, the Scottish minister for tourism, culture and sport, regarding creativity: "The creativity of Scots—from the classroom to the boardroom—is the edge we need in a competitive world. Our duty as an Executive is to create the conditions that allow that creativity to flourish—whether in arts, sciences, commerce or industry. Creativity is as valuable in retail, education, health, government and business as in culture. The cultural sector should become the national dynamo of the creative impulse that can serve all these areas" (p. 5). This was the precursor to the establishment of an independent Cultural Commission in June 2004, comprising representatives from various sections of the cultural sector and chaired by James Boyle, to refine the cultural and creative strategy for Scotland. The Cultural Commission's (2005) report includes a chapter focusing on education, which recommends that the curriculum for learners aged 3–18 should provide opportunities to learn in and through the arts and culture by promoting creativity among young people. The Scottish Executive's response to this was published in January 2006, and it made recommendations for linking creativity and culture at all levels in the curriculum for ages 3–18—a trend which is occurring alongside other initiatives to develop enterprise in schools and to develop teaching and learning to foster greater creativity. These latter approaches include a much greater emphasis on creative and cultural partnership with organizations beyond the classroom.

Similar arguments, perspectives, and strategic policy recommendations have emerged in many parts of the world since the early 1990s, as demonstrated by the following quotation from a Canadian Ministry of Education document: "In view of the new social and economic realities, all students, regardless of their immediate plans following school, will need to develop a flexibility and a versatility undreamed of by previous generations . . . [and] employ critical and creative thinking skills to solve problems and make decisions" (quoted in Woods 2002, 79). This trend continues, alongside the further development of partnerships with the arts and cultural sector, as reflected in initiatives such as one that was launched by the Academies for Arts, Humanities and Sciences in Canada in May 2007 to further explore such potential and possibilities. In the United States, the need for innovation, adaptation, communication, and connection in the workplace has long been advocated (Secretary's Commission on Achieving Necessary Skills 1991). In early 2005 came the announcement of a national inquiry project that would explore creativity, education, and the economy (Cultural Commission 2005). The case for fostering creativity in education is also made in the Far East. Ng and Smith (2004a, 2004b) report that in Singapore, pupils are expected by the end of their schooling (i.e., pre–higher education) to "have an entrepreneurial and creative spirit" (Ministry of Education 2004, n.p.). Richardson (2001) reports that an important element in achieving this goal is seen to be the integration of the arts and culture with education.

POLICY CONTEXT AND GLOBALIZATION

In addition to this shifting education policy context which recognizes a greater explicit role for creativity in the economy and in education, we have seen, particularly in the last 10 years, commentators and researchers exploring ways in which creativity and the economy interact and offering more and better strategies to increase productivity and, therefore, economic competitiveness in a global economy. For some, such as Sternberg and Lubart (1995), this means adopting the metaphor of the market as a way of explaining and exploring creativity. Their investment model of creativity involves buying low and selling high. As Sternberg and Lubart put it, *"Buying low* means actively pursuing ideas that are unknown or out of favor but that have growth potential, whereas *selling high* involves moving on to new products when an idea or product becomes valued and yields a different return" (p. 538; italics in the original). Sternberg (2003) later emphasizes the choice involved in creativity, describing investment theory as "the decision to be creative" (p. 206), underlining the significance of decision making in buying low and selling high.

For others, the market lurks in the background as an assumed "good." In discussing creativity and public policy, for example, Nagel (2000) suggests that "competitive business firms" and "increased national productivity" (p. 15) are key elements of public policies seeking to foster creativity. The implication is that this is appropriate and desirable.

Underlying such perspectives is the idea that performance in the marketplace is itself an indicator of creativity. Florida (2002, 2006) offers controversial comments on economic development. His argument is that the cultivation of creativity is increasingly highly valued globally. He claims to identify the phenomenon in North America of the growth of a *creative class* (i.e., engineers, architects, scientists, artists, educators, and entertainers) whose economic function is to create new technology, new creative content, and above all, new ideas. Florida argues that the growing size and influence of this sector of the population has a profound influence on work and lifestyle, derived from the characteristics of self-direction and high achievement. He claims that successful urban economic development relies on encouraging a diversity of population (e.g., attracting gays, bohemians, and ethnic minorities) on the basis that creative workers want to live in such places. His views have been influential in urban redesign and regeneration in the United States, although his thesis also has its critics, such as Malangi (2004), who questions the idea that creative workers are attracted to urban areas by tolerance, openness to creativity, and diversity. Malangi notes that some cities proposed by Florida as successful creative cities are underperforming, while some top creative cities do not appear to attract or retain residents. He suggests that Florida overemphasizes high-tech industries' contribution to the creative class, and he wonders why some cities which on other indices of economic growth have expanded quickly (e.g., Detroit) are omitted altogether, while other cities (e.g., New York, which Florida describes as one of the most creative cities) seem to produce fast-growing companies at less than half the rate of other big cities. Nevertheless, Florida's thesis remains influential, and the connection between the marketplace and creativity remains both visible and unquestioned in general parlance.

BLIND SPOTS?

This chapter seeks to highlight two blind spots in the creativity discourse. The first is culture. I argue that policy calls for creativity in some universalized form are made without reference to or regard for macrocultural or subcultural values and approaches to life. This type of approach has been described as *culture blind* (Ng 2003), in the sense that creativity is called for in the context of liberal individualism tied to a market economy, as if this were the only cultural context. The discourse around creativity is one in which high value is placed on individuality and being open to thinking generatively in ways that may involve challenging social and other norms. This discourse values highly innovative engagement in the economy as both a consumer and a producer.

The second blind spot relates to ethics and the environment, and it stems from the anchoring of creativity in the marketplace in this apparently culture-free way. What consequences flow from promoting so heavily the value of making and selling ideas and products? For the drive to innovate further becomes an end in itself within a culture which places high value and reward on continual market-orientated innovation. There is a danger—and plenty of evidence—that the re-use of old artifacts and ideas is a poor second best to shiny new profit-making novelty, an argument I make elsewhere (A. Craft 2006). Thus we find ourselves living in a unique and continually changing world of our own creation, but one where *new* is seen as being far preferable to *make do and mend*. Indeed, in order to maintain demand and therefore profit, many products and services appear to be designed with a short shelf life, ceasing to work after a short period—designed to be disposed of and replaced, rather than repaired or restored, or simply framed by advertising as being out of fashion.

This chapter asks: How desirable is the norm of innovation that the global economy demands? To what extent is it desirable to encourage and sustain the "disposable" culture, in which obsolescence is built in at the design stage of many consumer goods and fashion dictates the need for constant change and updating? But let's return to Blind Spot Number One—perhaps the most fundamental.

CREATIVITY AND CULTURAL CONTEXT

There is growing evidence that, since creativity is manifest differently according to culture, developing a *universalized* discourse around how creativity might be developed, one that implies a uniform model of and approach to creativity regardless of culture, is therefore both inappropriate and presumptuous. Differences in perspective on creativity, and how it may be manifested and fostered, reflect wider sociocultural values. While there is still much to explore regarding how these differences manifest themselves, there is plenty of evidence of differences between Eastern and Western views of creativity. For example, work by Ng (2003) suggests a striking emphasis within Confucian societies on the significance of the social group vis-à-vis the individual. In such systems, society is often tightly organized, and socialization of children focuses on fitting in with the in-group. The behavior of children and adults in these societies is governed by many social rules and regulations (Ng 2003).

This collectivist perspective on what it means to be a citizen contrasts strongly with Western individualism, which places far greater emphasis on the individual than on the social group (Bellah et al. 1985). In such societies, children and young people are socialized to develop as unique persons; they are expected to pursue their own interests and passions in life rather than complying so strongly with the in-group. This atmosphere is underlined by the work of Chao (1993), who found that 64% of Euro-American mothers felt that an important goal of childrearing was to emphasize and nurture the unique self of the child. This contrasted with just 8% of Chinese mothers emphasizing that particular goal in bringing up their children. Strongly individuated behavior seems typical of Westernized liberal individualism. Markus and Kitayama (1991, 1994) also discuss differences in socialization between individualistic and collectivistic cultures leading to very different self-constructs. They contend that individualistic (Western) socialization involves a view of self that is independent, distinct from the social group, and that involves direct expression of feelings and opinions together with behavior that is individuated. In contrast, collectivist (Eastern) socialization involves a view of self that is integrally related to the group, interdependent, and compliant in relation to the in-group and that involves conforming behavior. Markus and Kitayama highlight cultural differences in the ways in which validation is orientated, such that in a collectivistic society, the need for validation leans toward conformity with the social group, whereas in an individualistic society, the orientation and social pressure is toward differentiation and difference. Therefore, Western society encourages behavior which is individuated to a much greater degree. Added to this cultural frame, some studies document a pressure for acculturation to occur as cultural individualism rather than as cultural collectivism (Ng 2001; Smith and Bond 1993). Ng (2001) summarizes East/West differences as shown in Table 2.1.

Lim (2004), discussing Ng's work, suggests that "the Asian view traditionally emphasizes control by the environment so that the individual adapts; the Western view emphasizes the individual so that the individual changes the environment" (p. 4). Lim notes the Western emphasis on encouraging individuals to become themselves, thereby celebrating uniqueness. By contrast, the collectivist Eastern model tends to conformity, encouraging social cohesion and fitting in with the social group. The existence of what Lubart (1999) calls such distinct worldviews seems undisputed. He notes that examining differences in approaches to creativity can provide a magnifying lens for the wider culture. Drawing on Spindler and Spindler (1983), Lubart concludes that the U.S. worldview in particular is characterized by "individualism, a work ethic of

Table 2.1   Comparing and Contrasting Eastern and Western Cultures

East	West
Tightly organized, strong social rules and norms	Loosely organized, few social rules and norms
Emphasis on social group	Emphasis on individual
Hierarchical, distinctive ranks/status	Egalitarian, little distinction between superiors and subordinates
Emphasis on social order and harmony in family/society	Emphasis on open exchange of ideas between individuals
High value on gaining social approval of group	High value on realizing creative potential

SOURCE Adapted from Ng Aik Kwang, *Why Asians Are Less Creative Than Westerners.* Prentice Hall, Singapore, 2001.

achievement, a belief in progress and a better future" (p. 345). The U.S. emphasis on development and change as a good thing values creativity very highly. It is suggested that, by contrast, cultures placing a high value on adherence to tradition and conformity to the norm may in fact stifle creativity.

Studies exploring how such cultural values are played out in relation to creativity in teaching and learning (Martin, Craft, and Tillema 2002; Martin, Craft, and Zhang 2001; Ng 2002; Zhang et al. 2004) report that teachers in the Eastern tradition find greater difficulty than their Western counterparts in valuing creativity in the classroom. Eastern teachers tend to view children who diverge from the norm as disruptive; they tend to see creative behavior as disruptive (Ng and Smith 2004a). Ng and Smith argue that this is due to the emphasis on moral cultivation within the Confucian tradition in which the teacher serves as a moral exemplar. The appropriate student response, therefore, is to demonstrate respect through obedience. The increased emphasis in the creative classroom on responses running counter to the Confucian model of docile learner, who is submissive and conforming, encourages students to be argumentative, individualistic, and skeptical. For teachers socialized in the Confucian tradition, this poses actual and perceived challenges in classroom management and control.

Ng (2002) suggests that teachers' attitudes toward learners affect their effectiveness in fostering creativity. *Liberal-democratic* teachers seem to view their role as enabling each student to achieve his or her potential; thus divergent, or creative, behavior tends to be encouraged and rewarded more in their classrooms. Liberal-democratic teachers emphasize challenge, originality, and difference. *Conservative-autocratic* teachers, on the other hand, expect obedience and respect, and see themselves as the ultimate authority; thus creative responses are punished rather than rewarded.

Ng's (2002) findings have also been borne out in small studies by Martin, Craft, and Zhang (2001); Martin, Craft, and Tillema (2002); and Zhang et al. (2004). Findings suggest that Chinese teachers are far more likely to conform to perceptions of cultural norms (Martin, Craft, and Tillema 2002; Zhang et al. 2004).

Such East/West differences are explained by Nisbett's (2003) discussion of differences in values between Asians and Westerners. East Asian thought, characterized as *holistic*, focusing on the whole picture (quite literally in the case of looking at, say, a painting), generates dialectic reasoning, which seeks to find consensus, or a middle ground between opposing thoughts. Whereas Western thought, focusing on salient people or objects, categorizes these and then applies formal logic to explaining and understanding them. Having proposed differences in cognition between the two groups, Nisbett offers a social and economic account of the underlying causes, pointing to foundations laid in contrasting forms of social and economic organization in ancient China and Greece.[1]

It could be argued that the reification of the market (i.e., the Western capitalist model of "market as God") pervades the universalized notions of creativity that are apparent in Western policy and research literature. Given its cultural specificity, this notion may be inappropriately assertive over other values (A. Craft 2003, 2005, 2006). Clearly, values are culturally embedded, including the extent to which the observable outcomes of creativity are themselves valued. Lubart (1999) notes that an important feature of the Western conception of creativity is "its relationship to an observable product" (p. 339). This idea contrasts with the more inward conception held in the East, where "creativity involves a state of personal fulfillment, a connection to a primordial realm, or the expression of an inner essence or ultimate reality" (ibid, p. 340). Lubart does, however, note similarities between Eastern and Western humanistic views of creativity. In general, though, he suggests that the Eastern view of creativity is much more about spiritual expression than about producing something of external worth in some kind of judging field. He compares the frequently cited Western model of the creativity process (preparation, incubation, illumination, and evaluation/verification) with the Eastern model proposed by Maduro (1976) in a study of Indian painters. Maduro's model involved four similar but slightly different stages: preparation (in terms of contacting one's inner self), achievement of personal identification with the matter in hand, insight (focused on the personal rather than a product), and social communication of personal realizations. The Eastern process, Lubart (1999) notes, also involves looking inward and "the reinterpretation of traditional ideas—finding a new point of view," which contrasts with the Western approach in which "creativity involves a break with tradition" (p. 340). Lubart's perspective is echoed by Raina (2004), who adopts the traditional Indian metaphor of the garland as representing creativity to convey many diverse approaches to creativity coexisting—an inclusive perspective. This is echoed in the work of others, such as Sen and Sharma (2004), who also, however, discuss the perspective advanced by Bharati (1985) that there is evidence among the Indian population of people being both collectivist and individualist at the same time, acknowledging the dangers of oversimplifying cultural differences in a society which is itself plural and made up of many subcultural groups (Sen and Sharma 2004).

An approach to creativity which propagates lifestyles which rely on constant innovation and consumption is both born of and contributes to a global market economy, in which possible differences in cultural and subcultural perspectives are of little or no significance. There are, of course, difficulties with a simple categorization of Asian/Western, liberal individualist/collectivist. Both Nisbettt (2003) and Ng (2002) acknowledge the finer differentiations which may be invisible in a simple categorization describing these groups as polar opposites because, in a multicultural world, nationality does not necessarily represent cultural membership. And in a globalized world where acculturation occurs across national and cultural boundaries, it is not straightforward to make simple comparisons because the groups being compared with one another are not "pure." Also there may be a mix of cultures within one setting. China in the early twenty-first century, for example, is nurturing two contrasting sets of values: both the more closed, conformist tradition in which creativity is more likely to be stifled and a fast-growing mentality that values capitalism and demands innovation, creativity, and change. Cheung et al. (2004) cite recent large-scale far-Eastern studies of attitudes to creativity, reminding us that we may not always find what we expect in terms of values. Studies by Berndt et al. (1993) and Cheung et al. (1992), conducted in Taiwan, mainland China, and Hong Kong, revealed differences in adult attitudes toward creativity, the least positive of which was in fact demonstrated in Hong Kong—an unexpected finding. Other studies (e.g., Lau, Hui, and Ng 2004) reveal similar findings.

However—and here we come to the questions at the forefront of this book—if we are asking how we use our creativity wisely, and who are the trustees of generative thought in a globalized world in the early twenty-first century, we should perhaps question the appropriateness of fostering creativity as if we were culture-blind, that is, in a way which implies the imposition of one cultural model on another. When we consider this together with the power held by the teacher and the educational system over young people, in terms of defining what and how it is appropriate to learn, we recognize educators' immense responsibility for fostering pupils' creativity. One of the small studies discussed briefly earlier (Martin, Craft, and Zhang 2001; Zhang et al. 2004) noted that, following a short period of support to teachers, pupil behaviors and approaches were noticeably different; evidence showed acculturation to the universalized (i.e., Western) model of creativity and thus the (perhaps unwitting) domination of a particular model.

Clearly, there are other ways of interpreting the question of culture—from those such as Csikszentmihalyi's (1990) domain-situated notion, to the perspective of cultural capital and the creative and cultural agenda. The latter is perhaps particularly relevant in England at the present time, given the influence of the NACCCE (1999) report, which took the significant step of recommending a role for *artistic cultural achievement and development* in promoting pupil creativity through creative partnership, arguing that cultural and creative development should occur hand in hand. Roberts (2006), evaluating initiatives stemming from the NACCCE report, recommended continuation of such approaches in order to feed the *creative industries*.

For Culture with a large C, the creative and cultural sector is again situated in the values of the wider political and economic scene. And one aspect, of course, of situating culture is to consider what does and does not count as culture, who gets access to what culture, and which forms of cultural expression are valued. Some issues involved in broaching cultural boundaries are raised in a recent study exploring student participation in local cultural venues (A. Craft, Jeffrey, and Joubert 2004). Challenges included preconceived ideas held by students and teachers, ways in which schools described events and opportunities, and, by implication, what counted as culture. In a different study, Harland et al. (2000) found that success strategies included those by which students took on the role of *cultural mentor*. This study documented the importance of learners being able to make the transition across cultural contexts and different perspectives, but it also highlighted significant culturally based challenges in doing so.

The significance of culture is underlined by currently dominant sociocultural, constructivist approaches to learning, which underpin the practices of many (Western) teachers. Children's learning within this broad framework is construed as bound to context and as an inherently social and therefore cultural process (Vass 2004a, 2004b) in which cultural and social mediation (Crook 1994) plays a core role. A constructivist approach to learning may be viewed both as necessary to and demanded by promoting pupils' creativity, which automatically situates learning within the wider culture in various ways.

I want to touch on one other aspect of the sociocultural context: creativity and the socioeconomic context. The universalized creativity discourse may be saturated with social class–based assumptions, including strong individuation and self-reliance, future orientation, and persistence and control over one's environment (A. Craft 2002, 2005; Kluckhohn and Strodtbeck 1961). Clearly, this raises tensions and dilemmas for schools. The hegemonic dimension is problematic because when the so-called universalized concept of creativity is concerned with inclusion and opportunity for all, it sits uneasily with the power, authority, and control implied by imposing a creativity value set in the classroom which may in fact exclude some learners. However, and a similar argument has been invoked over the years in multicultural education (Banks 1997; M. Craft 1996), it could also be argued that educators and others have a significant responsibility to offer access to the *dominant* (in terms of social and economic) culture to pupils who might, without this, have little awareness of or access to it. Such an argument is based on the assumption that access to the dominant culture brings with it greater access to power and authority for those who may be otherwise more marginalized. Numerous programs aiming to foster creativity in education could be interpreted as emerging from this perspective. For example, Creative Partnerships, the English government initiative funded initially from 2002 to 2008, with its emphasis on working in areas of high urban or rural deprivation, can be seen in such terms. Another organization whose raison d'etre, for the first few years of its existence at least, was to stimulate and resource the creativity of young people as well as adults is the

National Endowment for Science, Technology and the Arts. Many of its early funded programs had social inclusion at their heart.[2] Of critical importance in such initiatives is undoubtedly educator sensitivity to the values students bring from the home, which may well be in tension with those of the classroom. This tension could be played out in the nursery, as discussed by Duffy and Stillaway (2004) regarding the parents who were concerned about their daughter performing on stage in front of others, or at a later age, as with refugee teenagers whose experiences influence their capacity to believe that they can achieve anything they wish to (Parkes and Califano 2004). So as educators, perhaps using our creativity with wisdom means being alert to the potential for unintentionally abusing the power that we hold in fostering the life-changing potential of generative creativity.

Before moving on from culture, a brief word on political context, since it provides another set of influences on the extent to which creativity is encouraged in the wider culture, in terms of peace and war, allies and enemies, perceived friendships and broken trust. I do not discuss these in depth in this chapter, nor the extent to which the wider cultural-political context affects people's experiences of what creativity might enable them to do in their lives, except to say that, at a micropolitical level, it may perhaps be easier to follow a personal and individualized path in an environment with multiple values and thus a plural context (e.g., a large city) than in a narrower context (e.g., a small village). It may also be easier to divert from the norm if one's own dominant values–identity is held in a pluralized space than if fundamentalism of any kind is part of one's values. Indeed, with fundamentalist belief as a core element of identity, being creative may seem less relevant, less desirable, less achievable, and possibly deeply inappropriate. In his work on changing minds, Gardner (2004) argues that a fundamentalist mind-set is antithetical to creativity. Gardner's view of fundamentalism is a broad one: "An adherent decides that he will no longer change his mind in any significant way" (p. 189); as a consequence, efforts are centered on rejecting nonconformist ideas. Gardner suggests that "the fundamentalist voluntarily suspends his imagination" (p. 189)—thereby undermining the possibility of creativity.

At a macropolitical level, it could be argued that democratic values and freedom of speech support the promotion of creativity in policy and practice. The expansion of the global marketplace has brought increasing wealth, enabling people in many parts of the world to make creative choices about their lives and providing sufficient resources to see these choices through (Ng 2001; Nisbett 2003). Yet the domination of the global marketplace, while appearing to generate many choices, also limits them because innovation carries such high value and is seen as preferable to the more resource-scarce perspective which says "make do and mend." A marketplace which creates and demands continual innovation and constantly shortens the shelf-life of products determines our choices within a specific framework of values which takes abundance, acquisition, and wealth for granted.

This brings me to the Blind Spot Number Two: linking creativity to ethics and the environment.

ENVIRONMENT AND ETHICS

Despite the evidence of the existence of both Eastern and Western models of creativity, the powerful global marketplace—thanks in part to growth in information and communication technologies—reaches far into people's lives, homes, and cultures, across the globe. Advertising bombards the individual, family, and community, shaping aspirations and encouraging acquisition of fast-evolving products and services with ever-decreasing fashion-lives. Persistent pressure to replace current goods and services with the latest model, toy, form of food, approach to entertainment, and lifestyle image conveys a model of creativity that is linked with the market. An implicit message appears to be that the universalized, free global market–linked version of creativity is a good thing and is superordinate to other possible societal values.

It is as though the market has taken on a divine force. What are the ethical and environmental implications and costs of giving such high value to the market in this way? An increasingly global lifestyle which encourages continual disposal and replacement of products fuels a ticking time bomb of environmental degradation. And we make our own contribution to the costs of creativity—as producers, consumers, parents, educators—each time we choose to purchase something we believe we need but in fact merely want. Looking behind the image and resisting market pressure is not fashionable; neither is asking ourselves seriously what kind of life we wish to lead at a more fundamental and global level. The drive to accumulate wealth and the belief that human beings can "have it all" are increasingly overwhelming. And yet there is growing evidence that our consumption is upsetting an ecological balance.

Of course, some innovation is actually responsive to environmental issues. Indeed some approaches to fostering creativity (e.g., Theory of Inventive Problem Solving) include in their processes a concern with environmental impact. A Canadian study (Hanel 2003) explored reasons why firms had introduced innovations. One in four innovators was motivated by high or very high concern to reduce environmental damage. And these firms retained a slight competitive edge over others.

Related to the environmental impact of market-hinged creativity is the spiritual exclusion that appears to accompany it. How far do we engage with the ethics involved? As I have argued elsewhere (A. Craft 2005), globalization and cultural imperialism may be partly responsible for global terrorism, because of its dismissiveness of continuity, tradition, and frugality, which in turn sparks a counterfundamentalist position leading to conflict.

Thinking of education, we might consider how far our reflectiveness about creative engagement translates to our behavior and to the explicit and hidden curriculum.

TENSIONS AND DILEMMAS FOR SCHOOLS

I have been exploring some significant ways in which the Western individualistic view of being and doing can frame the discourse around creativity in education. I have suggested that the apparent universalization of the concept of creativity implies the transcendence of this model, with implications for culture in a number of ways and for the wider ecological balance.

What Does This Mean for Schools?

Taking culture first, it could be argued (A. Craft 2003) that while there is a strong element of *cultural saturation* in the concept of creativity, the increasing global influence of Western culture, including its markets, means that the relevance of creativity as a universal concept may continue to grow. We might wonder whether, as educators, our role is to support this universalized approach to creativity, nurturing and nourishing a melting-pot approach which gradually rubs away cultural, political, and socioeconomic differences. In practice, this probably means doing nothing more than accepting and implementing the policy requirements and scaffolding offered to us as education practitioners.

But how *wise* and appropriate is it for us to do this without, at the very least, a plural context to our pedagogy? We do still live in a world where there are distinct cultural identities both within and between nation-states, as well as different traditions, value sets, and therefore motivations and preferences for learning and achievement. We are faced with the possibility that a universalized (and market-related) notion of creativity may in fact be perceived by some as exclusive.

It could be argued that the universalization of creativity in the current world is premature and inappropriate. Perhaps one of the biggest challenges we face as educators is the lack of a plural perspective on creativity in education and political policy. And yet, creativity does not necessarily have to be nurtured in this way. Indeed, by its very nature which embraces alternatives and possibilities, creativity offers inherent potential for evaluating the worth of any creative outcome by considering its implications or impact. Indeed, in England the Qualifications and Curriculum Authority (2005b) supports schools in this way by identifying critical evaluation within its Creativity Framework.[3] Thus, although creativity is always situated within a cultural context, by looking critically at it, the assumption of cultural universalism may be challenged and all perspectives, therefore, acknowledged or even celebrated. Perhaps *that* is the wise thing to do.

And What of Ethics and the Environment?

It could be argued that the purchasing of consumer and other items in a world where the market holds supreme value, as argued earlier, is in part a replacement for making existential meaning. The constant drive toward making and buying occurs at the same time as massive global population growth and a degraded physical environment. It could also certainly be argued that unless the most wealthy and educated parts of the world start to take less of the world's resources, there will be insufficient food and water at the most basic level, and certainly inadequate primary resources to draw on the way we currently do.

Starting to take or to consume less would mean viewing creativity as fulfilling a wider function in society. Rather than interpreting it in a value-neutral way and in the service of satisfying personal wants, it would mean taking a stronger perspective on its contribution to consumption—seeing creativity in perhaps a more spiritual way, emphasizing individual and collective fulfillment. It could thus mean a different existential view of life, recognizing the spiritual and environmental costs to the market-as-god model of existence. It certainly means asking questions about what kind of world we create when the market is reified. And it means providing chances for individuals, families, communities, and nations to find purpose, meaning, and connection when the market as a source of meaning is questioned. We might ask ourselves, then, what a marketized world does for retaining contact with an ethical dimension in life.

TOWARD CREATIVITY WITH WISDOM

In this chapter I have acknowledged the potential of creativity to act as a negative rather than a purely positive force, with what appears to be a life of its own, one which encourages innovation for innovation's sake and without reference to genuine need and presents wants as if they were needs. This notion runs counter to a culture of husbanding resources more carefully, despite the fact that, as Lane (2001) suggests, making do and mending may often require creativity of us.

And aside from the capacity of creativity harnessed by the market to generate a superficial existence predicated on being entertained[4] and keeping up with fashion, there is of course the question of creativity's destructive side. We know that as well as being capable of almost infinitely constructive possibilities, the human imagination is without doubt capable of incredible destruction. To what extent is it possible to generate systems which stimulate and celebrate creativity within a profoundly humane framework, integral to which is the critical awareness of values and culture in relation to the impact of creativity? The role of educators is perhaps to encourage students to examine the possible wider effects of their own ideas and those of others, and to evaluate both choices and worth in the light of this—in other words, to nurture wisdom and an orientation toward the responsible stewardship, or trusteeship, of ideas.

What might this mean in practice? As suggested in Chapter 1, the Berlin School and Sternberg's team offer a perspective on wisdom as multiple perspectives on knowledge, understanding, and experience translated into appropriate courses of action which take account of such multiplicity (Baltes and Kunzmann 2004; Baltes and Stange 2005; Baltes and Staudinger 2000; Sternberg 2003). Stated another way, wisdom is appropriate action taking account of not only multiple forms of understanding and knowledge, but also multiple needs and perspectives. From their studies of the emotional, motivational, and social dynamics of wisdom-related knowledge, the Berlin group suggests that while wisdom can be associated with aging, it is not an automatic outcome of growing older. These researchers propose the need for a range of supportive processes and conditions

relating to personality, cognitive capacities, environment, and life hist
nurture a person's capacity to orientate toward a *common-good* pers¡
opposed to adopting a more self-centered orientation.

However, while it may not be age-related, the development of wisdom may
be increasingly difficult to achieve in today's world due to the erosion of some
values by the capitalist marketplace. Such values include the notions of service,
responsibility to others, and even possibly, as Margaret Thatcher famously commented some twenty-five years ago, the very existence of society. Studies by the
research group at Harvard University known as the GoodWork Project (working in conjunction with researchers at Stanford and Claremont Universities),
from which Howard Gardner's contributions to this book are drawn, note a
decreasing tendency to prioritize the common-good perspective among ambitious young people seeking to excel in three professions studied (journalism,
science, and acting; Fischman et al. 2004). The research team identified common
threads across all three professions in the propensity to cut corners and bend
rules, and to see oneself as operating alone rather than as part of a community
in which peers and others including respected elders provide a set of reference
points which inform their actions.

Educators, then, face an interesting dilemma because with the impetus to
nurture creativity comes a set of assumptions which imply individual engagement and success. These may in fact run counter to *wise action*, as Sternberg puts
it (2003): "Wisdom is not just about maximizing one's own or someone else's
self-interest, but about balancing various self-interests (intrapersonal) with the
interests of others (interpersonal) and of other aspects of the context in which
one lives (extrapersonal), such as one's city or country or environment or even
God. Wisdom also involves creativity, in that the wise solution to a problem
may be far from obvious" (p. 152). While wise thought must be to a degree creative, he argues, creative thinking need not involve wisdom.

And this is the heart of the problem. This chapter has argued that, although
the policy perspective on the generation of creativity in classrooms appears to be
value neutral and lacks any moral and ethical framework, it nevertheless involves
cultural blindness and is derived from a cultural context which is overmarketized
at global, local, and personal levels. The very encouragement of creativity in education therefore raises fundamental questions and dilemmas. Creativity developed without wisdom may not serve children, their families, their communities,
and the wider social and cultural groupings to which they belong—and thus may
be seen as a questionable endeavor. Therefore, it is not clear what the trustee role
might involve with regard to fostering creativity with wisdom.

ORIENTING TOWARD TRUSTEESHIP?

It could be argued that practical approaches to nurturing wisdom in the classroom, such as Sternberg's (2003) *balance theory*, may offer practical assistance in
developing teaching and learning in classrooms. The balance theory proposes
wisdom in terms of successfully balancing interests; it recognizes that "wise

solutions are often creative ones" and proposes that wisdom is related to "creatively insightful thinking" (p. 158).

Balancing perspectives may mean, of course, attempting to balance the irreconcilable. It may also mean making a more strenuous effort to detach creativity from innovation. Because innovation, while involving creativity, is commonly thought of by commentators as distinct from creativity in that its focus is on bringing the ideas to market. And yet, we perhaps mix up our everyday conceptions creativity and innovation, resulting in a muddle of values around what is produced through creative effort and how that is evaluated. Although bringing ideas into the marketplace in some ways may add to the quality of the lived experience of all beings on the planet, very often this is not the case.

Perhaps as educators, we could usefully address how we can foster learner creativity, such that the potentially damaging cultural and environmental impact of generativity—creativity—is minimized, and positive impact maximized. In other words, we could consider how we might encourage a trusteeship-orientated attitude toward using our creativity wisely.

Starting Points for Discussion Among Teachers and Others

Philosophical/Foundational

- What do we mean by a wise use of creativity?
- Can an economic perspective with development at its heart ever by reconciled with a perspective that offers alternatives to it?
- What is the relationship between culture, creativity, and wisdom?
- Who are the trustees of wise creativity?
- Creativity is a natural ability of all people. Wisdom is not. Discuss.

Pedagogical

- What role should teachers have in encouraging a wise use of creativity?
- How can teachers encourage the trusteeship of creativity?
- What kinds of pedagogical strategies can be adopted in classrooms to encourage this?
- What implicit values are conveyed by our classrooms with respect to creativity, the marketplace, and culture?

NOTES

1. Ancient Greece valued individual freedom, individuality, and objective thought, and offered opportunities to respond to contradictions and dissonance. A maritime environment meant the development of trading led to the emergence of a wealthy merchant class which highly valued and could also afford education for its own sake (not simply as a ticket to wealth and power). By contrast, in ancient China, ethnic homogeneity and centralized political control meant little opportunity to deal with difference. As Nisbett (2003) writes, "the face-to-face village life of China would have

pressed in the direction of harmony and agreed-upon norms for behaviour" (p. 32). Given both absence of opportunities to explore differences and the sanctioning of these differences, finding means to resolve disagreement became more highly valued than did working out which proposition might be "true." Thus, ancient China would have been focused on finding the "Middle Way" (Nisbett 2003, 32). Nisbett argues that the underlying ecology of each region underpinned the economic, social, and political arrangements in the two ancient cradles of today's thought habits and patterns. In China, because the ecology lent itself to agriculture, cooperative social organization evolved. In contrast, in Greece, the ecology encouraged hunting, herding, fishing, trade, and piracy—none of which, Nisbett suggests, required the same degree of cooperation.

2. These included the East London Newham 6th Form College project (Jeffery 2005), the North London community arts project, Image Conscious (Camden Arts 2003), and the national Ignite! Programme (A. Craft et al. 2004). In each case, fostering the creativity of young people who were otherwise at least somewhat excluded from the game was of critical importance. Embedding this work explicitly within the home and community cultural values of the participant learners was vital to each (Davidson, Fell, and Jeffery 2004; Fell and Davidson 2005; Jeffery 2005).

3. The Qualifications and Curriculum Authority (2005a, 2005b) names the following elements in its framework for finding and promoting creativity: asking questions, making connections, using imagination, exploring options, and critical evaluation.

4. Fromm (1955) describes what we might now call *marketization* of society as likely to lead to mass conformity, arguing that this can only lead to an inability to make self-directed choices, being increasingly conditioned in response to a marketplace. Fromm does seem to have predicted accurately a world where a great deal of emphasis is placed on the surface, on acquiring, and on being entertained, rather than on much more fundamental and substantive issues. As Crichton (1999) rather depressingly puts it, being amused seems to drive loyalty at both a superficial level (e.g., brands, television channels) and a deeper one (e.g., political parties, loyalties). Whereas in previous centuries people wanted to be educated, to be saved, and to be improved, in the twenty-first century Westerners fear boredom and seek to be amused or entertained.

REFERENCES

Baltes, P. B., and U. Kunzmann. 2004. Two faces of wisdom: Wisdom as a general theory of knowledge and judgement about excellence in mind and virtue vs. wisdom as everyday realization in people and products. *Human Development* 47:290–99.

Baltes, P. B., and A. Stange. 2005. *Research project 6. Wisdom: The integration of mind and virtue.* Center for Lifespan Psychology. http://www.mpib-berlin.mpg.de/en/forschung/lip/pdfs/research_project_6.pdf.

Baltes, P. B., and U. M. Staudinger. 2000. Wisdom: A metaheuristic (pragmatic) to orchestrate mind and virtue toward excellence. *American Psychologist* 55:122–36.

Banks, J. 1997. *Educating citizens in a multicultural society.* New York: Teachers College Press.

Bellah, R. N., R. Madsen, W. M. Sullivan, A. Swidler, and S. M. Tipton. 1985. *Habits of the heart: Individualism and commitment in American life.* New York: Harper & Row.

Berndt, T. J., P. C. Cheung, S. Lau, K.-T. Nau, and W. J. F. Lew. 1993. Perceptions of parenting in China, Taiwan and Hong Kong: Sex differences and societal differences. *Developmental Psychology* 29:156–64.

Bharati, A. 1985. The self in Hindu thought and action. In *Culture and self: Asian and Western perspectives,* ed. A. J. Marsella, G. Devos, and F. L. K. Hsu, 185–230. New York: Tavistock.

Camden Arts. 2003. *Box.* London: Camden Arts Centre.

Chao, R. K. 1993. East and west: Concepts of the self as reflected in mothers' reports of their child rearing. Unpublished manuscript, University of California, Los Angeles.

Cheung, P. C., A. J. Conger, K.-T. Hau, W. J. F. Lew, and S. Lau. 1992. Development of the Multi-Trait Personality Inventory (MTPI): Comparison among four Chinese populations. *Journal of Personality Assessment* 59:528–551.

Cheung, P. C., S. Lau, D. W. Chan, and W. Y. H. Wu. 2004. Creative potential of School children in Hong Kong: Norms of the Wallach-Kogan Creativity Tests and their implications. *Creativity Research Journal* 16(1): 69–78.

Craft, A. 2002. *Creativity in the early years: A lifewide foundation.* London: Continuum.

———. 2003. The limits to creativity in education: Dilemmas for the educator. *British Journal of Educational Studies* 51:113–27.

———. 2004. Creativity in education: Challenges. Keynote address at the Plymouth Creative Partnerships Conference, Plymouth, England.

———. 2005. *Creativity in schools: Tensions and dilemmas.* Abingdon, England: Routledge.

———. 2006. Creativity and Wisdom? *Cambridge Journal of Education* 36:336–350.

Craft, A., B. Jeffrey, and M. Joubert. 2004. *Let's get going! Evaluation of the Schools and Cultural Venues Project.* London: Calouste Gulbenkian Foundation and Arts Council England.

Craft, A., D. Miell, M. Joubert, K. Littleton, P. Murphy, E. Vass, and D. Whitelock. 2004, September. *Final report for the NESTA's Fellowship Young People Project, Ignite.* London: National Endowment for Science, Technology and the Arts.

Craft, M., ed. 1996. *Teacher education in plural societies: An international review.* London: Falmer Press.

Crichton, M. 1999. *Timeline.* Alfred A. Knopf.

Crook, C. 1994. *Computers and the collaborative experience of learning.* London: Routledge.

Csikszentmihalyi, M. 1990. The domain of creativity. In *Theories of creativity,* ed. M. A. Runco and R. S. Albert, 190–214. Thousand Oaks, CA: SAGE.

Cultural Commission. 2005, June. *Our next major enterprise: Final report of the Cultural Commission.* http://www.culturalcommission.org.uk/cultural/files/Final%20 Final%20Report%20June%202005.pdf.

Davidson, K., R. Fell, and G. Jeffery. 2004. Building pathways into creativity: What do students and teachers need? Paper presented at the Economic and Social Research Council Seminar: Creativity, the Arts and Achievement, Canterbury, England.

Department for Education and Employment. 1997. *Excellence in schools.* London: Her Majesty's Stationery Office.

Duffy, B., and J. Stillaway. 2004. Creativity: Working in partnership with parents. In *Supporting children's learning in the early years,* ed. L. Miller and J. Devereux, 99–104. London: David Fulton.

Fell, R., and K. Davidson. 2004. Successful vocational learning for intermediate performing arts students: Key findings from the *Pathways into Creativity* research project. Paper presented at the British Educational Research Association Creativity in Education Symposium: Learners' Perspectives on Creativity, Manchester, England.

Fischman, W., B. Solomon, D. Greenspan, and H. Gardner. 2004. *Making good: How young people cope with moral dilemmas at work.* Cambridge, MA: Harvard University Press.

Florida, R. 2002. *The rise of the creative class: And how it's transforming work, leisure, community, and everyday life.* New York: Basic Books.

———. 2006. The future of the American workforce in the global creative economy. *Cato Unbound,* June 4. http://www.cato-unbound.org/2006/06/04/richard-florida/the-future-of-the-american-workforce-in-the-global-creative-economy.

Fromm, E. 1955. *The sane society.* London: Routledge and Kegan Paul.

Gardner, H. 2004. *Changing minds: The art and science of changing our own and other people's minds.* Cambridge, MA: Harvard Business School Press.

Hanel, P. 2003. *Note de Recherche: Impact of innovation motivated by environmental concerns and government regulations on firm performance: A study of survey data.* Quebec, Montreal: Centre Intrauniversitaire de Recherche sur la Science et la Technologie. http://www.cirst.uqam.ca/Portals/0/docs/note_rech/2003_08.pdf.

Harland, J., K. Kinder, P. Lord, A. Stott, I. Schagen, J. Haynes, L. Cusworth, R. White, and R. Paola. 2000. *Arts education in secondary schools: Effects and effectiveness.* Slough, England: National Foundation for Educational Research.

Jeffery, G., ed. 2005. *The creative college: Building a successful learning culture in the arts.* London: Trentham Books.

Kluckhohn, F. R., and F. L. Strodtbeck. 1961. *Variations in value orientation.* Westport, CT: Greenwood.

Lane, J. 2001. *Timeless simplicity: Creative living in a consumer society.* Dartington, England: Green Books.

Lau, S., A. Hui, and G. Y. C. Ng. 2004. *Creativity: When east meets west.* Singapore: World Scientific.

Lim, H. A. 2004. Creativity, culture, and entrepreneurialship. *Symbiosis* February:4–10.

Lubart, T. I. 1999. Creativity across cultures. In *Handbook of creativity,* ed. R. J. Sternberg, 339–50. Cambridge, UK: Cambridge University Press.

Maduro, R. 1976. Artistic creativity in a Brahmin painter community. Research Monograph 14, Center for South and Southeast Asia Studies, University of California.

Malangi, S. 2004. The curse of the creative class. *The Wall Street Journal,* January 19. http://www.opinionjournal.com/extra/?id=110004573.

Markus, H. R., and S. Kitayama. 1991. Culture and the self: Implications for cognition, emotion and motivation. *Psychological Review* 98:224–53.

———. 1994. A collective fear of the collective: Implications for selves and theories of selves. *Personality and Social Psychology Bulletin* 20:568–79.

Martin, D. S., A. Craft, and H. Tillema. 2002. Developing critical and creative thinking strategies in primary school pupils: An inter-cultural study of teachers' learning. *Journal of In-Service Education* 28:115–34.

Martin, D. S., A. Craft, and Z. N. Zhang. 2001. The impact of cognitive strategy instruction on deaf learners: An international comparative study. *American Annals of the Deaf* 146:366–78.

Ministry of Education (Singapore). 2004. *The desired outcomes of education.* http://www1.moe.edu.sg/desired.htm.

Nagel, S. 2000. Creativity and policy studies. *The Innovation Journal* 5(3). http://www.innovation.cc/discussion-papers/creativity-policy-studies.htm.

National Advisory Committee on Creative and Cultural Education. 1999. *All our futures: Creativity, culture and education.* London: Department for Education and Employment.

Ng, A. K. 2001. *Why Asians are less creative than Westerners.* Singapore: Prentice Hall.

———. 2002. The development of a new scale to measure teachers' attitudes toward students (TATS). *Educational Research Journal* 17:63–78.

———. 2003. A cultural model of creative and conforming behaviour. *Creativity Research Journal* 15:223–33.

Ng, A. K., and I. Smith. 2004a. The paradox of promoting creativity in the Asian class-room: An empirical investigation. *Genetic, Social, and General Psychology Monographs* 130:307–30.

———. 2004b. Why is there a paradox in promoting creativity in the Asian classroom? In *Creativity: When east meets west*, ed. L. Sing, A. Hui, and G. Ng, 87–112. Singapore: World Scientific.

Nisbett, R. E. 2003. *The geography of thought*. New York: Free Press.

Parkes, J., and A. Califano. 2004. *Home: An educational resource pack*. London: NewVIc New Media. http://www.newvic-creative.org.uk.

Qualifications and Curriculum Authority. 2005a. About QCA's creativity project. http://www.ncaction.org.uk/creativity/about.htm.

Qualifications and Curriculum Authority. 2005b. *Creativity: Find it, promote it*. London: Qualifications and Curriculum Authority.

Raina, M. K. 2004. I shall be many: The garland-making perspective on creativity and cultural diversity. In *Creativity and cultural diversity*, ed. M. Fryer, 25–44. Leeds, England: Creativity Centre Educational Trust.

Richardson, M. 2001. Singapore's reforms seek creative edge. *International Herald Tribune*, October 15. http://www.iht.com/articles/2001/10/15/rsinga_ed3_.php.

Roberts, P. 2006. *Nurturing creativity in young people: A report to government to inform future policy*. London: Department for Culture, Media and Sport.

Scottish Executive. 2004. *Cultural policy statement*. http://www.scotland.gov.uk/cultural commission/cultural/files/Cultural%20Policy%20Statement.pdf.

Secretary's Commission on Achieving Necessary Skills. 1991. *What work requires of schools: A SCANS report for America 2000*. Washington, DC: U.S. Department of Labor.

Seltzer, K., and T. Bentley. 1999. *The creative age: Knowledge and skills for the new economy*. London: Demos.

Sen, R. S., and N. Sharma. 2004. Teachers' conceptions of creativity and its nurture in children: An Indian perspective. In *Creativity and cultural diversity*, ed. M. Fryer, 153–70. Leeds, England: Creativity Centre Educational Trust.

Smith, P. B., and M. J. Bond. 1993. *Social psychology across cultures: Analysis and perspectives*. Hertfordshire, England: Harvester Wheatsheaf.

Spindler, G. D., and L. Spindler. 1983. Anthropologists view American culture. *Annual Review of Anthropology* 12:49–78.

Sternberg, R. J. 2003. *Wisdom, intelligence, and creativity synthesized*. Cambridge, UK: Cambridge University Press.

Sternberg, R. J., and T. I. Lubart. 1995. An investment perspective on creative insight. In *The nature of insight*, ed. R. J. Sternberg and J. E. Davidson, 535–58. Cambridge, MA: MIT Press.

Vass, E. 2004a. Developing creative writing through peer collaboration. Paper presented at the British Educational Research Association Conference, Manchester, England.

Vass, E. 2004b. Understanding collaborative creativity: An observational study of young children's classroom-based joint creative writing. In *Collaborative creativity*, ed. D. Miell and K. Littleton, 79–95. London: Free Association Press.

Woods, P. 2002. Teaching and learning in the new millennium. In *Developing teachers and teaching practice: International research perspectives*, ed. C. Sugrue and D. Day, 73–91. London: RoutledgeFalmer.

Zhang, N., L. Huang, D. S. Martin, A. Craft, and G. U. Lin. 2004. The impact of cognitive strategy instruction on deaf learners: An international comparative study. *Psychological Science* 27:193–97.

3

Wisdom

Advanced Creativity?

Guy Claxton

In a modern university if you ask for knowledge they will provide it in almost any form—though if you ask for out-of-fashion things they may say, like people in shops, "Sorry, there's no call for it." But if you ask for Wisdom—God save us all! What a show of modesty, what disclaimers from the men and women from whose eyes shine forth intelligence like a lighthouse. Intelligence, yes, but of wisdom not so much as the gleam of a single candle.

—Robertson Davies, *The Rebel Angels* (1981, 38)

It would be very unwise to try to legislate for an agreed or a canonical meaning of such an ambiguous and contested term as *wisdom*, so I shall not try. All I can do in this short chapter is to

- offer some guidelines for its exploration that I think might be productive;
- attempt to illustrate one legitimate—and I think core—sense of wisdom through three short narratives;
- extract from those some preliminary ideas about how wise action might be conceptualized in cognitive neuroscientific terms;
- offer some speculations about how, on this analysis, the propensity for wise action might possibly be cultivated through education.

The main point to emerge will be the suggestion that wisdom inheres not so much in a quality of thinking or cognition, but in the nature of the underlying *motivational vector* that drives cognition.

GUIDELINES FOR EXPLORATION

I think it is more productive to talk about wisdom as being an attribute of real, specific actions in real, lived situations than to try to define an abstract "quality" that people do or don't possess. This immediately narrows the field of inquiry in ways that some people might find too prescriptive, but that helps me focus on the practical, real-life aspect of wisdom that I think is the most important. The classical Greeks distinguished three types of wisdom: sophia, episteme, and phronesis. *Sophia* referred to the kind of insight that might arise as the result of specialized philosophical, contemplative, or spiritual practice. *Episteme* was the kind of empirical scientific knowledge given to those who made a detailed study of the way things worked. And *phronesis* was the quality possessed by "the statesman and lawgiver . . . that locates the prudent course of action and resists the urging of the passions and the deceptions of the senses" (Robinson 1990, 14).

The sense that I want to explore is closest to the latter, though I shall stretch the notion of phronesis to include even more localized and situated forms of wise action. I suspect that we are far better off talking, in a less grandiose fashion, about examples of "acting wisely," whereby wisdom is an adverbial quality that applies to specific actions in specific situations. As with other abstract nouns such as creativity or intelligence, the common compulsion to reify these adverbial qualities, turning them into hypothetical entities, sends people off on all kinds of unprofitable wild goose chases. This is due in no small part to the fact that reification suggests that the elusive quality under discussion is both separable from other cognate notions and homogeneous, rather than being an umbrella term that conceals a host of more specific attributes and abilities that overlap extensively with other concepts. It may be more profitable to look at the ways in which wisdom and creativity are both similar and distinct than to try to treat each *sui generis.*

I also think it is productive to leave open the question of the extent to which wise action or wise judgment has to draw upon deliberate, systematic, conscious, and even intellectual forms of thought. In the stories I cite below, it is moot as to how much conscious cogitation preceded the wise action, and indeed there are many examples of acting wisely in which the luxury of deliberation is precluded, for example, by the urgency of the situation. Wise action may manifest in a highly intuitive and spontaneous way, just as much as—or perhaps even more than—it requires explicit rationality. *Wise action,* at least as I use the term, often has a light and contingent quality that ponderous rationality—the methodical weighing up of pros and cons, and so on—often lacks.

As my selection of the stories highlighted in this chapter makes clear, I think wisdom manifests prototypically in the context of complicated human affairs.

As a rule, acting wisely means interacting with other people and their predicaments in such a way that multiple desiderata, often in the form of apparent conflicts and impasses, are satisfied, often in innovative and surprising ways. The timing of such interventions may well be at least as important as their nature. I suspect that acting wisely is underpinned more by an intuitive moral clarity than by analytical precision. The miscarriages of justice that are the regular outcomes of lengthy, clever, analytical argumentation are testament enough to the loose relationship between reason and wisdom. Politicians regularly make decisions that seem very far from wise.

I suggest that we use *wise* as an adjective to describe particular people only in the sense that they have arguably, over time, acted wisely more frequently or more reliably than most of their fellows. Calling someone wise is, at most, a prediction which is based on such observations or testimony that, faced with a morally or psychologically complicated situation in the future, that person's response stands a higher-than-average chance of being wise. Such a definition of *wise persons* does not, of course, say anything about their age, gender, or experience. The archetypal icons of wisdom, in Western society at least, tend to be male, bearded, and old—Gandalf, Obi-wan Kenobi, God—though we must remember that wisdom sometimes also arrives out of the mouths of babes and sucklings. However, whether there is indeed a correlation between the frequency of wise action and such characteristics is ultimately an empirical question.

I think that acting wisely can only be understood in light of a detailed appreciation of the full circumstances in which the act occurs, including both the explicit and the unstated hopes, fears, and expectations of all participants. If the actors do not have such an appreciation, their acts are very unlikely to be wise, and if the observers do not have such an appreciation, their judgments as to whether the act was wise are unlikely to be reliable. However—and here there is inevitable ground for disagreement—the attribution of wisdom to an action or a judgment reflects the values and perspectives of the attributor, and thus I doubt, as I said above, that there will ever be a consensus about any particular putative example. In my experience people tend to agree that the stories in the boxes describe plausible instances of wise action, but the judgment is by no means universal. It is always possible to attribute egocentric or even Machiavellian motives to the actors in such exemplary tales, and such attributions cannot ultimately be disputed. So I invite you, at least for the purposes of discussion, to give these stories and their protagonists the benefit of the doubt, but I cannot insist that you do so.

THE VALUE OF STUDYING WISDOM

It is helpful to bear in mind that the intellectual investigation of wisdom, whether empirical or conceptual, bears only the most tangential relationship to the cultivation of the ability to act wisely. These are the key educational questions: What conditions enable or encourage people to act more wisely? What conditions, over time, expand people's capacity and disposition to act wisely (regardless of whether the momentary conditions are conducive)? From this practical, educational point of view, conceptual discussions about the nature of wisdom are necessary only insofar as they facilitate exploration of the key questions. Some rough distinctions and working definitions may be needed to get you going; endless disputation about what is or is not a canonical case of wisdom is not, in itself, wise.

I find it salutary to bear in mind that studying wisdom courts the same kind of absurdity as studying humor or sexuality. Such study is an activity of interest to an intellectual minority that the vast majority of people find simply beside the point. For them, the proof of the pudding of humor, sexuality, or wisdom is in the eating of the momentary, lived experience. Jokes are funny when they are constructed and timed in such a way that they induce an abrupt, experiential shift of perception, accompanied by an explosion of bodily energy. Wise actions often have the same kind of immediacy and impact. Learned, articulate, scholarly people are no more conspicuously wise than anybody else, and there are those who would argue that—Socrates notwithstanding—they are likely to be less so.

It would, of course, be very easy to construct a syllabus that explored the concept of wisdom. There would be modules on the history of the idea, the etymology of the word, philosophical problems in the definition, anthropological studies of the various views of wisdom in different cultures, famous candidates for the title of "wise persons," and so on. But none of this need have any impact on the cultivation of the ability to act wisely in any of the students in such a course. It is an entirely empirical matter as to whether any such study (and which, if any, topics), taught through what sort of pedagogy, would have any effect on the growth of wise ability, rather than on mere knowledgeability.

Consider the following stories:

Story 1: The Unwise Hero

Back in the 1970s, American aikido student Terry Dobson was in Tokyo, putting in eight hours of intensive training a day. He was skilled and he was tough, but he hadn't yet grasped the central idea that aikido was, as his teacher put it, about resolving conflict, not starting it. One ordinary afternoon, on his way to training, the peace of the subway train was shattered by the arrival of a large, dirty, drunk Japanese laborer, swearing and lashing out at whoever got in his way—some old folks and a young mother and her baby. Dobson thought his moment had come, so he stood up, prepared to test his skill in real combat—with an impeccable moral rationale. "If I don't do something, people are going to get hurt," he said to himself.

Just as the drunk was gathering himself to rush Dobson, someone yelled "Hey!" and they both stopped in their tracks and looked down in surprise at a little old Japanese man sitting between them. Completely ignoring the American, he beamed up at the laborer and asked him what he had been drinking. "Sake," said the man, "and it's none of your goddamn business." Dobson hovered, ready to drop him if things got ugly.

"Oh that's wonderful," said the old man. "I love sake, too. Every night me and my wife—she's 76 you know—we warm up a little bottle of sake and take it out into the garden. We sit on our old bench and watch the sun go down, and we look to see how our persimmon tree is doing. My great-grandfather planted that tree, and we worry about whether it will recover from those ice storms we had a while back. . . ."

As the old man prattled on, the drunk's face began to relax and his fists to unclench. "Yeah," he said softly. "I love persimmons, too."

"And I'm sure you have a lovely wife too," said the old man.

"No," replied the laborer. "My wife died." He hung his head and began to sob. "I haven't got a wife. I haven't got a job. I've lost my home. You've no idea how ashamed I feel." A spasm of despair rippled through his body.

"My, my," said the old man gently. "That does sound terrible. Come over here and tell me about it."

Dobson hung his head in shame, too. As he puts it, "Standing there in my well-scrubbed youthful innocence, my make-this-world-safe-for-democracy righteousness, I suddenly felt dirtier than he was." As Dobson left the train at his stop, he looked back and saw the laborer sprawled on the seat, his head in the old man's lap. The old man was softly stroking the filthy, matted hair. A very chastened Dobson sat on a bench. "What I had wanted to do with muscle had been accomplished with kind words. I had just seen aikido in action, and the essence of it was love."

Adapted from *Soul Food*, edited by Jack Kornfield and Christina Feldman. Harper San Francisco, 1996.

Story 2: More Antagonism Reframed

Eighty people are sitting in the big vestibule at Leiston Hall in Suffolk, home to Summerhill School. They are gathered for the weekly *moot*, the school's governing body. The youngest is 4 years old, and the oldest over 60. Everyone from the newest arrival to the founder of the school, A. S. Neill, has an equal voice and a single vote. Decisions about almost every aspect of school life are made democratically in this forum.

On this occasion, a group of teenage girls is complaining that they are being harassed by a group of boys, who insist on flicking them with wet towels whenever they get the opportunity. The moot is discussing what punishment the boys deserve. Neil and his wife Eva both sit there patiently with their hands up, waiting to be called on by the 10-year-old who is chairing the meeting. Eva's turn comes first. "Just think how dull your lives would be if you *didn't* have these boys to harass you," she says, and everyone laughs.

A little later it is Neill's turn. In his soft Scottish burr, he simply says, deadpan, "I don't think the meeting has any right to interfere in a love affair." Again everyone laughs. The girl who has been complaining most vociferously looks at the ringleader of the boys and blushes. He looks away with a silly smile on his face. The meeting decides to give the boys a stiff warning, and business moves on.

Story 3: A Question of Wisdom

There's a nun who will never give you advice, but only a question. I was told her questions could be very helpful, so I sought her out.

"I am a parish priest," I said. "I'm here on retreat. Could you give me a question?"

"Ah, yes," she answered. "My question is, 'What do they need?'"

To tell the truth, I came away disappointed. I spent a few hours with the question, writing out answers, but finally I went back to her.

"Excuse me," I said. "Perhaps I didn't make myself clear. Your question has been helpful, but I wasn't so much interested in thinking about my congregation during this retreat. Rather I wanted to think seriously about my own spiritual life. Could you give me a question that will help?"

"Ah, I see," she said. "Then my question for you is, 'What do they *really* need?'"

Adapted from *Soul Food*, edited by Jack Kornfield and Christina Feldman. Harper San Francisco, 1996.

WHEN DOES ACTING WISELY MATTER?

In the boxes are three cases that might enable us to reflect on what it is to act wisely and on how easy or difficult it is to make that judgment in particular cases. I have also chosen them to suggest the kinds of situation in which wisdom, at least of a particular kind, seems to me to be most relevant. We do not normally talk about making the tea or feeding the cat wisely, nor is the word commonly applied to practical problem solving (fixing the plumbing) or to matters of aesthetic taste (redecorating the spare room). We do make wise or unwise investments and wise or unwise career decisions, but what George Kelly (1955) called the *focus of convenience* of the concept of wisdom seems to be complicated human, and particularly interpersonal, affairs. The old man on the Tokyo subway, the wily old nun, and A. S. Neill, in their different ways, seem to me to be acting wisely in the face of situations of apparent conflict, confusion, or entrenchment. Both the old man and Neill act in a way that takes the heat out of the situation, and the nun gently guides the priest toward a deeper appreciation of his own dilemma. All three also act in a way that subtly reframes the perception of the parties involved in a manner that seems to offer new opportunities for productive progress and/or resolution—possibilities that had not been apparent from their previous perspectives.

WHAT IS IT TO ACT WISELY?

Can we also extract from these examples some tentative indications of what it is to act wisely? Let me offer for discussion some possible features of wise action.

First, wise action seems to have an essentially moral quality that distinguishes it from other actions we might call *cunning, smart, expedient,* or merely *intelligent.* Acting for short-term personal gain, especially if one's own long-term goals or others' concerns and well-being are neglected or jeopardized in the process, would not be called wise. Wisdom takes account of the greater good and of one's own higher, deeper, or more lasting values. Terry Dobson describes the old man as operating on the basis of a kind of selfless love. Indeed, in Buddhism, compassion is seen as the inseparable companion of wisdom.

Thus, second, acting wisely seems to require a degree of disinterestedness on the part of the actor which enables him or her to stand back from the fray and to see the predicament more objectively and in more of its all-round complexity. Complementary perspectives that perhaps, on the face of it, seem irreconcilable can be entertained simultaneously and in such a way that a more all-encompassing metaperspective may emerge. Interestingly, A. S. Neill, passionate though he was about his students and his work, described himself as having a quality of benign indifference in his dealings with young people. One could say that he cared deeply about them but did not need anything from them or require them to be anything in particular. Of course, people deceive themselves about their degree of disinterest all the time, and it is always possible to project a cynical view onto any such examples.

So wise actors appear not to muddy the situation by bringing much in the way of their own ego-based hopes, fears, and expectations with them. Just as a counselor or mediator is able to see a conflict more clearly than can the warring combatants, so the wise actor does not distort the situation by being partial, impatient, or eager to demonstrate his or her own effectiveness (or indeed wisdom). The young American has something to prove, and his desire to be a hero and to have a legitimate excuse to try out his aikido skills "for real" lead him to inflame the situation, even as he tries to deal with it. The old man's freedom of maneuver is greater. He does not seem to be afraid of the drunk, so is not acting out of self-protection. He does not seem to be using the incident to prove anything to himself or others. And his unself-consciousness allows him to babble on in an inconsequential way that looks, to begin with, quite irrelevant and self-indulgent, yet reveals itself to be a very astute and effective way of calming the angry laborer and opening up more productive ways to proceed. (Whether he was conscious of the need to teach the young American a lesson, as well as to enable the drunk to feel inward rather than act out, we do not know. Perhaps the old man was a plain-clothes Zen master, a sort of spiritual guardian angel protecting subway passengers as much from self-important foreigners as from indigenous hooligans.)

Implicit here, third, is the ability of the wise actor not only to get out of the way, but also to empathize—to put him- or herself in other people's shoes and see the world as they see it, without becoming captured by the hurts or desires that, to those others, shine so blindingly bright. The old man is able to see through the laborer's anger to the distress below and, by skillfully indicating his recognition of it, allows it to surface. Neill was able to help his adolescent students recognize themselves more clearly and thus to move beyond the level of antagonism in which they had become temporarily stuck. It is said of Gandhi that, when he was facing a difficult decision, he would look at it first through Hindu eyes, then from an Islamic perspective, and finally from the point of view of the British—and only when he had coactivated, as it were, all three complementary stances did he feel able to formulate what might be a wise course of action.

In the somewhat more oblique story of the nun and the priest (and, as ever, giving the nun the benefit of the doubt), the nun's re-emphasizing of her original question invites the stressed priest to challenge his assumption that his own well-being is being drained, rather than fed, by his ministry. Ultimately, do his own real needs compete for attention with those of his flock—as he seems to assume—or is it possible that his own deepest nurturance and fulfillment comes through the exercising of his compassion? One is reminded of Rabindranath Tagore's small poem: "I slept and dreamed that life was joy. I woke, and found that life was service. I meditated, and behold! I found that service was joy."[1]

PUTATIVE DISPOSITIONS FOR WISDOM

Such a line of thought leads to a kind of short list of personal traits or dispositions that, taken together, might provide the psychological platform from which wise actions can be launched. I prefer to think of *dispositions* rather than *skills* because wise actions will not be produced spontaneously unless a person is disposed toward them, that is, inclined to see appropriate occasions and to act on them. To be wise, I think you have to be ready and willing, as well as able.

What might some of these putative dispositions for wisdom be? It follows from the discussion above that one has to be interested and engaged in human affairs. At the same time, one has to be disinterested—ready, willing, and able to see situations in a way that is unclouded by one's own motivational agendas. I could argue that one has to be more generally perceptive, disposed to take account of the unique constellation of patterns, considerations, and details that are actually present, rather than to look through perceptual filters that neaten or distort things. And this may well require the capacity to tolerate things that do not "fit" with normal expectations—ambiguities, contradictions, and apparently irresolvable uncertainties. John Keats (1899) called this disposition *negative capability*: "being in uncertainties, mysteries, doubts, without any irritable reaching after fact and reason" (p. 277).

Part of the complexity that the wise person typically has to deal with is the fact that different protagonists hold different value systems and different points of view, so wisdom would seem to require a capacity for empathy: being able to put oneself in the shoes of several others simultaneously—and yet to look beyond, for the time being, as much as possible, one's own values and perspectives. Allied to this might be the ability to take time—when there is time—and to patiently allow situations to reveal themselves in all their complexity, before attempting to formulate action. Yet at the same time, one needs to be able to act decisively when the moment is judged to be right, and often to be willing to act on the basis of intuition, before a defensive portfolio of explicit justifications has been prepared. The fact that wise interventions are often simultaneously subtle, surprising, and incisive suggests the wise actor might need to be open to and trusting of such intuitive promptings.

To act wisely might well take a degree of courage: daring to intervene in situations that are emotionally fraught or downright dangerous, rather than hanging back or merely theorizing or pontificating from a position of personal safety, and to do so in ways that others might find strange. This might, in turn, require a degree of indifference to public opinion—reflecting a secure sense of self, perhaps—and a commitment to doing what feels right rather than what looks good.

As I say, such a list of *protosagacious dispositions*—traits that incline a person toward wise action—has a degree of face validity, in terms of the approach to wisdom that I have adopted, but no more than that. It would require an extensive research project to establish the empirical robustness of such suggestions. Such an approach to wisdom may well bear fruit in the future.

WISDOM: ADVANCED CREATIVITY?

It is no coincidence that many of the traits that may be associated with wisdom have also been connected with creativity. Tolerance for complexity and uncertainty, perspective taking, assumption questioning, negative capability, independence of mind, and courage have all been proposed as characteristics of the *creative mind* (see Sternberg 1999).

But while wise actions are often creative, creativity is not always wise. Wisdom and creativity differ in two important respects: morality and humanity. As I use the term, *wisdom* has a necessarily moral quality. It functions for the greater good, rather than for the personal advantage or ego satisfaction of the wise actor. *Creativity*, on the other hand, is associated with the production of something novel and valued, or the innovative solution of a tricky problem, regardless of the moral dimension of the problem or the ego motivation of the creator. Designing new weapons of mass destruction or ingenious forms of torture could very well be called creative, within the normal meaning of the word; but no one would call them wise, I think. Creativity is judged primarily by pragmatic, aesthetic, or cognitive standards, not by moral ones. Likewise, creativity is not especially associated with the resolution of complex human or emotional predicaments. It might as well concern the design of a new gizmo or a film script. Wisdom, I think, is centrally concerned with the skillful conduct of human affairs and the resolution of complex human predicaments. So I would argue that the cognitive aspect of wisdom is very similar to the cognitive aspect of creativity. But wisdom has moral, motivational, and social aspects with which creativity does not necessarily concern itself.

IS THE BRAIN NATURALLY
WISE AND COMPASSIONATE?

> *Perowne's reduced defence feels very much the nub of* Saturday: *no single course of action, including taking no action, is without ramifying consequence, potential casualty or guilt.*

> —James Urquhart (2005, ¶ 8) on Ian McEwan's *Saturday*

In a nutshell, this kind of wise action seems to emerge in the absence of an all-too-familiar backdrop of complex, anxious self-regard and self-concern. In its place comes a kind of clear, uninhibited moral clarity that leads to action which is often surprising or creative and achieves a degree of reconciliation, insight, and a lightening of mood—in others as well, perhaps, as in oneself. It would be absurd to try to offer a neural account of wise action; theoretical fools rush in where angels wisely fear to tread. But a brief Just So Story might serve to illustrate the lines along which a more sophisticated train of neural thought might eventually run.

Human beings are social animals, and like all such, their portfolio of survival strategies comprises both selfish and altruistic actions. For such animals, recurrent conflicts are bound to occur. Do I attend to my own blood-sugar levels by taking the last banana, or do I service the *web of social reciprocity*, as Bruner (1966) called it, by offering the banana to the alpha male or to the female with whom I hope to mate? Both are potentially intelligent actions in terms of my own well-being, but I cannot do both. I have to choose, and if I am to choose wisely, my brain has to make the most accurate calculation it can of all possible costs and benefits, both short- and long-term. And the parameters of this computation are personal and contingent. There is no rule book for wise action. The wise decision about the banana may be very different for a healthy newcomer to a social group than for a well-esteemed but diabetic old-timer.

One of the primary functions of the brain is to seek optimal resolution of such motivational conflicts and complexities. "What to do for the best?" is its perpetual problem, and the subjectively optimal solution is always relative to the momentary configuration of active concerns, both sociable and selfish: physical needs, desires and values, ongoing goals and interests, perceived threats and risks. The more complex this motivational force field, the harder it is to discover a course of action that satisfies every possible concern. Integrating all desires into a single motivational vector that points the way to optimal action may even, on occasion, turn out to be impossible—in which case action may be suspended completely, paralyzed in a paroxysm of self-consciousness (as in the case of McEwan's protagonist, neurosurgeon Henry Perowne). Such paralysis is usually, of course, a dysfunctional response. Animals seem only to freeze when faced with an overwhelming threat. Politicians may do so when asked a tricky question from which they can see no safe way out (though usually they have trained themselves to cover the panic quickly with a veneer of anodyne blather).[2]

One of the brain's methods of simplifying the motivational force field to the point where it becomes tractable is to subtract some of the most inconvenient motives from the mix; it can do that by muting or inhibiting them. Indecision can be resolved, in other words, by effectively denying the genuine motivational complexity of the situation. For example, in the classic Good Samaritan experiment, in which participants find themselves near a person in apparent distress, people tend to resolve any motivational discomfort—"I'd like to help, but it would make me late for the meeting"—by denying or downgrading their natural concern for a distressed human being. "One of these other people will be sure to help" or "She's probably just drunk, or acting the fool," they say to themselves. Through denial or rationalization of this kind, the awkward concern is removed from the functional motivational tangle that the brain is trying to resolve.

But while this maneuver may ease the momentary problem of what to do next, such suppression seems only to disconnect, rather than deactivate, the awkward concern, and it therefore goes unrequited. A small, unattended deposit of guilt may accrue and be carried forward, consciously or unconsciously, into the next computation. Unwise action, in this simple picture, reflects an intuitive misjudgment of one's true long-term interests through over- or underestimating the motivational value of some subset of concerns. We may care for others too much, to the detriment of our own health. We may act selfishly and fail to recognize the long-term damage this does to trust and goodwill. We may respond only to the most immediate concerns and neglect to activate those that are more long-term. We may lose sight of what truly matters to us most. In all these cases, acting unwisely is not the same as acting unintelligently. What matters when it comes to wisdom, I suggest, is not the astuteness of cognition per se, but the nature of the underlying motivational vector that is driving cognition.

Another way in which the motivational force field can be simplified is if other people's motivational worlds are neglected. Without imagination or empathy, self-interest can be placed in the foreground without being subverted or confused by taking into account other people's legitimate agendas or the likely effect our actions will have on them. There is a possible analogy here with the two complementary visual systems which neuroscientists now distinguish: the egocentric and the allocentric systems (Gray 2004). The *egocentric* system places the self at the center of the world, and external objects are located at the ends of rays of possible interaction that radiate from the self as the origin. *Allocentric* space, on the other hand, "utilises a map in which the relationships between locations of objects can be specified independently of the location of the observing subject, who himself has a location on the same map" (Gray 2004, 97). If we replace these literal representations of physical space with the idea of motivational spaces, then egocentric space puts myself and my concerns squarely at the middle of all that goes on. Allocentric motivational space allows for a decentering and a kind of relativism in which other people's concerns have equal status, and my own personal portfolio of desires does not constitute the reference point against which all else is measured. Wise action, I suggest, can be seen as originating from such an allocentric viewpoint, in which a long-term appreciation of the good of all supplants the perspective of narrow, egocentric self-interest.

CAN WISDOM BE CULTIVATED?

Does this preliminary analysis of wisdom give us any handle on whether it may be cultivated, and if so, how? First, we might observe that it throws some light on the question of whether wisdom is associated with aging and the elderly.

The empirical evidence is inconclusive, but my approach implies that there may at best be only a loose correlation between wisdom and age, mediated by the factors outlined above. The approach suggests some hypotheses that may be worthy of further investigation. For example, if empathy is a component disposition of wisdom, then age-related variations in empathy will affect the ability to act wisely. (It is alleged that older people can become less able to bear the cognitive load that is required to hold someone else's perspective in mind, which would militate *against* a positive correlation between age and wisdom.)

On the other hand, it is also alleged that older people may lose many of the self-referenced motivations that once seemed so important, thus clearing the space for greater motivational clarity. In addition, wise intuitions may only emerge from a rich, experiential database of complex, value-ridden situations as well as both personal and vicarious observations of more or less successful ways of resolving them. Such a database probably takes a good many years to accumulate. Further, wise options may only become apparent in these memories to someone who has developed the ability to inhabit an allocentric rather than an exclusively egocentric motivational frame of reference—and here again, time is on the side of the older person.

Which of these factors predominate and how they interweave are ultimately matters for empirical investigation. I think it is clear, however, that whether people tend to get wiser as they get older may well depend on the developmental trajectories of a range of other factors, especially the protosagacious dispositions which I reviewed earlier. The question is: what factors influence whether people get more or less empathic, patient, or capable of disinterest, for example, as they age? But can we now say anything new about how these trajectories are influenced—hopefully for the good—through education? One implication could be that, as with creativity, teachers are better advised to think of cultivating *component dispositions* and *precursors,* rather than grandly aiming at teaching the concept of wisdom itself.

The disposition toward empathy could be one such candidate. Can it be cultivated? Some teachers think so. In a social studies lesson in a comprehensive school in Cardiff, Wales, the class of 11-year-olds thinks about the causes of the Iraq War. They wear spectacles cut out of blue cardboard. These are their *empathy specs,* which magically enable them to look at events through different people's eyes. What do things look like to George Bush? To Tony Blair? To the sister of a soldier? To a widow in Fallujah? To the chief executive of BP? Of course, no magical advantage is conferred by wearing the specs; all that happens is that empathy is highlighted as a valuable ability, and by turning it into an entertaining activity, the ability is stretched and the disposition strengthened. That, at least, is the intention—and the results of this small pedagogical experiment suggest that it can be successful (see Claxton 1999, 2002).

Cultivating motivational clarity in young people would probably be a very difficult task. Adolescence is a time in which motivational portfolios are becoming, for most young people, significantly more complex and conflictual. The demands of school, family, and friends continually collide, and a variety of motivational stances are tried on for size. At one moment, a blank look or a facial blemish can matter terribly; at another, it can seem as if it is overridingly cool to care about nothing at all. Perhaps the most that teachers can hope to do is offer young people models of people who manifest a degree of motivational clarity. These could be the heroes and heroines of history, contemporary figures whose heroic (or otherwise) actions are up for discussion, and even, perhaps, teachers' own conduct. It may be that the casual sowing of such seeds is as much as can be done. But the idea that wisdom is a hybrid quality that emerges from the deployment of a range of less exotic—and therefore perhaps more teachable—dispositions might give some clues as to how to cultivate it more effectively.

It could be that the ability to adopt a kind, wise, and disinterested perspective itself grows out of the development of empathy. As one masters the ability to look at the world through the eyes of an increasing range of other people, it becomes possible to partial out the particulars of individuals' motivational perspectives and approximate more and more closely to the view from "nowhere." One is able to adopt the perspective of the other—but of no particular other. And from that position of relative objectivity, one can learn to look back at oneself and see one's own motivational perspective, as it were, from the outside. This is the knack that is cultivated, allegedly, by the Buddhist meditative practice of *mindfulness* (see Claxton 2006) or by the practice of *bracketing* advocated by phenomenologists such as Husserl (see Varela, Thompson, and Rosch 1992).

CONCLUSION

Many approaches can be taken to investigate the relationship between wisdom and creativity. In this chapter, I have mapped out an approach that relies on the identification of the putative array of personal dispositions that might underpin both wisdom and creativity. I have argued that such an approach reveals a good deal of overlap between these dispositional sets, but that there are two areas that distinguish wisdom from creativity. The first is wisdom's close concern with the domain of complex and seemingly intractable human affairs. The second is the necessity for an act to be wise, for the actor to be able to achieve a degree of motivational clarity in which his or her ego needs and perspectives are temporarily subordinated to a broader, more *value-fair* form of perception. From the perspective of such a fair witness, the actor is able to see his or her own set of beliefs and motives as one among many—all with an equivalent validity—rather than, as is more normally the case, imbuing (and therefore skewing) his or her own perception with largely unacknowledged sets of biases, beliefs, and preferences.

It seems that some of the dispositions that make up a mind that is *sagacity prone* are capable of being deliberately nurtured in the context of education. The development of others, however—such as the capacity for the kind of objectivity just described—may well only be possible, or more appropriate, later in the life span.

ACKNOWLEDGMENT

I am grateful to Jonathan Rowson for his substantial and insightful comments on an earlier draft of this paper.

NOTES

1. Like all such stories, this one can be read on many levels. Jonathan Rowson reminded me that the force of "really" could also be to draw the priest's attention to the universality of the deepest human needs—and thus to the possibility that, by answering the nun's question, he will also have answered his own. Indeed, part of the nun's wisdom lies in her appreciation that it may be easier to arrive at this realization if we begin by considering others' concerns. If we start with ours, all kinds of more superficial, ego-related concerns can cloud our vision and obscure the enquiry.

2. For paralysis followed by blather, see the example of George W. Bush when asked to describe what mistakes he thought he had made—or indeed his seven minutes of inaction on September 11, 2001, when told, in front of a class full of children, of the first plane crash into the World Trade Center.

REFERENCES

Bruner, J. S. 1966. *Toward a theory of instruction.* Cambridge, MA: Harvard University Press.

Claxton, G. L. 1999. *Wise up: The challenge of lifelong learning.* London: Bloomsbury.

———. 2002. *Building learning power: Helping young people become better learners.* Bristol, England: TLO.

———. 2006. Mindfulness, learning and the brain. *Journal of Rational-Emotive and Cognitive-Behavior Therapy* 23:301–14.

Davies, R. 1981. *The rebel angels.* Toronto: Macmillan of Canada.

Gray, J. A. 2004. *Consciousness: Creeping up on the hard problem.* Oxford, UK: Oxford University Press.

Keats, J. 1899. *The complete poetical works and letters of John Keats.* London: Houghton Mifflin.

Kelly, G. A. 1955. *The psychology of personal constructs.* New York: Norton.

Robinson, D. N. 1990. Wisdom through the ages. In *Wisdom: Its nature, origins, and development,* ed. R. J. Sternberg, 13–24. Cambridge, UK: Cambridge University Press.

Sternberg, R. J., ed. 1999. *Handbook of creativity.* Cambridge, UK: Cambridge University Press.

Urquhart, J. 2005, January 30. Saturday by Ian McEwan: The brain inside the skull beneath the skin. *The Independent.* http://arts.independent.co.uk/books/reviews/article17578.ece.

Varela, F., E. Thompson, and E. Rosch. 1992. *The embodied mind.* Cambridge, MA: MIT Press.

4

Creativity, Wisdom, and Trusteeship[1]

Howard Gardner

After several decades of research in cognitive psychology, developmental psychology, and education, I turned my attention in the 1990s to the area of professional ethics. I undertook a joint research project with my colleagues Mihaly Csikszentmihalyi and William Damon, both psychologists. Initially, we decided to investigate whether it is possible for an individual to be both creative and humane; that is, whether the desire to be innovative could reside comfortably with a desire to behave in an ethical, responsible, humane way. Indeed, we initially termed our project The Humane Creativity Project, which closely echoed the title of the symposium in which I participated at Cambridge University on April 22, 2005.

The research project, which is still ongoing, evolved considerably over the next decade. We changed the name to the GoodWork Project; we shifted the investigative lens from creativity, in a strict sense, to a study of high-level professionals. And we eventually refined our research question to read as follows: How is it possible for individuals who desire to do good work—work that is excellent in quality, ethically oriented, and meaningful to the practitioner—to succeed at a time when things are changing very quickly, markets are very powerful, and there are few if any counterforces to the market (such as potent religious, ideological, or communal forces)? We have approached this project through in-depth interviews with leading practitioners who are reflective and who are considered by their colleagues to be good workers. So far, we have interviewed over 1,200 Americans in nine different professions, ranging from law to philanthropy to higher education. The results of our studies have been presented in several books, dozens of articles, and many national and international forums. For an introduction to the project, see our book, *Good Work: When Excellence and Ethics Meet* (Gardner, Csikszentmihalyi, and Damon 2001), and our Web site, www.goodworkproject.org.

At the aforementioned Cambridge conference, I spoke informally about our project and its results to date. Before the conference, I also circulated two papers. *The Ethical Responsibilities of Professionals*, drafted initially in 2000, focuses on our studies of science (particularly genetics) and precollegiate education and describes some of our initial conclusions. The second paper, *Can There Be Societal Trustees in America Today?*, presents some recent work on the issue of trust. While the latter paper chronicles a decline within the United States in the incidence of individuals who are trusted broadly across the society, the phenomenon described therein may well be discernible in other societies.

In my oral presentation at the conference, I spoke about different classical models of the origins of society. On the one side, we have Thomas Hobbes's (1651/1886) infamous description of the state of nature as "nasty, brutish, and short" (p. 64). From across the channel come the words of Jean-Jacques Rousseau (1762/1998): "Man is born free, and everywhere he is in chains" (p. 5). I expressed my own conviction that societies today are best crafted according to the original state portrayed by the twentieth-century American philosopher John Rawls (1971). What kind of society would we want to live in, asked Rawls, if we were covered by a veil of ignorance? That is, if we did not know the combination of talents, luck, and experiences with which we happened to be endowed? I believe that most people would like to live in a society that features good work and that has trustees on whom people could call at critical times.

These papers present two snapshots of the state of professional ethics at the present time. In the United States, and perhaps elsewhere, there is plenty of reason for concern. However, there are countless individuals who are still carrying out good work, and many of them have the potential to become societal trustees. At the least, our GoodWork Project helps bring current trends to the attention of a wider public. And perhaps, in due course, the project will also point the way to a society that would meet Rawls's desires—an abundance of good workers and a cohort of able trustees.

THE ETHICAL RESPONSIBILITIES OF PROFESSIONALS

In the middle of the nineteenth century, a serious proposal was made to close the U.S. Patent Office because it was felt that all inventions of significance had been made. In light of the subsequent appearance of the telegraph, the telephone, the radio, the television, airplanes, and computers, we now laugh at the naiveté of this proposal. A few years ago, an American journalist named John

Horgan (1996) wrote a book titled *The End of Science*, in which he speculates that the important questions about the nature of matter and life have been answered and that most other questions about nature and mind are not susceptible to scientific answer. A century from now, the suggestion that science was effectively at an end in the 1990s is likely to seem as ill informed as the proposal to close the Patent Office.

To be sure, we cannot predict particular advances in science and technology. At the end of the nineteenth century, who could have anticipated the theory of relativity, plate tectonics, or quantum mechanics? Turning from the physical to the biological world, who could have foreseen the revolution in molecular biology, the nature of genes and chromosomes, or the structure of DNA, let alone the fact that scientists can now clone entire organisms and will soon have within their grasp the power to transform the human genetic sequence and control heredity? And in light of the progress being made in the neural and cognitive sciences, investigators will continue to unravel the mysteries of thinking, problem solving, attention, memory, and—the most elusive prize of all—the nature of consciousness. The result of this work is likely to be of singular importance for all of us who are engaged in teaching and learning across the life span.

It is hard to deny the excitement of these enterprises. So many issues and questions that were once the lot of poets and armchair philosophers have already been answered by scientists, or at least hover within their grasp. Mysteries have now become problems, and problems are susceptible to solution. And yet, it is dangerous to adopt a Pollyannaish view. Science marches on, smartly but blindly. There is no guarantee that such a sequence from mystery to soluble problem will naturally contribute to the good of the public or that it will prove to be a benevolent force in the future.

Science—indeed, scholarship more generally—is morally neutral. It represents the best efforts of human beings to provide reliable answers to questions that fascinate us: Who are we? What is the world made of? What will happen to it? When? (Should I put the date on my calendar?) What kind of creature would ask such questions?

But what happens when these questions are answered? Sometimes, the answers simply satisfy human curiosity—an important and valid goal. But at other times they lead to concrete actions—some inspiring, some dreadful. Einstein's seemingly innocuous equation $E = MC^2$ stimulated many outcomes, which ranged from powering cities with nuclear energy, to detonating nuclear devices at the cost of thousands of lives in Hiroshima and Nagasaki, to spreading fallout after the Chernobyl disaster. Following the discoveries of antibiotic agents, we behold the production of wonderful drugs that can combat dread diseases as well as the emergence of new toxic organisms that prove resistant to the effects of antibiotic medication.

Again, scholarship itself cannot decide which applications to pursue, and which not to pursue. These decisions are made by human beings, acting in whichever formal and informal capacities are available to them. Einstein is a good case in point. It is doubtful that he thought about the applications of atomic theory when he was developing his ideas about the fundamental properties of the physical world. By the time the politically attuned physicist Leo Szilard approached the aging propounder of relativity theory in the late 1930s, it was already apparent that nuclear energy could be harnessed to produce very powerful weapons. Einstein agreed to sign a letter to U.S. President Franklin Roosevelt, and that action, in turn, led to the launching of the Manhattan Project and the building of the first atomic weapons. After the end of World War II and following the detonation of nuclear devices over Japan, Einstein became a leader in the movement toward peace and eventual disarmament.

Such choices and dilemmas are not solely the province of those in the so-called hard sciences. For most of the twentieth century, psychologists were involved in efforts to measure individual differences in human intelligence. Most psychologists feel comfortable using the intelligence test—an instrument developed over a century ago to help predict success or failure in school—but among the issues faced by researchers is whether to investigate group differences in intelligence (e.g., between men and women, among races).

Some scholars have stayed away from these issues for one reason or another. Others have focused on them. Richard J. Herrnstein and Charles Murray (1994) devote a portion of their provocative book *The Bell Curve* to a discussion of the long-standing and widely reported difference of 15 points (one standard deviation) between intelligence test scores of Americans of Caucasian and of African American descent. Herrnstein and Murray believe that it will be difficult to eliminate that difference and that it probably does not make sense to try. Others believe that intelligence in general can be raised and that these group differences can be narrowed or perhaps eliminated (Neisser 1998). Even a person who believes that it is difficult to raise intelligence still faces a choice: either elect not to devote resources to such an effort, or elect to direct sizeable resources to it. None of these decisions can be dictated by science; they all involve judgments of value.

In the past, scientists argued that their job was to add to permanent human knowledge and understanding, not to make decisions about policy and action. But what factors, then, have prevented the random use, misuse, or frank abuse of technology—the so-called fruits of scientific progress?

We can identify three factors that have traditionally served as a restraint on the misapplications of science. First of all, there have been the values of the community, in particular religious values. For example, in principle a scientist could conduct experiments in which prisoners are exposed to certain toxic agents, but religion counsels the sanctity of all human life. A second balancing force has been the law. In many nations, prisoners are protected against unusual forms of treatment or punishment. Third, there is the sense of a calling, or ethical standards, that professionals have. For example, a scientist might take the position that a contribution to knowledge should not be secured at the expense of human or animal welfare; indeed, some scientists have refused to make use of findings obtained by the Nazis as a result of immoral experiments. Or the warden of a prison might refuse to allow his prisoners to participate in studies using inhumane treatments, even in the face of social or financial pressures to do so.

Each of these restraining factors remains operative, but, alas, each seems reduced in force nowadays. At a time of rapid change, values are fragile and religious creeds may seem anachronistic. Laws remain, unless they are over-turned, but often events move so quickly that the law cannot keep up. And dur-ing an era when the market model has triumphed in nearly every corner of society, it is often quite difficult for individual professionals to uphold the stan-dards of their calling. In the 1980s, physicians in France colluded in the sale of blood that they knew to be tainted by HIV virus. It is probable that their sense of calling was not potent enough to combat financial and societal demands for the blood.

Market pressures are becoming all too familiar to educators, too. More and more, education is justified in terms of its economic leverage. Powerful politi-cians and policymakers call for vouchers, charters, and other market mecha-nisms as a means of permitting families to select schools. The arts are justified for their potential contributions to learning in skills useful in business rather than for their inherent worth. Colleges compete with one another through advertising, scholarships, and high salaries for star faculty. It is difficult to dis-cern voices that invoke forces other than the bottom line. Nowadays, few edu-cators underscore the intrinsic value of education or highlight the need for noncommercial communal values.

Thus we encounter an impasse. On the one hand, science and innovation proceed apace, ever conquering new frontiers. On the other hand, traditional restraints against wanton experimentation or abuse appear to be tenuous. Must we leave events to chance, or are there ways to pursue science and education—and, more broadly, professional life—in a responsible way?

Enter the ethical responsibilities of a professional. I contend that a new covenant must be formed between professionals and the society in which they live. Society makes it possible for scientific professionals to proceed with their work—by the funding of science as well as by cooperation in its execution. In return, I submit, scientists must take on an additional task: they must relinquish the once-justifiable claim that they have no responsibility for applications and undertake a good-faith effort to make sure that the fruits of science are applied wisely, not foolishly. So it must be for all professionals, including those in education.

Let me introduce an example from my own work as a cognitive psycholo-gist. In the early 1980s, I developed a new theory of intelligence, called the theory of multiple intelligences (Gardner 1983). While I thought that this theory would be of interest primarily to other psychologists, I soon discovered that it was of considerable interest to educators as well. Educators began to make all kinds of applications of the theory. I was intrigued and flattered by this inter-est. Yet, like most scientists, I felt little personal involvement in these applica-tions. Indeed, if asked, I would have responded, "I developed the ideas and I hope that they are correct. But I have no responsibility for how they are applied—these are 'memes' that have been released into the world and they must follow their own fate" (cf. Dawkins 1976).

About 10 years after my book *Frames of Mind* (Gardner 1983) was published, I received a message from a colleague in Australia. He said, in effect, "Your Multiple Intelligence ideas are being used in Australia and you won't like the way that they are being used." I asked him to send me the materials and he did so. My colleague was absolutely correct. The more I read those materials, the less I liked them. The so-called smoking gun was a sheet of paper on which each of the ethnic and racial groups in Australia was listed, together with an explicit list of the intelligences in which a particular group was putatively strong as well as the intelligences in which members of that group were putatively weak.

This stereotyping represented a complete perversion of my personal beliefs. If I did not speak up, who would? Who should? So I went on television in Australia and criticized that particular educational endeavor as "pseudo-science." That critique, along with others, sufficed to result in the cancellation of the project.

I do not hold myself up as a moral exemplar. It was not a job-threatening choice to appear on a television show in a far-away country, and I was not doing work in biotechnology or rocket science—work that can literally save or destroy lives. Yet the move that I made in my own thinking was crucial. Rather than seeing applications as the business of someone else, I had come to realize that I had a special responsibility to make sure that my ideas were used as constructively as possible. And indeed, ever since that time I have devoted some of my energies to supporting work on multiple intelligences of which I approve and critiquing or distancing myself from work whose uses are illegitimate or difficult to justify (Gardner 1995).

What can be done to forge a new covenant between professionals and the larger society? To my mind, the current impasse calls for greater efforts by each party to make clear its needs and its expectations. Professionals must continually be willing to educate the public about the nature of their enterprises and about what is needed for good work to be done within their domains. Professionals have a right to resist foolish misunderstandings of their own enterprises and to fight for the uncensored pursuit of knowledge. At the same time, they must be willing to listen carefully to reservations about their work from nonprofessionals, to anticipate possible misapplications of the work, and to speak out forcefully about where they stand with respect to such reservations, uses, and misapplications.

Ordinarily, neither professionals nor the general public should block the road of inquiry. Assuming that they do not harm others, individuals must have the right to follow their questions and curiosity wherever they lead. Occasionally, however, professionals may want to consider not exploring certain questions, even though they may be personally curious about the outcomes. In the case of my field, I do not condone investigations of racial differences in intelligence because I think that the results of these studies are likely to be incendiary. Many biological scientists are extremely reluctant to engage in experiments of genetic engineering or cloning of human beings, not because of lack of curiosity about the results, but rather because some of the implications of this work could be very troubling. It is not difficult to envision serious psychological or medical problems in light of these experiments; it is even possible to imagine how genetic experiments gone awry might threaten the viability of the species.

STEPS TOWARD RESPONSIBLE ACTION

If they believe that my claim has merit—if they believe that professionals generally should become more deeply involved in ethical considerations—how might individuals act upon that belief? This is the question I have been pondering with my close colleagues Mihaly Csikszentmihalyi of the University of Chicago, William Damon of Stanford University, and several other researchers in our laboratories (Gardner, Csikszentmihalyi, and Damon, 2001; Gardner 2007). We are trying to understand how leading practitioners—individuals doing cutting edge work—deal with the various invitations and pressures in their domains. We have been observing and interviewing scientists and professionals in other rapidly changing domains, such as journalism, business, and the arts. We want to know how their present work situations appear to such individuals "in the trenches," and we want to identify individuals and institutions that have succeeded in melding innovative work with a sense of responsibility for the implications and applications of that work.

While our study is far from complete, let me make a few comments about our findings thus far, with a particular eye on education. To begin with, professionals are not naïve about their situation. They are aware of the great pressures on them and the hegemony of the market model at the beginning of the twenty-first century. They want to be ethical persons in their professional and private lives. They recognize the pressures that make it difficult for them always to do the right thing and to avoid crossing tempting lines.

Yet clear differences can be observed in how successful these innovative individuals are in maintaining an ethical sense. Not surprising, early training and values are important, and that includes a religious affiliation in many cases. Opportunities to work in the laboratory of an ethical scientist, to spend time in a truly distinguished institution, or to be surrounded by colleagues with impressive values are equally important formative factors.

Once they have begun their careers in earnest, creative individuals are aided by two factors. The first is a strong sense of internal principles—lines that they will not cross, no matter what. If a scientist says—and believes—that she will never put her name on a paper unless she has reviewed all of the data herself, that virtually eliminates the likelihood that she will be an accessory to the reporting of fraudulent data. The second factor is a realization that the profession does not have to be accepted the way that it is today: as a human agent, a person can work toward changing that domain. Suppose, for example, that it has become routine practice, in the writing of grants, for the head of a laboratory to propose work that has in fact already been carried out but has not yet been published. A scientist could decide henceforth not to do so and work with colleagues to change the reigning but flawed procedures in the domain. Indeed, the installation of a process through which senior scholars apply for support by describing work that has recently been completed, rather than work that might be carried out in the future, would represent a significant alteration in the customary practices of a domain.

Similar examples can be gleaned with reference to the applications of creative work. A researcher could decide, for example, that all of his work is in the public domain and thus refuse to patent any findings. Here an internal principle wins out over the desire for personal profit. Or he could insist that science take the public interest into account. One way to do that would be for every laboratory voluntarily to set up an advisory committee consisting of knowledgeable individuals from neighboring domains and laboratories. This advisory group would inform itself about the work of the lab, critique it when appropriate, and make suggestions about benevolent and possibly malevolent uses of findings.

THE RESPONSIBLE EDUCATOR

Plunging directly into the matter of education, let me attempt to apply the present analysis to a teaching professional who wants to devote her energies to the inculcation of disciplinary understanding in her students.

Let us suppose that you are a teacher of American history in the 10th grade. You take your calling very seriously. You have decided that you want to bring about deep understanding of historical thinking in your students. And you believe the best way to do this is to study a few topics in considerable depth—say, the American Revolution, the Civil War, and immigration at the beginning of the twentieth century. Your students will work with original documents, ponder essential questions, and be expected to argue about current events (e.g., recent immigration to California, the Civil War in the former Yugoslavia) on the basis of their newly acquired historical understandings. You want them to understand the difficulty and the power of the venerated discipline of history.

Enter the frameworks developed in the community or state in which you reside. Working together, politicians and educational policymakers have developed a curriculum and a required set of tests for all 10th-grade students. The curriculum features a text that is rich in facts and figures but unsettlingly thin in ideas. The tests match the curriculum. There is no room for engaging in thoughtful analysis, for raising new questions, for applying historical insights to the current situation, for acknowledging the fragility of the historical record. Instead, the high performer is the student who—shades of television quiz shows—knows the names and dates of hundreds of politicians, military leaders, treaties, laws, and disputes.

What should you do as a professional, imbued with a strong sense of calling? Should you succumb to these new frameworks, actively fight them, conduct some kind of a guerrilla activity, or begin to scan the want-ad section (or Web site) of your local newspaper? Circumstances and personalities differ, and no solution to this conundrum will work for every professional. Our study has yielded two ways of thinking about these issues that may be appropriate.

One approach could be to think about which stance you wish to assume toward the domain in which you work—in this case the teaching of American history. Recalling the reasons for your original choice of career, you could elect to pursue the domain as you initially learned it. Alternatively, recognizing the pressures of the moment, you could accept the definition of the domain imposed by others—in this case, those who write the laws and regulations and pay the salaries. Or you could attempt to modify the domain—for example, organizing teachers and parents to develop an alternative view of the 10th-grade curriculum, complete with its own set of standards or assessments. Yet another stance could be to try to recreate the domain in a new setting—for example, by deciding to work for, or create, a textbook company, a Web site, a cable television program, a new kind of testing, or an afterschool program in which you teach history and current events in a quite different way.

A second way to approach this issue is to think about your responsibilities. In our view, every individual has a set of at least five responsibilities among which he or she must continually negotiate. One responsibility is to yourself— your own goals, values, and needs, both selfish and selfless. A second responsibility is to the people around you—your family, friends, daily colleagues. A third responsibility is to your calling—the principles that regulate your profession—in this case, what it means to teach a discipline to students. A fourth responsibility is to the institution to which you belong: the particular school or perhaps the school system or network of schools of which you are a member. A final responsibility is to the wider world—to individuals you do not know, to the safety and sanctity of the planet, and to those who will inherit the world in the future. As the American historian Henry Adams (1918) powerfully phrased it, "a teacher affects eternity; he can never tell where his influence stops" (p. 300). We suggest that the thoughtful professional is always wrestling with these competing responsibilities and, insofar as possible, trying to meet each reasonably well (cf. Gardner 2007).

Whether sage or scientist, lawyer or layperson, parent or teacher, all of us must negotiate our way among these strong and sometimes competing responsibilities. We are helped by religion, ethics, friends, and colleagues, but in the end we must do the balancing ourselves. Personal responsibility cannot be delegated to someone else. Those who have the special privilege of educating the young have an obligation to be reflective about their stance toward teaching and their negotiation of these competing responsibilities. At a time when there is so much to learn, so many new media to master, and such pressing needs in the world, these responsibilities can seem awesome. Greater mindfulness about our responsibilities has become a necessity if we are to pass on to our progeny a world that is worth inhabiting.

CAN THERE BE SOCIETAL TRUSTEES IN AMERICA TODAY?

In earlier times, select American citizens were well known, widely respected, and thought to be nonpartisan. For a variety of reasons, these *trustees* appear to have been a casualty of the 1960s. Is there a contemporary equivalent of the trustee? If so, who are the current trustees? If not, what individuals or institutions can or should play the role of trustees in the coming years? Or is the trustee a concept whose time has come and gone? In what follows, I introduce the concept of *trustee*, review a pilot study carried out some years ago, and outline some promising lines for future investigations.

Background

In traditional societies, particularly aristocratic ones, certain individuals are imbued with the power to make consequential decisions for the rest of the society. In democratic societies, far more influence is ceded to the broader population. Nonetheless, in European, Asian, and American democratic societies, certain individuals have over the years been invested with considerable advisory or decision-making powers, on account of their background, expertise, connections, or a combination of such factors.

The changing situation in America over the last half century has been effectively conveyed in three books. In *The Wise Men* (1986), Walter Isaacson and Evan Thomas describe six men who formed a policy establishment in the post–World War II era. Dean Acheson, Charles Bohlen, Averell Harriman, George Kennan, Robert Lovett, and John McCloy forged a Cold War consensus and were consulted regularly by leaders of both parties. In *The Guardians* (2003), Geoffrey Kabaservice portrays Yale President Kingman Brewster and five close associates: McGeorge Bundy, John Lindsay, Paul Moore, Elliot Richardson, and Cyrus Vance. In background and aspiration very much like the earlier generation, these men each were jolted by the domestic and foreign events of the 1960s and 1970s. Their careers ended on notes of disappointment and unfilled promise. In *The Paradox of American Democracy* (2000), John Judis documents the turbulent events of the 1960s. The various revolutions of that decade undermined the authority of the best and the brightest and led to a society in which few, if any, leading figures embody the combination of features characteristic of a societal trustee.

Over the past decade, in our GoodWork Project, we have asked over 1,200 professionals drawn from nine domains to discuss the contours of their careers. We found that most of the older individuals were able to name figures whom they held in high regard. Journalists cited figures like Katharine Graham,

Edward R. Murrow, and I. F. Stone; lawyers mentioned persons like Archibald Cox and Edward Levi; scientists picked out Barbara McClintock and Francis Crick. Such highly regarded trustees were less frequently cited by subjects below the age of 50. When they were mentioned, mentors were more likely to be local figures; numerous young subjects lamented the lack of heroes or mentors.

As described in our book *Making Good* (Fischman et al. 2004), young professionals would like to carry out work that is both excellent and ethical. Yet, determined to succeed, many feel that they cannot afford to behave in an ethical manner because so few of their peers do. They say that they will become good workers *after* they have achieved success—a classic sacrifice of means in favor of ends. Both the decline of respected figures and the inclination of young workers to set their own standards are chillingly described by David Callahan (2004) in his recent book *The Cheating Culture*.

Intrigued by these trends, I began to ask associates and younger persons whom they regarded as trustees. The responses surprised me. Some older central banking persons mentioned Alan Greenspan, though clearly the domain of his expertise is circumscribed. Several young persons mentioned Jon Stewart, someone I had never heard of. Stewart is a comedian who is featured on *The Daily Show*, on which he pokes fun at all manner of political figures and events. Some persons mentioned Americans whose greatest influence is overseas, such as Jimmy Carter and George Soros. Probably the most cited person was Oprah Winfrey—a person who in terms of race, gender, and expertise would have been inconceivable as a trustee 50 years ago.

A Pilot Study

On the basis of these readings, reflections, and casual impressions, Jessica Sara Benjamin and I decided to conduct an empirical investigation of the phenomenon of societal trusteeship. During the summer of 2004, we carried out a pilot study which shed light on how contemporary citizens view trusteeship.

Methods

We interviewed two groups of individuals: 20 community leaders and 25 average citizens. About 60% of the subjects approached in each group agreed to participate in the study. Most lived in the Philadelphia area or surrounding states. The community leaders were contacted by phone or e-mail and asked whether they would be willing to participate in a study on trusteeship. We briefly described the concept of trusteeship. If the community leaders agreed to participate, they were then interviewed either in person (14 people) or by phone (6 people). Interviews lasted on average 30–45 minutes, but ranged anywhere from 20 minutes to two and a half hours. The mean age of the community leaders—comprising 2 women and 18 men—was 58 with a standard deviation of 8. The interviewees encompassed a diverse spectrum of occupations, from entrepreneurs to educators, politicians to leaders in the media.

In the aggregate, the leaders had a high degree of education, were well-off, and had contributed to the community in a significant way. As a token of appreciation, each interviewee received a book on the GoodWork Project.

The average citizens were interviewed at various shopping malls throughout the suburbs of Philadelphia, a location that offered an abundance of both people and stores. For this reason, we offered gift certificates to Marshalls, Bloomingdale's, Borders, or Starbucks. The gift certificates provided both an incentive for participation and (because participants could choose the store whose gift certificate they would receive) an unobtrusive measure of socioeconomic status (SES). The SES of each individual was also determined by appearance, manner of speaking, and answers. Overall, in our rough-and-ready assessment, the majority of people were middle SES (19), with a few high SES (3) and a few low SES (3) as well. The mean age of the average citizens was 55 with a standard deviation of 15, and there were roughly equal numbers of women (13) and men (12). The interviews with average citizens lasted approximately 10–20 minutes, with a few outliers at either end.

For both of the groups we began with a brief explanation of the study and a brief definition of trusteeship. Both groups were asked the same four questions, in this order:

1. Do you feel that there has been a decline in trusteeship in America over the past half century?

2. If so, is this a positive or negative situation for America?

3. Who, if any, might be some modern-day trustees of America and why?

4. If one were to resurrect the role of trustee, how might it best be fostered in the America of the early twenty-first century? Do you believe that this is desirable or even possible?

The interviewees were encouraged to elaborate on any or all questions. With the community leaders there was more time and therefore more room for digressions and exploration of related topics.

Findings

Five sets of findings emerged from the study:

1. *Common themes and explanations across groups.* There was surprisingly little variation between the community-leader and average-citizen groups; differences that emerged were, for the most part, expected. There was an overwhelming consensus that trusteeship had in fact declined over the past half century, and the reasons offered were similar.

Most interviewees felt that America is more fragmented today as a result of immigration, assimilation, and greater mobility; this fragmentation may catalyze polarized public sentiments. As society becomes more complex and differentiated, it is increasingly difficult for a single individual to know enough to make judicious recommendations on a range of issues. During the Cold War, for example, it was possible to think in terms of a bipolar world; such expertise is less likely to be adequate in a multipolar world. Similarly, as the federal government grows in size and is involved in hundreds of domains, it is more difficult for individuals to possess expertise across the domestic front. The sheer speed of change and the deluge of information also undermine a common knowledge base and a collective will.

Both the community leaders and the average citizens felt that the media bore significant responsibility for the decline in trusteeship. Informants cited media scrutiny as something that discourages quality people from running for top positions due to fear of irreparable damage to their reputations as well as the sheer hassle of negative press. The infiltration of the media into every aspect of life, coupled with their unrelenting muckraking, has also bred distrust and dissent among the public. This situation stimulates desire for self-reliance and independence of thought; for better or worse, the individual becomes his or her own best "wise man."

2. *Choice of trustees.* When pushed or probed for trustees, interviewees gave generally similar responses. Within both groups journalists came first (e.g., Tom Brokaw, Thomas Friedman), followed by politicians (e.g., Jimmy Carter, Ralph Nader, Senator John McCain) and then a mix of business (e.g., Bill Gates), media (e.g., Oprah Winfrey), and religious figures (e.g., Pope John Paul II).

There were some differences, however. Compared to leaders, the average citizens were more likely to mention well-known television personalities and more local news media. The community leaders were more fluent in their abilities to name organizations and foundations (e.g., government agencies such as the Food and Drug Administration, nongovernmental organizations like the Brookings Institution). They were also more likely to suggest practical solutions to the problem of declining trusteeship (including the promotion and encouragement of good works; the creation of more nonprofit organizations; the emphasis of public speaking, to encourage greater communication and leadership, and, somehow, the reform of the media).

3. *Contrasting views of the decline.* One perhaps more surprising difference between the two groups was the fact that the community leaders regretted the loss or lack of trusteeship more so than did the average citizens. The average citizens were more likely to discern positives in the lack of traditional trustees of influence and the advantages of increasingly diverse sources of information and democratic institutions. The contrasting sentiment may be due to the community leaders' greater knowledge of past events and deeper understanding of the detrimental effects of a lack of trusteeship. However, community leaders may also be lamenting their own loss of power.

4. *Shifts in the nature of trustees.* Both groups identified three major shifts that have occurred in the past half century: from national trustees to local trustees, from universal trustees to specialized trustees, and from educated trustees to celebrity trustees. Provoked by debacles such as Watergate and the Vietnam War, respondents ceased to trust national political figures; instead they

sought more familiar and trustworthy (hence, local) trustees. Additionally, we now live in a celebrity culture. The best-known individuals are not political figures like Dean Acheson or educators like Kingman Brewster. Rather, entertainers, athletes, and individuals famous for being famous populate mass circulation magazines and the airwaves. The election to high office of Senator George Murphy, President Ronald Reagan, and most recently California Governor Arnold Schwarzenegger documents this shift in the capacity to command public attention and respect.

Again the media were identified as the chief culprit in the shift from ivy-educated generalists to trained specialists and, increasingly, widely recognized celebrities. Two features associated with the mass media may undermine the possibility of trusteeship. One is the contentious atmosphere promoted by the media—the screaming heads that Deborah Tannen (1999) has chronicled in *The Argument Culture*. Also discouraging trusteeship is the recent trend toward *pathographies*: biographical portraits that focus on the weaknesses and foibles of the well known. Had the wise men or the guardians thought that every peccadillo would be broadcast or transmitted on the Web, they might have elected to pursue other avenues.

5. *Nostalgia for traditional values.* There was nostalgia among both groups for "simpler times"—even if these times are in part mythical—especially on the part of the older subjects. Traditional values were seen to be eroding. *Values* seemed to refer both to a familial component (the traditional nuclear family) and an ethical component (greater sense of integrity and helpfulness). Some blamed the media for undermining these values, while others acknowledged that the media simply reveal things today that would have been censored a half-century ago.

Comment

To this impressive analysis by our subjects, I add two additional points. First, I call attention to a paradox: subjects regularly denigrated the media, and yet many of the named trustees were either journalists or celebrities who were regularly featured on the media. Second, I note the role played by the amount of money an individual can amass and the uses to which that money is put. Recently, I engaged in a discussion of trusteeship with a group of school teachers in Texas. They all nominated wealthy individuals who had donated buildings or other public gifts. The source of the money was not discussed. I wondered whether, a few years ago, Kenneth Lay of Enron might have headed the list.

LINES OF INVESTIGATION

I believe that the phenomenon of societal trusteeship is well worth further systematic exploration. Such investigation should begin with historical and empirical descriptions. Ultimately it should lead to recommendations and demonstrations based on the results of the studies and also on an explicit statement of values. I outline six possible avenues of study:

1. *Expanded replication.* Our pilot study had numerous limitations. It focused on one area of the country, highlighted middle-aged persons and male community leaders, and gathered little additional information on the subjects. We should revise and expand the protocol and administer it to a larger population. Among the variables that we should examine are age, socioeconomic background, religious orientation, occupation, and racial/ethnic background. Such a study might also be carried out on the Internet.

2. *In-depth probing of mental models.* Inspired by the work of cognitive scientist George Lakoff (1990), students of public opinion have begun to investigate the mental models that underlie conceptualization of important topics. By mental models, I refer to the often unconscious ways in which individuals think about issues like communication, power, and trust.

Consider, for example, the question of how individuals think a society should decide about a complex issue like the prevention of terrorism or the advisability of genetically modified food. Individuals might think about decision making as occurring in a top-down manner; through open, cross-fire debate between individuals who hold opposing positions; through democratic sharing of information among neighbors or in a chat room; through the caricaturing of various positions; or by other means. Such an investigation can occur through an examination of spontaneous language or through responses to dilemmas or probes. It may well yield new and unsuspected approaches to the issue of trusteeship.

3. *Investigation of trusteeship in constrained domains.* While societal trusteeship may be on the wane, it is possible that trusteeship is still viable in more constrained domains or institutions. The GoodWork Project serves as a point of departure for such a study. Also relevant is an investigation of trusteeship in the traditional sense (e.g., members of boards of nonprofit institutions) and its relation to the broader form of trusteeship examined here.

4. *Trusteeship at other times and in other places.* Clearly, trusteeship has existed—and persists—in many other societies, so it is germane to gather information on the status of trustees in other societies. By the same token, the trajectory of trusteeship in American society needs study. It may be that the rise and fall of trusteeship is cyclical—consider the rise of Jacksonian democracy in the period after the Founding Fathers had passed from the scene. But it might also be the case that certain contemporary trends render trusteeship unlikely in the future.

5. *Technology and trusteeship.* Building on the pioneering work of Marshall McLuhan (1964), a number of observers have put forth an intriguing possibility: perhaps persons (especially young persons) who are deeply involved in the new technologies may process and exchange information in ways that are

fundamentally different from those used by persons reared in a more top-down, linear, and print-oriented culture. Such a perspective might reveal new forms that can replace traditional trusteeship. Of possible importance are once-obscure bloggers who gain a surprisingly large following in a short period of time and a general shift to reliance on Internet sources and "trust" indices.

6. *The training of trustees in the future.* I believe that traditional trustees served an important societal function. The disappearance of the traditional trustee may have been warranted, but one cannot replace something with nothing. Our empirical and historical investigations should reveal which approaches to trusteeship—or its contemporary equivalent—make the most sense in the twenty-first century. A final goal for this project is to identify the most promising approaches to trusteeship for today and tomorrow, and to help construct institutions and career paths that lead to a society that is well guided and functions productively.

NOTE

1. This chapter comprises a contextual note, followed by two short papers which were discussed at the Economic and Social Research Council–funded seminar Creativity and Wisdom at the University of Cambridge in April 2005.

REFERENCES

Adams, H. 1918. *The education of Henry Adams: An autobiography.* Boston: Houghton Mifflin.

Callahan, D. 2004. *The cheating culture: Why more Americans are doing wrong to get ahead.* New York: Harcourt.

Dawkins, R. 1976. *The selfish gene.* New York: Oxford University Press.

Fischman, W., B. Solomon, D. Greenspan, and H. Gardner. 2004. *Making good: How young people cope with moral dilemmas at work.* Cambridge, MA: Harvard University Press.

Gardner, H. 1983. *Frames of mind: The theory of multiple intelligences.* New York: Basic Books.

———. 1995. Reflections on multiple intelligences: Myths and realities. *Phi Delta Kappan* 77(3): 200–209.

———, ed. 2007. *Responsibility at work.* San Francisco: Jossey-Bass.

Gardner, H., M. Csikszentmihalyi, and W. Damon. 2001. *Good work: When excellence and ethics meet.* New York: Basic Books.

Herrnstein, R. J., and C. Murray. 1994. *The bell curve.* New York: Free Press.

Hobbes, T. 1651/1886. *Leviathan or the matter, form and power of a commonwealth, ecclesiastical and civil.* London: Routledge.

Horgan, J. 1996. *The end of science.* New York: Broadway Books.

Isaacson, W., and E. Thomas. 1986. *The wise men: Six friends and the world they made.* New York: Touchstone.

Judis, J. 2000. *The paradox of American democracy: Elites, special interests, and the betrayal of the public trust.* New York: Routledge.

Kabaservice, G. 2003. *The guardians: Kingman Brewster, his circle, and the rise of the liberal establishment.* New York: Henry Holt.

Lakoff, G. 1990. *Women, fire, and dangerous things.* Chicago: University of Chicago Press.

McLuhan, M. 1964. *Understanding media.* New York: McGraw-Hill.

Neisser, U. 1998. *The rising curve.* Washington, DC: American Psychological Association.

Rawls, J. 1971. *A theory of justice.* Cambridge, MA: Harvard University Press.

Rousseau, J.-J. 1762/1998. *The social contract.* Hertfordshire, England: Wadsworth.

Tannen, D. 1999. *The argument culture: Moving from debate to dialogue.* New York: Random House.

PART TWO

Response Chapters on Creativity, Wisdom, and Trusteeship

5

Creative Wisdom

Similarities, Contrasts, Integration, and Application

Dean Keith Simonton

One of the pleasures of becoming a senior member of an academic profession is that I increasingly encounter invitations to apply whatever expertise I have accumulated over the years to book projects such as this one. This particular volume holds especial interest because its expressed subject matter is both provocative and important: creativity and wisdom, two exceptional human assets. Moreover, the chapters in the book attack the topic in rather divergent ways. Anna Craft begins by discussing creativity and ends up encompassing wisdom, whereas Guy Claxton begins his essay with a treatment of wisdom and then brings in the subject of creativity in the context of wisdom. Then to augment the heterogeneity of perspectives all the more, Howard Gardner contributes not one but two essays dealing with what could be considered unrelated topics. Although all of these four analyses can be said to deal with the overall topic of Creativity, Wisdom, and Trusteeship in Education, they also put rather contrasting emphases on each of the subtopics. Therefore, I have to consider my own commentary as a major intellectual challenge. I must write an educational piece with all the creativity and wisdom I can muster.

What makes my task all the more challenging is the superficial disconnect between two key concepts. In truth, *creativity* and *wisdom* are not two words that go together in psychological research. This fact was revealed by conducting a key-word search of the literature using PsycINFO. Of the 14,901 publications on creativity and the 2,622 on wisdom, only 107 were identified as covering both subjects. In other words, less than 1% of the publications on creativity also concern wisdom, while about 4% of the publications on wisdom also concern creativity. Although this overlap is very small, it is also not zero. Hence, some kind of connection exists between the two. However, as suggested by some of the target chapters in this volume, the connection can be antagonistic rather than supportive. Therefore my main goal in this commentary is to examine the similarities and contrasts between the two concepts. From there I discuss how the two concepts might be integrated, and then I close with an application of that discussion.

SIMILARITIES?

Although people in general tend to view creativity and wisdom as rather distinct human traits, these two concepts also have a certain amount of overlap. For instance, both bear some relationship with intelligence (Sternberg 1985). It presumably requires some degree of intelligence to be creative, and some degree of intelligence to be wise, albeit intelligence may be more critical for creativity than for wisdom. Whereas creativity is often associated with genius, wisdom does not have to be, and it can even be associated with the apparent opposite—such as the wisdom of naive children or the wisdom of fools.

Even though psychologists also tend to keep the two concepts distinct, researchers occasionally connect the two. Illustrations can be found among the leaders of the Humanistic Psychology movement that began in the 1960s. Both creativity and wisdom were seen as good things possessed by individuals who managed to fully realize their potential. For instance, Maslow (1970) makes this manifest in his description of the *self-actualizing person*. On the one hand, self-actualizers tend to be more creative (see also Maslow 1959); in fact, much of Maslow's data came from scrutinizing the lives of such eminent creators as Albert Einstein, George Washington Carver, William James, Ralph Waldo Emerson, Johann Wolfgang von Goethe, John Keats, Robert Browning, Walt Whitman, Pierre Renoir, Camille Pissaro, and Franz Joseph Haydn. On the other hand, self-actualizers have many characteristics that could be considered representative of wisdom; for example, they are able to transcend their own egos and social conventions to look at themselves and others in a much broader, more inclusive, even emphatic view. Indeed, some of the famous self-actualizers that Maslow (1970) studied could be considered exemplars of wisdom: Thomas Jefferson, Eleanor Roosevelt, Frederick Douglass, John Muir, Jane Addams, Albert Schweitzer, Benjamin Franklin, Baruch Spinoza, Martin Buber, and Aldous Huxley.

Although Maslow's research was qualitative, even impressionistic, rather than objective and quantitative, some empirical research indicates some overlap between wisdom and creativity. Both characteristics appear to be associated with a certain degree of intelligence, cognitive flexibility, openness to experience, relativism in the sense of the perception of alternative perspectives, and the tolerance of ambiguity or uncertainty (Baltes and Freund 2002; Baltes, Glück, and Kunzmann 2002; Simonton 2002, 2004; Sternberg 1985). Of course, the correspondence in traits is not so strong that the two human virtues become equivalent. On the contrary, each asset has correlates that are not shared with the other asset, and even those correlates they do share may have distinctive weights. So now we must turn to the dissimilarities that render wisdom and creativity very distinct phenomena.

CONTRASTS?

The positive psychology movement views both creativity and wisdom as representing important human virtues or character strengths (e.g., Seligman and Peterson 2004). Yet as Bacon (2005) has well argued, there are actually two kinds of strengths: focus strengths and balance strengths. Creativity exemplifies the former, and wisdom the latter. Thus, whereas creativity requires concentration on the development of very specific expertise, wisdom requires the mastery of much more generalized knowledge about human life. Whereas creativity is required to solve domain-specific problems in the arts or sciences, wisdom is required to solve the far broader but perhaps more urgent problems of everyday life.

It should be clear that as alternative forms of expertise, creativity and wisdom are not just different but even antithetical. According to empirical literature on expertise acquisition, world-class creativity demands that the individual devote the minimum of a decade to extensive learning and practice within a specific domain (Simonton 2000a). This has been called the *10-year rule* (Ericsson 1996; Hayes 1989). Yet by concentrating on such a narrow domain of expertise, the individual must necessarily diminish the scope of less-specialized experience and information. Nor is that the only potential source of conflict. In the first place, the very cognitive and dispositional attributes that creativity and wisdom appear to have in common tend to be differentially applied. For example, creative individuals may be able to entertain alternative perspectives with respect to their domain of expertise, but with regard to more mundane affairs be no different than persons far less creative (see, e.g., Feist 1994).

Worse yet, highly creative personalities are prone to feature character traits that may actually be negatively associated with wisdom. Most conspicuously, creativity tends to be positively correlated with elevated scores on the clinical scales of the Multiphasic Personality Inventory (MMPI; Barron 1969) as well as higher-than-normal scores on the psychoticism scale of the Eysenck Personality Questionnaire (EPQ; Eysenck 1995). Insofar as mental illness can be considered the antithesis of wisdom, these correlations must be considered a bit disconcerting. This opposition becomes more obvious with the observation that the MMPI subscales include depression, hypochondriasis, hypomania, hysteria, paranoia, psychopathic deviation, and schizophrenia, while those who score high on the psychoticism scale of the EPQ tend to be aggressive, cold, egocentric, impersonal, impulsive, antisocial, unempathetic, and tough minded as well as creative. Few if any of these attributes appear very conducive to wise thought, feeling, and action. Yet these same traits may be highly supportive of creativity, particularly genius-level creativity (Eysenck 1995). For example, research on the differential eminence of great philosophers has shown that the most illustrious thinkers in Western civilization tend to take extremist positions on various intellectual questions, to argue for beliefs that are often seemingly inconsistent, and to push ideas that depart significantly from the prevailing views of the philosophical tradition (Simonton 1976). These attributes appear somewhat incompatible with wisdom—an incongruity that must be considered ironic insofar as philosophy etymologically signifies the *love of wisdom*.

One final disparity between creativity and wisdom deserves mention: their life-span developmental progress (Simonton 1990). They do not appear to have the same trajectories. On the one hand, wisdom is expected either to increase with age or at least not to decrease with age (Baltes, Glück, and Kunzmann 2002). Indeed, because a key component of wisdom is life expertise, it is hard to imagine how wisdom could exhibit any decline except under the most extreme circumstances, such as organic brain disorders. On the other hand, creativity has very different longitudinal distribution: it first rises to a peak sometime in the late 30s or early 40s and thereafter gradually declines (McCrae, Arenberg, and Costa 1987; Simonton 1988, 1997). This single-peak function holds for both psychometric measures (creativity tests) and behavioral indicators (productivity counts). Furthermore, this differential distribution closely parallels that for fluid versus crystallized intelligence and that for general creativity versus practical problem solving (Simonton 1990), suggesting that the contrast in trajectories is truly fundamental. Hence, from the perspective of an entire human life, creativity and wisdom appear to be quite distinct.

INTEGRATION?

In the first section of this chapter, I specified some similarities between creativity and wisdom, whereas in the second section I indicated some disparities between the same human strengths. But can the two virtues be integrated in some way? To answer, we should consider three factors that moderate the relationship between creativity and wisdom:

First, creativity researchers often distinguish between two grades of creativity (Simonton 2000b). On the one hand is *little-c* creativity, which concerns mundane problem solving—such as that which takes place in the home and at work. On the other hand is *big-C* creativity, which entails genius-level contributions to a given domain—usually in the form of major discoveries, inventions, or compositions that earn considerable recognition. It is the latter form of creativity that seems most inconsistent with the acquisition of wisdom. That is, it is genius-grade creativity alone that requires focused domain-specific expertise and somewhat psychopathological inclinations. More commonplace creativity, in contrast, seems more compatible with wisdom, at least insofar as such creativity involves successful adaptation to life. Consistent with this connection, problem-solving ability concerning issues of everyday life tends to peak at a later age than does performance on standard creativity tests (Cornelius and Caspi 1987). Moreover, this later peak is especially strong when the problems involve interpersonal content (Thornton and Dumke 2005), the kinds of problems about which we also expect wise solutions.

Second, creativity is commonly defined as the joint product of two separate components (Simonton 2000b). First, an idea must be original, novel, or surprising. Second, an idea must be functional, workable, or adaptive. If both of these characteristics can be assessed on a ratio scale, then $C = O \times F$, where $O = 0$ signifies zero originality (e.g., a cliché) and $F = 0$ signifies zero functionality (e.g., an airplane made out of cinder blocks). If either component equals zero, then $C = 0$. The first component can be considered a fairly well-defined, even objective feature of the idea. For instance, it can be assessed in terms of how many others would come up with the same problem solution. Yet the second component has much more ambiguous status. What can be considered workable, functional, or adaptive depends on the criteria applied to the problem. These criteria are usually provided by the specific domain (e.g., logic in science, symmetry in art), but can also be imposed by the sociocultural system (e.g., Socialist Realism must show happy workers, Islamic architecture cannot show representations of Muhammad). This openness means that the second component can incorporate criteria that would meet some accepted standard of wisdom. By this route scientists can be legitimately asked to treat each experimental subject—whether animal or human—with a respect that honors each subject's rights as a living creature.

Third, according to the formula $C = O \times F$, creativity can be increased by raising the value of either component. Thus, the same level of creativity can be attained in two different ways. One idea might be highly original but less functional, another highly functional but less original—but both could be considered equally creative. Yet the relative importance of the two components tends to vary across distinct sociocultural systems (Simonton 2005). In cultures that place a strong emphasis on individualism, as holds in Western civilization, the originality component tends to assume the greater significance, so much so that sometimes creativity and originality are equated. This emphasis makes sense because individuality requires the demonstration of personal uniqueness and because originality provides an obvious means to establish that uniqueness. In other cultures where the values are more collectivistic, such as many Asian civilizations, it is the functional component that carries more weight. This shift in emphasis arises because ideas are not considered adaptive if they disrupt the social order, whether at the family level or at the level of the political system.

APPLICATION?

I would now like to apply the foregoing discussion to some of the issues raised by the target chapters. Let me begin with Claxton's query about whether it is possible to accelerate the growth of wisdom. My analysis suggests that educational measures that are designed solely to increase the development of creative potential will at best prove irrelevant and at worst prove detrimental to the acquisition of wisdom. As noted earlier, whereas wisdom is a balance strength, creativity is a focus strength (Bacon 2005). Accordingly, gifted and talented programs that place the greatest emphasis on helping youths develop highly domain-specific expertise may actually hinder the development of wisdom. The extreme case of such asymmetrical growth is seen in those child prodigies who combine adult-level expert performance with almost infantile social skills and emotional intelligence (see, e.g., Montour 1977). Hence, the promotion of big-C creativity may conflict with the acceleration of wisdom.

The educational enhancement of little-c creativity, while not an outright hindrance, may not be much help either. In particular, programs that focus on improving student performance on so-called creativity tests or measures of divergent thinking cannot be expected to have positive transfer on behalf of wisdom acquisition. The cognitive skills necessary to generate numerous and varied uses for a toothpick or a paper clip are only weakly connected with the intellect required for true wisdom. Only if the tests concerned practical problems of everyday life—and especially interpersonal relationships—would we anticipate any meaningful correspondence. To be wise, problem-solving expertise must deal with people, not things.

This brings me to some issues raised by both Craft and Gardner. The former is concerned with making creativity wiser, while the latter is concerned with increasing the ethical responsibility of professionals, including creative individuals such as scientists. Both concerns can be addressed in terms of my earlier discussion of the formula $C = O \times F$ (creativity equals originality times functionality). Although creativity researchers and practitioners tend to concentrate on the originality component, I have argued that the functionality component is no less critical in this multiplicative relationship. Hence, creativity can be enhanced by placing more focus on how to make ideas more functional, adaptive, or workable. Furthermore, this shift in emphasis can incorporate the fundamentals of moral behavior and social responsibility. Both scientists and artists must learn to consider the social ramifications of their ideas, not just whether those ideas display sufficient novelty to attract professional attention. Although contemplating such ethical constraints might stifle personal originality to some degree, we must remember that an enhancement of this functional component can actually compensate for a corresponding loss in the originality component, leaving the total amount of creativity unscathed. What may be lost in individualistic self-expression would be gained in collective utility. Such wiser creativity can then make the world a better place.

This argument may seem excessively collectivistic rather than individualistic. Some degree of personal originality may have to be sacrificed for the general good. At the very least, that originality should not overstep the boundaries that divide the adaptive from the maladaptive, the functional from the dysfunctional. Nevertheless, I would argue that the individual creator has something to gain from this concession. It is striking that those domains with the fewest constraints on originality are precisely those with the highest rates of psychopathology (Ludwig 1998; Simonton 2004). Scientific creators are less prone to mental illness than are artistic creators, and even within the arts, those who are restricted to formal styles tend to be more mentally healthy than those who can engage in unconstrained expressionism. Perhaps when creators indulge in the extravagancies of their uniqueness, they become more estranged, more alienated from social support; their ideas reduce to vain, autistic attempts to communicate what few others can share—or even comprehend. By altering the balance of originality and functionality, particularly by obliging that functionality include social value and moral principles, not only may the society at large be better off, but so will the individual creators. Rather than a compromise, this sounds like a win-win outcome.

As a pure rather than applied researcher, it is difficult for me to make highly specific recommendations about instructional implementations. So I can only hope that these remarks on the target chapters make some positive contribution to the development of any innovations. In particular, I would like to be assured that any novel attempts to increase both creativity and wisdom will be based upon assumptions that are both creative and wise.

Creativity and Wisdom Compared and Integrated

Similarities

- Both are considered "good things" (i.e., virtues or character strengths) that can converge in single individuals (e.g., self-actualizers).
- Both are positively related to intelligence, cognitive flexibility, openness to experience, flexibility, relativism in the sense of the perception of alternative perspectives, and tolerance of ambiguity or uncertainty.

Contrasts

- Creativity constitutes a focus strength, whereas wisdom represents a balance strength.
- Creativity usually requires domain-specific expertise, whereas wisdom requires broader knowledge about everyday life.
- Creativity is positively associated with personal attributes that are negatively associated with wisdom (e.g., elevated scores on the EPQ's psychoticism scale).
- Creativity usually declines in the latter part of life, whereas wisdom does not.

Integration

Wisdom overlaps more with little-c (everyday) creativity than it does with big-C (genius-level) creativity; however, even this statement is tempered by the following two points:

- If creativity is defined as the product of originality and functionality (i.e., $C = O \times F$), then wisdom has a place in the determination of what is functional (e.g., requiring that scientific research be ethical as well as new).
- Moreover, according to this product definition, creativity may be increased by raising either originality or functionality separately; the former approach is favored by individualistic cultures, the latter by collectivistic cultures, which leaves more latitude for wisdom in the latter.

REFERENCES

Bacon, S. F. 2005. Positive psychology's two cultures. *Review of General Psychology* 9:181–92.

Baltes, P. B., and A. M. Freund. 2002. The intermarriage of wisdom and selective optimization with compensation: Two meta-heuristics guiding the conduct of life. In *Flourishing: Positive psychology and the life well-lived,* ed. C. L. M. Keyes and J. Haidt, 249–73. Washington, DC: American Psychological Association.

Baltes, P. B., J. Glück, and U. Kunzmann. 2002. Wisdom: Its structure and function in regulating successful life span development. In *The handbook of positive psychology,* ed. C. R. Snyder and S. J. Lopez, 327–47. New York: Oxford University Press.

Barron, F. X. 1969. *Creative person and creative process.* New York: Holt, Rinehart and Winston.

Cornelius, S. W., and S. Caspi. 1987. Everyday problem solving in adulthood and old age. *Psychology and Aging* 2:144–53.

Ericsson, K. A. 1996. The acquisition of expert performance: An introduction to some of the issues. In *The road to expert performance: Empirical evidence from the arts and sciences, sports, and games,* ed. K. A. Ericsson, 1–50. Mahwah, NJ: Lawrence Erlbaum.

Eysenck, H. J. 1995. *Genius: The natural history of creativity.* Cambridge, UK: Cambridge University Press.

Feist, G. J. 1994. Personality and working style predictors of integrative complexity: A study of scientists' thinking about research and teaching. *Journal of Personality and Social Psychology* 67:474–84.

Hayes, J. R. 1989. *The complete problem solver.* 2nd ed. Hillsdale, NJ: Lawrence Erlbaum.

Ludwig, A. M. 1998. Method and madness in the arts and sciences. *Creativity Research Journal* 11:93–101.

Maslow, A. H. 1959. Creativity in self-actualizing people. In *Creativity and its cultivation,* ed. H. H. Anderson, 83–95. New York: Harper & Row.

———. 1970. *Motivation and personality.* 2nd ed. New York: Harper & Row.

McCrae, R. R., D. Arenberg, and P. T. Costa. 1987. Declines in divergent thinking with age: Cross-sectional, longitudinal, and cross-sequential analyses. *Psychology and Aging* 2:130–36.

Montour, K. 1977. William James Sidis, the broken twig. *American Psychologist* 32:265–79.

Seligman, M. E. P., and C. Peterson, eds. 2004. *Character strengths and virtues: A handbook and classification.* Washington, DC: American Psychological Association.

Simonton, D. K. 1976. Philosophical eminence, beliefs, and zeitgeist: An individual-generational analysis. *Journal of Personality and Social Psychology* 34:630–40.

———. 1988. Age and outstanding achievement: What do we know after a century of research? *Psychological Bulletin* 104:251–67.

———. 1990. Creativity and wisdom in aging. In *Handbook of the psychology of aging,* 3rd ed., ed. J. E. Birren and K. W. Schaie, 320–29. New York: Academic Press.

———. 1997. Creative productivity: A predictive and explanatory model of career trajectories and landmarks. *Psychological Review* 104:66–89.

———. 2000a. Creative development as acquired expertise: Theoretical issues and an empirical test. *Developmental Review* 20:283–318.

———. 2000b. Creativity: Cognitive, developmental, personal, and social aspects. *American Psychologist* 55:151–58.

———. 2002. Creativity. In *The handbook of positive psychology,* ed. C. R. Snyder and S. J. Lopez, 189–201. New York: Oxford University Press.

————. 2004. *Creativity in science: Chance, logic, genius, and zeitgeist.* Cambridge, UK: Cambridge University Press.

————. 2005. Creativity (in the arts and sciences). In *New dictionary of the history of ideas,* vol. 2, ed. M. C. Horowitz, 493–97. New York: Charles Scribner's Sons.

Sternberg, R. J. 1985. Implicit theories of intelligence, creativity, and wisdom. *Journal of Personality and Social Psychology* 49:607–27.

Thornton, W. J. L., and H. A. Dumke. 2005. Age differences in everyday problem-solving and decision-making effectiveness: A meta-analytic review. *Psychology and Aging* 20:85–99.

6

Creativity and Wisdom

Are They Incompatible?

David Henry Feldman

Three unusually stimulating chapters comprise the set under discussion. Only one of them (Craft) takes up the relationship between creativity and wisdom directly, this in the context of an educational movement now underway in the United Kingdom. A second (Claxton) is about wisdom, not creativity, and not their relationship. Claxton tries to illustrate what is meant by *wisdom* by providing three compelling examples and some helpful clarifying distinctions; separately, he explores underlying brain processes that might be involved in wise activity. The third chapter (Gardner) does not deal directly with either creativity or wisdom (something of a surprise given his long history in the field). Gardner presents some findings from his recent GoodWork Project with Csikszentmihalyi and Damon on high achievement as it confronts ethical issues. He separately discusses a proposal for constituting a new version of a Sanhedrin or council of elders to help guide society toward ethically admirable goals and practices.

In this brief response I could not possibly do justice to even one of the target chapters, so I focus on a single theme that, to varying degrees, runs through each of them. This theme is expressed as *universalized creativity* in Craft's chapter; as the diversity of examples of wisdom in Claxton's; and in Gardner's, as the fact that good works require different sets of capabilities, sensibilities, proclivities, and responsibilities depending on the field. Being a "good" (i.e., ethical) journalist, for example, is not the same as being a "good" scientist, which is not the same as being a "good" artist.

The theme discussed here, then, is based on the fact that we have come to understand that there are varieties of both creativity and wisdom, and that our current challenge is to clarify the different forms and specify possible relationships between and among them. This work must take place in the context of the histories, traditions, beliefs, customs, and practices of different cultural groups (see Greenfield 2004) and should begin to explain how policies, decisions, choices, and changes of direction can be understood within and across groups involved in one or more creative domains.

The specific question for this brief chapter is whether creativity and wisdom are fundamentally incompatible, that is, if their relationship is always antithetical. The answer I propose is that it depends on what kind of creativity and what kind of wisdom we are talking about. While most known forms of creativity seem to require a disrespect for wise and judicious action, there are certain forms that may actually depend on a deep and abiding respect for and understanding of traditions and sociocultural contexts.

ONE VERSUS MANY CREATIVITIES

For most of its history, creativity research has tended to conceive of creativity as a single trait, or at least to study it as if it were. The "creativity" tests that marked the beginning of the field's resurgence in the 1950s in the United States reflected the view that a single measure could capture a person's creative potential and that a score on a creativity test was a reasonable estimate of that person's promise for doing creative work (Getzels and Jackson 1962; Guilford 1950; Torrance 1966; Wallach 1971; Wallach and Kogan 1965).

In more recent years, there have been efforts to differentiate creativity into several different forms; with these more differentiated notions of creative accomplishment comes the possibility of a more systematic discussion of how creativity and wisdom might (or might not) be related (see Csikszentmihalyi 1999; Gardner 1993; Morelock and Feldman 1999; Sternberg 2003a).

For most known varieties of creative achievement, wisdom would seem to play a minor role, if it plays any role at all, in forming and fashioning a transformational work. But for at least one kind of creative endeavor, wisdom may be essential. The kind of creative effort I refer to is one that radically transforms a social or political environment (e.g., the sort brought about by Gandhi; cf. Gardner 1993) or a religious movement that transforms the fundamental forms of spirituality (as Christianity did from its root religion, Judaism).

I did a brief Internet search using the key words *creativity and wisdom,* which turned up many sites. Most were spiritual/religious sites, but several were business sites, and for these the emphasis was understandably different. For the spiritual/religious uses of creativity with wisdom, most referred to finding ways to sustain and/or transform belief and faith in the face of seemingly overwhelming forces that might undermine those commitments to a particular religious doctrine. Pleas are made to the faithful to be resilient and innovative in coming up with reasons for continuing to adhere to traditional religious beliefs and for religious communities to generate innovative plans to sustain their viability in the face of increasingly challenging threats to faith.

Business Web sites tended to pair the creative and the wise in terms of understanding the changing marketplace, its history, and traditions, and to better anticipate what kinds of business ventures and products might have the best chance to succeed. Learning from past efforts, the rules and principles of successful product development, service delivery, competitive edge, differentiation from existing products or services, and how to best motivate and reward employees would lead to "creative" and "wise" practices. An example of a business-oriented use of creativity with wisdom is the TechnoRising Star Awards presented to minority- and women-owned businesses by the Maryland Department of Business and Economic Development. These awards "recognize creativity, wisdom and innovation, the very same characteristics that define Maryland's technology-driven economy" ("State Honors Minority, Women-Owned Tech Firms" 2002, ¶ 3).

Creativity researchers have rarely studied creativity within spiritual and religious contexts (see Scarlett 2006), but some have been interested in business and creativity, particularly in light of the ever-growing global marketplace and the increasingly competitive technological and scientific markets (see Amabile 1988; Sawyer 2007). *Creativity* and *innovativeness* are essentially synonyms in the context of business.

When discussing the more profound manifestations of creative activity, wisdom in the usual sense of thoughtful, reflective, balanced, and circumspect effort often runs counter to the process. To achieve great creative works, it is usually necessary to break from established knowledge, traditional paradigms, long-held assumptions, and entrenched authority. Indeed, *conventional wisdom* is often used to refer to what must be transcended if a major transformation in a field is to be achieved. There are numerous examples of individuals who defied convention, would not accept that certain things were true and proven beyond doubt, and like Copernicus, Darwin, and Galileo, have risked persecution or death to find a new and better truth—hardly wise in any pragmatic sense.

Creativity of the most profound sort has more to do with unwise risk than it does with being wise by moving within established parameters, boundaries, and conventions. If Picasso and Braque had been wise in their choice of techniques with which to represent three-dimensional space, would the cubist movement have been started? If Darwin (and Lord Wallace) had not embraced a thoroughly natural form of change, would evolution by natural selection have been proposed? If Stravinsky had adhered to musical convention, would we have ever listened to *The Rite of Spring*? What is creativity of the most profound sort if not a fundamental break with the past, a dramatic change of direction, a path not known to exist—or if it is known, is seen as so dangerous and fraught with peril that only the most intrepid of voyagers might choose it?

Yet even in the most extreme instances of creative revolution, the past is hardly ignored, nor are the great advances in a field dismissed out of hand. In every known instance of great creative transformation, those who brought about that transformation have been steeped in the traditions of their domain, schooled in the knowledge and, yes, the wisdom of a field, and trained to follow the contemporary paradigms. Mozart's father, for example, his primary teacher throughout his musical apprenticeship, had nothing more in mind for his talented son than to see him compose and perform in the service of the church or the political powers-that-be in Salzburg (Ostwald and Zegans 1993).

Natural scientists are now trained in the laboratories of their sponsors and are required to demonstrate their skills in research using known techniques (Dunbar 2000; Root-Bernstein, Bernstein, and Garnier 1993). Visual artists for most of Western history were made to serve a decade or longer in an apprenticeship in an established atelier, with no encouragement to break with the established techniques and accepted products of their employer (Csikszentmihalyi 1999). Societies have always created structures to control and channel the drive toward change, the desire to bring about transformation, the tendency to deconstruct and reconstruct that is often at the core of great creative advance. It is as if there is a kind of wisdom at the cultural level which, on the one hand, recognizes that innovation, change, even revolution must be allowed to take place under certain circumstances, but only when absolutely necessary. Societies that set overly strict controls on change run the risk of being displaced, superseded, or conquered. Societies that put too few constraints on change run a different set of risks: self-indulgence, low standards, or change for change's sake. At the sociocultural level, then, we can assume that a form of wisdom as balance must operate, although it might be difficult to specify the parameters of such balanced ways of managing, channeling, and occasionally encouraging major change (Feldman 1994). It is this function that animates Gardner's call, in his target chapter, for a council of wise elders.

CREATIVITY THAT REQUIRES WISDOM

Finally, there are some forms of extreme creativity that seem to depend on a deep understanding and appreciation of a society's control mechanisms and power structures—a kind of political and cultural wisdom in people who might choose to seek major changes in those mechanisms and structures. Gandhi was, along with his satyagraha movement, responsible for one such set of political changes in his native India, finding the pressure points and sustaining the tensions along the appropriate fault lines at just the right times to generate maximum leverage. Gandhi led the first known nonviolent revolution and was a catalyst for the first intentional transformation of a society that did not require armed and violent forces to bring it about (Gardner 1993). In this form of creativity, it is impossible to explain what was achieved without recourse to both fundamental processes of transformation in thought and action as well as wise understandings of the people, political structures, traditions, and practices that his movement was designed to transform.

With an example like Gandhi, have we moved adjacent to, if not into the orbit of, religious and spiritual transformations? If we can call Gandhi and the satyagraha movement creative, as we can indeed do within the more differentiated conceptions of creativity now gaining acceptance in the scholarly field, then it is not too much of an extension of our expanding conception of creativity to consider religious and/or spiritual movements, too. For these contributions, wisdom of the sort that Gandhi possessed must be involved, but perhaps so, too, should wisdom of another sort. To bring about a profound religious or spiritual transformation, a deep appreciation of the unmet needs, deepest fears, and impossible hopes of a society or group of societies is a creative work and must be better captured in the proposed framework than the existing one to be replaced. Imagination is surely called for in creative works such as that which became the protestant transformation. Indeed, to a less profound degree, any act of religious belief must be an act of imagination (Scarlett 2006).

Have we come to the conclusion, then, that there is no "universal" creative process, no generalized meaning to the term *creativity* itself? Perhaps so, but there is at least one possibility for a universal process that is, if not creativity itself, surely a prerequisite to it. Elsewhere I have referred to this process as *the transformational imperative*, a unique human tendency to become dissatisfied with the world as it is (Feldman 1994). The transformational imperative appears to be a unique epistemological stance that allows human minds to disrespect what is known and what has been established. There is apparently no other creature that takes this particular stance toward the world.

Even so, minds vary in how strongly they react with impatience and dissatisfaction to the known and accepted as well as in the range of things that arouse their distaste and objection and thus lead to transformation, that is, to creative efforts to change the world (Feldman, Csikszentmihalyi, and Gardner 1994). It may well be that all normal human minds participate to some degree in the transformational imperative, in this sense a universal creative process, but they do so to varying degrees and across varying numbers of fields.

In the end, the brief Internet search that started this chapter may have helped identify one of the domains where creative and wise insights are jointly essential. If a major change in religious doctrine is to come about, a new set of beliefs and/or ideas about human life and how it is to be organized can be successfully established only if the new form engages and transcends the traditional forms that it aims to replace. In so doing, it furthers the contemporary effort among creativity scholars to describe the many forms of creativity and the key dimensions along which they vary. This, in turn, appears to be a wise goal for the field of creativity studies. Even if all minds are capable of taking liberties with the world, it is more often than not unwise to do so. Knowing the difference in all fields requires a more differentiated notion of creativity than we currently tend to use.

EDUCATIONAL IMPLICATIONS

What can we say about these matters as they relate to how students are taught and how schools are advised to do their vital work? It should be obvious that no single formula for discovering creativity and fostering wise decision making is likely to be of much use. If there is anything that follows from our discussion for practice, it is that the approach will vary depending upon a number of things: what kind of creativity has been targeted for cultivation, what issues are important for the community and/or the student at a given moment, the student's profile in terms of openness to change versus resistance to change, the student's specific strengths, what kinds of resources are available and can be accessed for that student, how skilled and well trained the teachers are in fostering various forms of creative development, and no doubt others.

Perhaps our goal should be to recognize that creativity is complex, that wisdom is not the same from one context to another, and that different schools and communities may choose to emphasize different aspects of creativity and wisdom for different students under different circumstances. To be sure, this is not a relativist, anything-goes, vacuous invocation that everything depends on local conditions. A great deal *does* depend on local conditions, particularly the distinctive qualities of each student, each teacher, and each school, but there are also general aspects of understanding creativity and wisdom that can inform and guide practice at local levels. However, it is important to recognize that a formulaic and singular approach to fostering creativity and/or wisdom is likely to miss the mark in most instances. It is equally important to recognize that the field of scholarship is in an early phase in its understanding of the diversity of creativity and how it can be fostered (Craft 2005)—and of wisdom, even more so.

REFERENCES

Amabile, T. 1988. A model of creativity and innovation in organizations. In *Research in organizational behavior,* vol. 10, ed. B. M. Staw and L. L. Cunnings, 123–67. Greenwich, CT: JAL.

Craft, A. 2005. *Creativity in schools: Tensions and dilemmas.* Abingdon, England: Routledge.

Csikszentmihalyi, M. 1999. Implications of a systems perspective for the study of creativity. In *Handbook of creativity,* ed. R. J. Sternberg, 313–35. Cambridge, UK: Cambridge University Press.

Dunbar, K. 2000. What scientific thinking reveals about the nature of cognition. In *Designing for science: Implications from everyday, classroom, and professional settings,* ed. K. Crowley, C. D. Schunn, and T. Okada, 115–40. Hillsdale, NJ: Lawrence Erlbaum.

Feldman, D. H. 1994. Mozart and the transformational imperative. In *On Mozart,* ed. J. M. Morris, 52–71. Cambridge, UK: Cambridge University Press.

Feldman, D. H., M. Csikszentmihalyi, and H. Gardner. 1994. *Changing the world: A framework for the study of creativity.* Westport, CT: Praeger.

Gardner, H. 1993. *Creating minds.* New York: Basic Books.

Getzels, J. W., and P. W. Jackson. 1962. *Creativity and intelligence: Explorations with gifted students*. New York: John Wiley.

Greenfield, P. M. 2004. *Weaving generations together: Evolving creativity in the Maya of Chiapas*. Santa Fe, NM: School of American Research Press.

Guilford, J. P. 1950. Creativity. *American Psychologist* 5:444–54.

Morelock, M. J., and D. H. Feldman. 1999. Prodigies and creativity. In *Encyclopedia of creativity*, ed. M. Runco and S. Pritzker, 1303–10. San Diego, CA: Academic Press.

Ostwald, P., and L. S. Zegans, eds. 1993. *The pleasures and perils of genius: Mostly Mozart*. Madison, CT: International Universities Press.

Root-Bernstein, R. S., M. Bernstein, and H. Garnier. 1993. Identification of scientists making long-term, high-impact contributions, with notes on their methods of working. *Creativity Research Journal* 6:320–43.

Sawyer, R. K. 2007. *Group genius: The creative power of collaboration*. New York: Basic Books.

Scarlett, W. G. 2006. Toward a developmental analysis of religious and spiritual development. In *The handbook of spiritual development in childhood and adolescence*, ed. E. C. Roehlkepartain, P. E. King, L. Wagener, and P. L. Benson, 21–33. Thousand Oaks, CA: SAGE.

State honors minority, women-owned tech firms. 2002, December 4. *Baltimore Business Journal*. http://www.bizjournals.com/baltimore/stories/2002/12/02/daily20.html?f=et52.

Sternberg, R. J. 2003. The development of creativity as a decision-making process. In *Creativity and development*, ed. R. K. Sawyer, V. John-Steiner, S. Moran, R. J. Sternberg, D. H. Feldman, J. Nakamura, and M. Csikszentmihalyi, 91–138. Oxford, UK: Oxford University Press.

Torrance, E. P. 1966. *Torrance tests of creative thinking: Norms/technical manual*. Princeton, NJ: Personnel Press/Ginn.

Wallach, M. A. 1971. *The creativity-intelligence distinction*. New York: General Learning Press.

Wallach, M. A., and N. Kogan. 1965. *Modes of thinking in young children: A study of the creativity-intelligence distinction*. New York: Holt, Rinehart and Winston.

7

How Are We Disposed to Be Creative?

Jonathan Rowson

I t is a great pleasure to have the opportunity to respond to the three papers presented at the Cambridge Conference on Creativity and Wisdom in Education. Anna Craft highlighted the need to problematize the place of creativity in education, while Howard Gardner and Guy Claxton offered rich lateral and comparative perspectives on creativity within our wider social fabric, examined in terms of trusteeship, professional ethics, and wisdom.

On the face of it, Craft's aspiration to foster creativity in education with wisdom feels unsettling, because it is not initially obvious why doing so is necessary or what such an aspiration amounts to. Creativity is complex at a purely conceptual level, in terms of what we mean when we call something creative, and becomes even more challenging when we think about why we value creativity personally, or at a socioeconomic level, and what this implies for its place in education. Introducing wisdom into this equation is ambitious but emerges from Craft's observation that there has been a progressive commodification of creativity in postindustrial societies, to the extent that we are losing sight of its broader importance and emancipating potential.

The value of thinking of creativity in terms of wisdom is that wisdom is usually thought of as a distinctly human quality, grounded in the challenges of being human, in a way that intelligence, for instance, need not be. Our task therefore amounts to finding a way to continue to promote creativity while being mindful of the human values that we want creativity to implicitly propagate, including open-mindedness, self-expression, and insight. In this respect, highlighting the wider significance of creativity is a way of challenging the existing emphasis on innovation and is part of a wider struggle to protect the integrity of education from the collateral damage caused by attempts to create ever more productive human capital.

There are many valid approaches to the question at hand, but it seems particularly important not to speak of creativity and wisdom in education as "things" to squeeze into a bloated timetable. Perkins (1992) describes how doing so can lead to the *token investment strategy*, whereby overburdened teachers heroically do a little bit of everything to preemptively defend themselves against the charge of ignoring important aspects of education. Educators need a perspective on creativity that allows them to understand and promote it in a more integrated way, and that is what I hope to offer in this chapter.

One promising approach is to think of creativity at the most intimate human level, where our creative impulses begin to manifest, long before a polished solution, performance, or product takes shape. At this level of response, we are framing a situation and gauging what it means for us; there is not yet any creative output, but our acquired attitudes, beliefs, abilities, and values are already influencing our propensity to be creative and, I suggest, the ethical direction of our creative thought and action. This approach is consonant with Sternberg's (2003) claim that "creativity is as much a decision about and an attitude toward life as it is a matter of ability" (p. 98).

This way of thinking about creativity emerged from reflecting on Claxton's reference, in his target chapter, to "the nature of the underlying *motivational vector* that drives cognition" (p. 36); this is an enigmatic expression that hints at the values and motivations that shape our actions at a very general level, but also at a generative level, and one that is therefore relevant not only to wisdom, but also to creativity and to "good work." The level of analysis may seem abstract at first, but the aim is actually to move the conceptual discussion toward a more experiential approach to creativity, whereby we observe the creative impulse, or lack of it, in ourselves and reflect on what is happening at that level in terms of the values and motivations that we bring to our creative acts. The analytical framework used for this task is the interplay of affordances (stimuli perceived as opportunities for action) and dispositions (our inclination to act in certain ways based on our attitudes and experience). This framework is applied to creativity and wisdom in an effort to clarify the scope that educators may have to develop both, and perhaps find some sort of synergy of the two.

MOTIVATION: THE GAP BETWEEN CREATIVE CAPACITY AND CREATIVE ACTS

I believe the most fundamental reason we value creativity is that we tacitly associate it with the experience and expression of free will. Our creativity often manifests as a capacity, within the systems, structures, and events that shape us, to go beyond our conditioned reactions and be more effectively responsive within those constraints. Yet having the capacity—being able—is not always enough because we don't always make use of our capacities. For instance, if we are given a set of paints, an empty page, and plenty of time, most of us would be inclined to paint something, but if we encounter a problem opening an e-mail attachment, we might give up if it doesn't open properly with the standard procedure that we are used to, when a more creative approach might have worked. We might behave this way because we do not see the situation as an opportunity to be creative, perhaps because the undercurrent of the action is the belief that "I am not a computer person," thus robbing ourselves of the motivational fuel required to think creatively about the problem.

One reason this type of behavior persists is that we tend to talk about motivation primarily as something quantitative, which is reflected in the widely used expressions *highly motivated* and *lacking in motivation*. However, my impression is that insufficient attention has been given to the nature and quality of motivation and how this underpins our propensity to think and act in certain ways. For instance, one conventional way to unpack motivation is to distinguish extrinsic motivation, whereby we are motivated by the results of our actions, from intrinsic motivation, whereby we are motivated by the rewarding experience of the action itself. While this distinction can be useful from a descriptive point of view, the motivation required to fuel creativity with wisdom may come from a different dimension altogether.

Claxton's emphasis in this volume on *egocentric* and *allocentric* motivation is useful because it goes beyond the relationship between interest in the experience of a task and interest in the rewards of a task; it also speaks to the psychological and ethical underpinnings of the interest itself, in particular how this interest leads us to frame situations that involve wider interests, and to act within them. However, many, if not most, creative acts comprise aspects of intrinsic, extrinsic, egocentric, and allocentric motivation without necessarily integrating them in any ethically progressive way. For instance, a child writing a poem about world peace may be not only deeply absorbed in the task and genuinely care for the subject matter, but also strongly motivated by the prospect of winning a poetry prize and being thought of as a great poet.

Perhaps we need a wider perspective to understand motivation in a qualitative way. In this respect, youth community projects like those documented in Shirley Brice Heath's documentary *ArtShow* suggest that there can be a constructive fusion of intrinsic and extrinsic motivation. My impression of these projects, which tend to involve individuals doing self-sustaining creative work toward a community goal, is that they are highly effective in broadening motivation away from self-interest. At the beginning of these projects, participants can be observed competing for attention and fighting over shared resources. However, over time, individual identities and preferences are gradually transformed by the shared sense of purpose, until activities that were initially undertaken only as a means to obtain extrinsic rewards begin to become valuable for their own sake. What seems to be happening in these projects is that participants' sense of self seems to change and expand. If you feel that you have an important contribution to make to a group project that you care about, and sense that your overriding goal is shared by everybody else, the experience of your contribution becomes both its own reward and a means to a greater end (Heath 2006).

The main implication for educators is to not take motivation for granted. Claxton is right to suggest that achieving greater motivational clarity is a demanding task, especially in adolescence, but in principle I think it is worth striving for. For instance, if you feel that a student could try harder, it should be possible for you to suggest why and how in a way that makes sense to the student. This could amount to simply making students aware that it is normal for things to seem difficult or boring at times, but that the experiences of boredom or difficulty are not necessarily reasons to lose interest; rather, they can also be opportunities to make sense of material by bringing it to life in a distinctive way. At such moments, there is an opportunity for a good teacher to model or scaffold the kinds of creative processes they hope to inculcate in their students. More generally, it would be useful to periodically discuss different levels and kinds of motivation in class and place greater emphasis on motivation in summative and formative assessments.

DISPOSITIONS

When Claxton refers to the *underlying motivational vector* that drives cognition and *motivational force fields*, he is alluding to the relationship between the values and attitudes that are tied up in our motivation and how they are unpacked in what we do. Figuratively, these expressions imply that cognition is given *direction* by motivation. Our thoughts and feelings about a situation are *carried* by the way we frame that situation. The source of this motivation is a self: a person with a unique history, with projects, purposes, and goals. Such motivational influences are sometimes revealed explicitly in terms of goals we are trying to achieve, but often they are revealed implicitly in what we care about, what holds our interest, and the way we treat other people. Thus a person's propensity to be creative is often coextensive with the propensity to act casually or callously, or, preferably, with care and consideration for others.

I am therefore seeking a way to pinpoint a complex interplay of motivation, values, habit, and freedom. The challenge of finding a word to capture this combination goes back to Dewey's (1922) writing on habits: "We need a word to express the kind of human activity which is influenced by prior activity and in that sense acquired; which contains within itself a certain ordering or systematization of minor elements of action; which is projective, dynamic in quality, ready for overt manifestation; and which is operative in some subdued subordinate form even when not obviously dominating activity" (quoted in Ritchhart 2002, 19). More recent work suggests that the word best suited for our task is *disposition* (Perkins 1995; Ritchhart 2002).

Perkins (1995) describes dispositions as the *soul of intelligence*. Our dispositions are formed over time by the way our motivations feed into our actions and, in turn, receive feedback from those actions. We might be disposed, to a greater or lesser extent, to be curious, suspicious, reflective, cautious, mindful, analytical, critical, and creative. For instance, teachers are typically disposed to react to disruptive students in a certain way, perhaps very strictly and punitively, or perhaps in a more tolerant way. This disposition depends on their view of themselves as teachers, their assumptions about the students involved, their view of what the atmosphere in the classroom should be like, how much order is required for learning, and so on.

Such dispositions become habitual, but they are not merely habits. To have a habit, good or bad, is to be conditioned to react in a way that is reinforced by familiar stimuli. Our habits come naturally in situations we experience as normal. Dispositions lie closer to our experience of freedom and reflect our readiness to *choose* to respond in certain ways. This is particularly important in light of what Craft, in her target chapter, argues about choices being determined by the market, because choosing to be creative often amounts to reframing the choices offered and finding alternatives to the initial choices that seemed to be available.

But if the educational aim is to foster desirable dispositions, such as the disposition to be creative, how are we to do it? Perhaps this is too general a question, but trying to bridge the gap between *can do* and *do do* should be a central aim for any educator. There is no easy answer here, but my impression is that teachers make most impact at the dispositional level when students are stretched in such a way that their habitual way of making sense will no longer suffice and their meaning-making capacity has to expand. What is distinctive about this kind of learning experience is that it belongs to the students in some way. As Lipman, Sharp, and Oscanyan (1980) put it, "meanings cannot be dispensed. They cannot be given or handed out to children. Meanings must be acquired; they are *capta*, not data. We have to learn how to establish the conditions and opportunities that will enable children, with their natural curiosity and appetite for meaning, to seize upon the appropriate clues and make sense of things for themselves" (p. 13).

My suggestion is that dispositions are only marginally and gradually influenced by data, but are more profoundly altered by capta. In a classroom context this means giving students, as much as possible, time to think for themselves about things that matter to them. This might mean that within any given subject matter students are given the necessary support to relate what they are learning to their own lives and aspirations, even if such links will inevitably seem tenuous at times. By repeatedly asking "What does this remind you of?" and "Give me an example of how this might influence your life?" teachers run the risk of adulterating the subject matter being taught. But by consistently encouraging students to reflect on the relevance of what they are learning and to make connections that only they could have thought of, teachers help them develop their imaginations and increase the chance that learning will become dispositional, rather than merely add to the sum of their inert knowledge.

IS CREATIVITY AFFORDABLE?

At an abstract level, a creative act emerges from the interaction of a person and some sort of stimulus—whether a problematic situation, a musical instrument or even just a thought—and the focus of concern here is how the person perceives that stimulus. There is good reason to believe that we do not perceive things purely in sensory terms (e.g., colors, shapes), but in terms of what they are *for*—our opportunity to use or interact with them. So we see a door as a thing for opening, a chair as a thing to sit on. Our perceptual worlds do not consist merely of objects that we passively imbibe, but of affordances that lead us to think and act in certain ways depending on what they mean for us. We have aims, and we direct our attention accordingly. We are, as Claxton (2006) recently put it, always up to something. There is insufficient space to argue for this view of perception here, but it grows out of Gibson's (1979) ecological view of perception and is grounded in more recent work on embodied, situated, or enactive cognition (A. Clark 1997; Lakoff and Johnson 1999; Varela 1999, 2000; Varela, Thompson, and Rosch 1991).

Varela's (1999) work is particularly relevant because he argues for a link between embodied cognition and the experience of *the virtuality of self*, which he sees as a precondition for wise action. His view is informed by Buddhist epistemology, and the role of affordances in Western thought is comparable to the role of *rupas* in Buddhist psychology, which places a more explicit emphasis on the way we reinforce our sense of self through our perceived opportunities for action: "We commonly impose distortion on to the object world. We take it as implying ourselves, and in the process create self-material in relation to it. . . . We see in the object signs that lead us to construe a self, and from this create a sense of self. We can say that the object is an indicator of that self. The object is called a rupa" (Brazier 2003, 62). The implication is that rupas constrain creativity because the boundaries of the self become the limits of a person's creative potential.

It is worthwhile to extend this account of perception beyond objects to situations. Viewed as opportunities for action (including inaction), many situations afford the opportunity to be creative and wise, but only if we are disposed to see them in that way. For example, Perkins (1995) gives the amusing example of a group of friends who sat down to have bread and cheese at a picnic, only to discover that there was no knife to cut the cheese. After the initial disappointment, one of them took out his wallet and cleanly cut the cheese with one of his credit cards. Perkins suggests that he managed to do this because he was not limited by *functional fixedness* (a knife is for cutting, a credit card is for paying), and in this case he was not only capable but also ready and willing to reframe the situation appropriately.

With this view of perception in mind, perhaps the most important role for an educator is to make students aware of their creative freedom where they are least likely to suspect it. One way of doing this is to try to combat functional fixedness in the classroom. A chair is for sitting on, but it can also be a door stop, a prop to reach the top shelf, a goal post, and a multitude of other things. The students passively know this already, but it is not part of their perceptual apparatus. By repeatedly reinforcing the idea that there are multiple uses for a single object, the educator reinforces the importance of seeing things from multiple perspectives, and new affordances will thereby emerge in the students' perceptual field in everyday life. Indeed, it is important to understand that those present at the above-mentioned picnic will *literally* never see a credit card in the same way again.

GANDHI'S SECOND SANDAL

> *Experience is not what happens to you; it is what you do with what happens to you.*
>
> —Aldous Huxley (1932, 5)

A striking example of what it means to be *disposed* to be creative is provided by the story of Gandhi's second sandal, all the more so because the creative act also appears to be wise. As Gandhi hurriedly boarded a train that was beginning to depart, one of his sandals fell onto the tracks, and he immediately responded by taking off his second sandal and throwing it onto the tracks, so that later somebody would find both sandals and have a pair to wear.

What is arresting about this example is the speed with which Gandhi acted. It seems that he immediately reframed the situation from being one of personal loss to being one of someone else's gain and was therefore in a position to act effectively. I imagine many people might think of the solution, but only several minutes later when it would be too late. However, Gandhi was ready, willing, and able to act creatively and in a manifestly wise way when it mattered, and how this kind of disposition emerges is of central concern here.

A full discussion of the formation of Gandhi's character is beyond the scope of this chapter, but noteworthy here is Gandhi's response when asked, just before his 70th birthday, to single out the most creative experience of his life:

> Seven days after I had arrived in South Africa the client who had taken me there asked me to go to Pretoria from Durban. It was not an easy journey. On the train I had a first-class ticket, but not a bed ticket. At Maritzburg, when the beds were issued, the guard came and turned me out. The train steamed away leaving me shivering in cold. Now the creative experience comes there. I was afraid for my very life. I entered the dark waiting room. There was a white man in the room. I was afraid of him. What was my duty; I asked myself. Should I go back to India, or should I go forward, with God as my helper and face whatever was in store for me? I decided to stay and suffer. My active non-violence began from that day. (Gandhi, 1994, 165–73)

Clearly the creative *experience* of being thrown off a train is markedly different from the creative *act* of throwing one's own sandal off a train, but there is an important link between the two. The salient point is Gandhi's capacity to repeatedly milk his own experience in order to reaffirm values, direct motivation, and thereby strengthen dispositions. It was through his response to situations such as these that he acquired not only the capacity but also the readiness and willingness to act spontaneously in an effective and ethical manner.

In my experience, some people are immediately awestruck by the story of Gandhi's second sandal, while for others the context seems so unfamiliar and the action so counterintuitive that it takes a while to appreciate why the behavior is supposed to be impressive. Many more such scenarios broaden our horizons in this way. Some arise in famous books or films, and some in our everyday lives. Educators could consider collecting examples like this and using them as a basis for class discussion. There might also be value in asking students to find such examples or indeed to devise for themselves situations that seem to call for creative or wise action.

WHAT MAKES ACTION WISE?

Why does man not see things? He is himself standing in the way: he conceals things.

—Friedrich Nietzsche (M. Clark and Leiter 1997, 187)

Advancing chronological age is often assumed to be concomitant with growing experience, but if experience is viewed as what you do with what happens to you, there is no necessary connection. Indeed, arguably it is because skill and persistence are necessary to turn raw experience into personal development that wisdom is only loosely correlated with age (Jordan 2005). Examples of wise action tend to involve protagonists who may be incidentally old, but are necessarily experienced, and call upon their experience to find apposite courses of action.

In the Tokyo subway story in Claxton's target chapter, the old man's intervention was certainly effective, but it was noticeable that many members of my discussion group at the Cambridge conference were not convinced that his behavior was wise. Many felt that "trying something like that" would be highly risky and might needlessly endanger people. At the level of behavior, this is certainly a valid and important point, but the wisdom is not manifest directly in the behavior of the old man, rather from the old man's framing of the situation that led to it. Indeed, it would be foolish to try to "teach" wise action at a behavioral level because it is highly context sensitive and typically arises from a set of dispositions cultivated over a period of time.

A deeper problem is that the loosening of egocentricity is central to wisdom. This can be felt by reflecting on the fact that the statement "I am wise," like "I am humble," sounds like a performative self-contradiction. This feature of wisdom, which is not at all peripheral, is not syntonic with our current cultural climate in which self-interest is pervasive and self-esteem is prized. This is not to say that wisdom implies meekness, just that the very idea of promoting wisdom on a large scale is difficult, and perhaps even unwise.

Unlike creativity, which can directly impact productivity, wisdom has little or no policy impact. By its very nature, wisdom cannot be readily appropriated or measured and is therefore difficult to make tractable at an institutional level. These thoughts developed in response to a discussion with Howard Gardner, who remarked that educators should take note of the implicit messages in a culture. In this respect, creativity is already implicitly valued and promoted and doesn't need explicit support. However, there is some value in finding a way to promote wisdom because this is not being done at the cultural level.

The heart of this challenge is that wise action is inimitable. What makes an action wise is not a set of behaviors that can be promoted or measured, but behavior that arises from acute sensitivity to context, flowing from a set of wisdom-related dispositions. To be disposed to act wisely is to be capable of viewing complex and morally charged human situations as affordances for a certain kind of intervention, but in a manner that is typically highly nuanced. This point can be illustrated by analyzing the Tokyo subway story in more depth (see Dobson n.d. for a full version of the story, with vivid contextual details).

Terry Dobson and the old man saw the same set of circumstances, but they were disposed to view them differently in terms of affordances. The underlying motivational vector driving Dobson seems to be "How can *I* improve the situation?" while we can imagine that the equivalent for the old man might be "How can the situation be improved?" What drives Dobson is a narrative of self-creation, and the action that is about to take place is a response to what he sees as an affordance for his aikido aptitude, rather than an affordance for compassion in terms of the suffering of the drunk.

Although it appears that the old man is just blathering, his action is highly sophisticated. Claxton remarks: "The old man is able to see through the laborer's anger to the distress below and, by skillfully indicating his recognition of it, allows it to surface" (p. 41). As a result of his age and the fact that he remains seated, he is not an affordance for the drunk's aggressive disposition. Moreover, his tone of speech is friendly, signaling to the drunk that he does not view him as an enemy. Asking the drunk what he has been drinking highlights that the old man sees him as a person with preferences, and saying "I like sake, too" creates space for mutual recognition and empathy to emerge. "She's 76 you know" and "my great-grandfather planted that tree" introduce people, references, and images that continue to widen the perspective of the drunk and dilute his volatile state. Finally, the passively framed question "And I'm sure you have a lovely wife too" suggests that the drunk is viewed as a person of value who has significance beyond his recklessness in the given situation.

For those listening to Claxton tell this story, it was striking that he appeared to be very moved toward the end. I cannot speak for Claxton, but what I find moving is not so much the skill of the old man, but the rueful reflection of Dobson after he steps off the train, because I think anybody who cares about education can identify with Dobson's predicament. At a basic level, he wants to use what he has learned to help other people. He does not appear to be naïve or selfish; on the contrary, he is brave and cares deeply about improving the situation. However, Dobson's reflection on the incident highlights that we often imperceptibly get in the way of our own ideals.

The importance of not getting in the way of what we are trying to achieve brings us back to creativity because it is consonant with Amabile's (1998) research on the factors that can stifle creativity, including surveillance, competition, time pressure, and evaluation. However, the *self getting in the way* issue is a particularly complex one to tackle in practice. For most of us, our egos form a large part of our self-confidence and motivation to learn, and any attempt to directly undermine egocentricity will be met with a robust, defensive response. Helpful in this respect is Kegan's (1982) claim that self-esteem tends to be a misnomer in educational circles, in that most children of school age derive self-esteem from the attention and praise of others rather than any autonomous sense of self. These two points together suggest that any loosening of egocentricity is a complex social and psychological process that should be left to unfold over time. Moreover, given the prevalence of egocentricity and self-interest, it is important that these motivational vectors are not demonized, but rather seen as natural and understandable, yet also profoundly limiting and problematic, and something we should aspire to gradually transcend.

Insofar as educators should try to facilitate this process, there is value in regularly encouraging students to see things from perspectives other than their own. One way to do this is to examine stories or films in which the protagonists pursue their own interests in fairly reasonable ways, but ways that ultimately lead to undesirable consequences. There are many such examples, but I have in mind two fairly recent films (suitable for older children): *The House of Sand and Fog* and *Babel*. At any given point in these films, it seems to me that the protagonists are acting appropriately given their sense of self and perceived responsibilities, yet at some point they lose control of the situation and disaster results. Such examples of things going terribly wrong are very useful for highlighting the importance of creativity and wisdom because students will relate to moments when characters needed to call upon a qualitatively different way of thinking or acting but didn't. Moreover, through projective identification, students might enjoy imagining how things would have been different if they had been in the story instead.

CONCLUSION

The primary aim of this chapter was to introduce a fresh way of looking at the challenge of how to foster creativity with wisdom, rather than to propose detailed changes at the level of policy and practice. It is useful to think about creativity at a dispositional level, and educators interested in this path need to develop a rich qualitative account of motivation, encourage students to move beyond functional fixedness, ensure that learning involves capta as well as data, and examine well-selected stories and scenarios from multiple perspectives. The deeper question regarding wisdom concerns the loosening of egocentricity, and I suggest that any approach to this delicate task has to be suitably careful and considerate.

I hope the foregoing discussion is useful in making sense of how people are disposed to be creative, because this underlying issue will continue to be relevant regardless of changes in education or the world at large. However, education now takes place within a media-saturated culture in which students are bombarded with formative images and effectively sold identities. In this context, a mischievous question occurs to me. What should we say to somebody who asks, "How will being creative and wise help me become rich and famous?"

REFERENCES

Amabile, T. 1998. How to kill creativity. *Harvard Business Review* 76(5): 76–87, 186.

Brazier, C. 2003. *Buddhist psychology: Liberate your mind, embrace life*. London: Constable and Robinson.

Clark, A. 1997. *Being there: Putting brain, body, and world together again*. Cambridge, MA: MIT Press.

Clark, M., and B. Leiter. 1997. *Nietzsche: Daybreak: Thoughts on the prejudices of morality*. Cambridge, UK: Cambridge University Press.

Claxton, G. 2006. *Learning to learn: Educational and biological perspectives*. Paper presented at Neuroscience and Education: Conjoining Theoretical Perspectives, Nottingham, England.

Dobson, T. n.d. *A short story by Terry Dobson—a master of akido and conflict resolution*. http://www.wattstapes.com/dobson.htm.

Gandhi, M. 1994. *The collected works of Mahatma Gandhi*, vol. 68. New Delhi: Publications Division, Ministry of Information and Broadcasting, Government of India.

Gibson, J. J. 1979. *The ecological approach to visual perception*. Hillsdale, NJ: Lawrence Erlbaum.

Heath, S. B. 2006. *Vision, language and learning: Why creativity is really about sustainability*. Plenary session at the This Learning Life Conference, Bristol, England.

Huxley, A. 1932. *Texts and pretexts: An anthology of commentaries*. London: Chatto and Windus.

Jordan, J. 2005. *The quest for wisdom in adulthood: A psychological perspective*. In *A handbook of wisdom: Psychological perspectives*, ed. R. J. Sternberg and J. Jordan, 160–88. New York: Cambridge University Press.

Kegan, R. 1982. *The evolving self: Problem and process in human development*. Cambridge, MA: Harvard University Press.

Lakoff, G., and M. Johnson. 1999. *Philosophy in the flesh: The embodied mind and its challenge to western thought*. New York: Basic Books.

Lipman, M., A. M. Sharp, and F. S. Oscanyan. 1980. *Philosophy in the classroom*, 2nd ed. Philadelphia: Temple University Press.

Perkins, D. 1992. *Smart schools: Better thinking and learning for every child*. New York: Free Press.

———. 1995. *Outsmarting IQ: The emerging science of learnable intelligence*. New York: Free Press.

Ritchhart R. 2002. *Intellectual character: What it is, why it matters, and how to get it.* San Francisco: Jossey-Bass.

Sternberg, R. J. 2003. The development of creativity as a decision-making process. In *Creativity and development,* ed. R. K. Sawyer, V. John-Steiner, S. Moran, R. J. Sternberg, D. H. Feldman, J. Nakamura, and M. Csikszentmihalyi, 91–138. New York: Oxford University Press.

Varela, F. J. 1999. *Ethical know-how: Action, wisdom, and cognition.* Palo Alto, CA: Stanford University Press.

———. 2000. Steps to a science of inter-being: Unfolding the Dharma implicit in modern cognitive science. In *The psychology of awakening: Buddhism, science, and our day-to-day lives,* ed. G. Watson, S. Batchelor, and G. Claxton, 71–89. York Beach, ME: Samuel Weiser.

Varela, F. J., E. T. Thompson, and E. Rosch. 1991. *The embodied mind: Cognitive science and human experience.* Cambridge, MA: MIT Press.

8

Good Thinking

The Creative and Competent Mind

Helen Haste

How far should we seek to reconcile the three different takes on creativity, ethics, and wisdom in the chapters by Howard Gardner, Guy Claxton, and Anna Craft? To what extent should we recognize that they are legitimately different perspectives? Gardner concentrates on the responsibilities of those who create or innovate to ensure the ethical application of their work. Claxton asks "What is wisdom?" and in so doing more implicitly informs us about what is creative in wise behavior and thinking. Craft addresses ethical issues within a cultural context; her argument is that the purposes or desired outcomes of creativity are culturally embedded and that cultures vary in how they foster creativity (or not). In industrialized Western societies the *cult of the new* is integral to a go-getting, material-rewards version of creativity that is implicit in the ethic of individualism.

I argue in this chapter that the concept of *competence* may be a route to fruitful synthesis. Explicit in Craft's and Claxton's analyses, and more implicit in Gardner's, are four common themes: *flexibility, critical evaluation, taking multiple perspectives,* and *exploring nonobvious options.* All of these imply getting outside both the frame and one's preconceptions, and considering the larger human and ethical implications—which may not always be obvious, as Claxton's three vignettes show. These themes relate to something we might call *generative adaptation*: a creative response to the management of inevitable ambiguity and uncertainty.

In any discussion of creativity, or indeed of competence, there is an assumption of successful productive future output, effective adaptation to available resources, and innovative problem solving. However, emphasis on creativity as innovation—the cult of the new that Craft critiques—misses an important issue. Focusing on innovation leads us to ask primarily how people deal with novelty and the unfamiliar, which involves the implication that the new replaces the old. In practice, the real tension is between managing continuity and change at the same time; this is a problem both for culture and for the individual. It has become increasingly apparent that the traditional problem-solving model, which seeks a single take on the multiple perspectives that we face in contemporary society, does not work. We must instead find ways of dealing constructively with *irreconcilable* multiple perspectives.

A few years ago I was part of an Organisation for Economic Co-operation and Development brainstorming seminar on the competencies that would be needed in the twenty-first century (Haste 2001). The term *competence* itself implies "good enough" functioning, rather than innovation. Also, in the context of education, the implication of identifying competencies is that they should guide all education, not only education for the creative, exceptional, or groundbreaking. A competence is not merely a collection of skills; it is a way of approaching problems and issues, within which certain skills are required. The conclusion I have drawn in working on these ideas is that many of the competencies we have been teaching require not just modifying, but quite substantially rethinking.

THE PROBLEMS OF PREDICTION

Part of this is about taking the future seriously; in all aspects of education, it is the future to which we direct our sights. But future-gazing is fraught. Our immediate tendency is to extrapolate from the present. The control theorist William Gosling (1994) identifies three different ways in which we think about technological change, but these also extend very aptly to much wider areas of the human condition—and profoundly reveal the problems of prediction and planning. The first kind of change is *more of the same*; it changes little and assumes that things will continue very much as they are now, with perhaps minor tweaking. This model informs most of our predictions. The second kind, *quantity into quality*, is the gradual process by which incremental changes accumulate to make an eventual qualitative difference. This is more difficult to imagine but is still within the skills of the particularly farsighted. In thinking about the future, most scenario builders work with a model that implies more of the same, or very occasionally quantity into quality.

The third and truly transformational kind of change is *the knight's move*. It shocks our assumptions and the frames of thought and action that we take for granted. In technology, this type of change is often the consequence of a major invention (e.g., the microchip) which revolutionizes both our artifacts and the social practices associated with them. In education, we often deal with the fallout, the dramatic changes in social practices, that such technological change brings. It is almost impossible for even the most creative person to make a knight's move in thinking about the future because it is so difficult to anticipate the unexpected development—and even more difficult to anticipate the social consequences. That this should be so is a salutary thought for educational policymakers. Yet the competencies we require are the very ones that can enable us to deal with a knight's move, even if we cannot predict it in advance.

PRESENTING FIVE KEY COMPETENCIES

Education of the twenty-first-century child does not simply need a few additional add-on skills—more of the same. It requires the capacity for creative transformation. Based on this notion, I conceptualized five key competencies, and I argue that each competence involves both cognitively creative and ethically creative dimensions.

Managing Ambiguity and Diversity

We have come to understand diversity particularly in the context of a multicultural society, and one of the tenets of this understanding is tolerance. However, numerous writers have pointed out that tolerance may require little actual cognitive work because it does not require a shift in perspective-taking per se; one can tolerate others' views or lifestyles while making no dent in one's one assumptions. To recognize the validity of another's perspective—to manage diversity effectively—one must be able to put oneself in that person's place, at the very least to see how one's own position looks from another point of view.

The challenge of managing ambiguity, however, is broader and in some ways more profoundly novel (and also perhaps ultimately more creative) because it is not about the *content* of thinking—the potential clash of values— but the *process* of thinking. There is a cultural message frequently transmitted in education which favors linear thinking, linear logic. This is purveyed through such adages as "Stick to the point," "Don't be distracted by irrelevancies," and "Look for the single correct answer." In this context, Craft's comparisons with the more holistic perspectives of Asian thought are salient. The reason that this is important in relation to the process of managing ambiguity lies in the way that it engenders anxiety. If children are reared to seek the single right answer and to avoid the messy and the ambiguous, they will become uneasy when confronted with multiple options and solutions. The pursuit of closure and a deep discomfort with the relativistic or pluralist are the likely outcomes of exposure to such a cultural message.

But in many areas of life, the mundane as well as the creative, the most effective problem solving comes through recognizing and using multiple possible solutions. The power of cultural representation and how it can mislead our evaluations can be seen in the example of multitasking. Once this was an

unremarked feature of the largely devalued, inevitable routin/
realm of female life. Now it has become recognized as an essen
for all, in both the public and the private sphere. In a world that
ticultural in terms of ethnicity but also multidimensional in terms of
and social demands which we recognize in wide swaths of our lives, the inability to manage ambiguity is manifestly disabling.

So far I have concentrated on the cognitive-creative aspects of managing ambiguity and diversity, but the ethical implications are also very significant. In extreme form, fundamentalism, whether political or religious, reflects a total intolerance of ambiguity and diversity. The psychological inability to manage uncertainty was, of course, a cornerstone explanation in early work on the psychology of authoritarianism. But recognizing ethical ambiguity is not ethical relativism; it is the ability to appreciate the diversity of ethical perspectives—and one's own position, and positioning, within them. Claxton's vignette of the young aikido expert shows just such a creative switch of ethical perspective taking.

Embracing Agency and Responsibility

This competence refers to the ability to see oneself as an active agent in one's cognitive, social, and moral world and to take the responsibilities that go with that agency. It is a competence that depends on developing a sense of efficacy, a belief that one can have an effect. Research from developmental psychology indicates that this comes from having early experience taking responsibility and being effective, and being in an environment in which there is routine expectation that one will be effective (Haste 2004).

This is first and foremost an ethical competence. Its creativity lies in being able to position oneself *appropriately* in relation to not only moral dilemmas and responsibilities but also ethically relevant domains such as the community and sociopolitical issues. In relation to appropriateness I again turn to Claxton's apparently highly *agentic* aikido expert. Research on the factors which predict taking responsibility in the community, and making one's voice heard in relation to issues such as social injustice, indicates that the development of agency and responsibility can involve major shifts in perspective taking and positioning. Yates (1999) and others (e.g., Haste 2004, 2006; Kahne and Westheimer 2003) have shown that participating in community service that is initially motivated by helpfulness can result in an increased awareness of the social and political conditions which create disadvantage and deprivation, leading to a sense of personal responsibility to challenge injustice.

However, the competence to exhibit agency and responsibility is not solely ethical. The capacity to meet the challenges of the social and physical world require more cognitive versions of creative fixing and *bricolage*—a general propensity, for example, to master alien subway systems, to find the right tools or artisan when things break down, to negotiate a turgid bureaucracy, to know how to assist the sick stranger in the street as well as feeling that one should do so.

Finding and Sustaining Community

In the twenty-first century, this competence goes beyond calling on one's neighbors and remembering one's friends' birthdays. Most obviously, it involves the technological communication resources that are now available, but managing these is a multilevel task. Face-to-face communication is but one of the routes. Connecting to strangers via a variety of media, and maintaining boundaries around the self within these media, are skills that even children need. Lamentations about loss of face-to-face communication (and the skills thereof) ignore their replacement or augmentation by technological routes, and the skills that go with this development.

Apart from obvious technological skills, wherein lies the competence—and the creativity? First, it lies in managing the considerable diversity of contacts, keeping track of one's virtual friendship world. Second, it lies in incorporating and using cultural resources; we must not forget that connecting with someone also means finding shared cultural experience and constructing shared meaning. In both new and long-standing relationships, we position ourselves, and are positioned by, the way we do or do not access shared cultural symbols, resources, and narratives, that is, how we do or do not find common ground (Clark and Brennan 1991; Edwards 1997). One blatant fallout of globalization is the universality of young people's sartorial and musical tastes; thanks to MTV, teenagers from almost any culture can find common ground instantly at least in some areas of consumption. Another interesting example is a recent brilliant (and richly informative) advertising campaign by HSBC which capitalizes on the dangerous significance of different cultural meaning, showing us how a polite gesture in one culture is seriously offensive in another.

Managing Emotion

Here is an area in which both (Western) culture and science have seen changes in recent decades. Within the dualistic metaphor that suffuses Western culture are purveyed variations of the theme that emotion and reason are distinct and antithetical—such that one poses a threat to the other (Haste 1994). Different variations—stories—operate in different subcultures. As we move between these, we adjust competently to their requirements, but I would argue that most are ultimately not a competent way to live either ethically or cognitively.

One story is that emotion *disorganizes* reason. Accordingly, the most effective form of knowing is logical reasoning; emotion is not a trustworthy source of knowing, and it distorts reason. Competence here would be to separate thinking and feeling, and suppress feeling where possible. A second story is that while reasoning is paramount, emotion is needed to energize cognition. Good emotion here is the appropriate motivation enabling one to carry through one's thinking into action. Competent emotion management, therefore, is the ability to direct one's affect toward following through the tasks that one's cognition has set—willpower, in other words. But reason is still master, and passion is suspect.

A third story privileges emotion over reason; it is the Romantic story. True knowledge comes from listening to the heart; the head's knowledge is cold and narrowly focused. The Romantic version surfaces at various times in history. In Europe, the Enlightenment—a triumph of reason over passion—met resistance from those who saw what we would now call science as something that would destroy the beauty and meaning of the universe. The more common-sense view is that if one does not feel, one cannot understand other people or recognize one's moral obligations to them. In the decades after World War II, the Romantic story reemerged in humanistic psychology, which was trying to find a richer concept of the human than that offered by "sterile" cognitive science. Competence within this story meant getting in touch with one's feelings— which itself presupposes that one has lost touch with them through being brainwashed by the story that valorizes reason alone.

A breakthrough story comes from neuroscience, particularly the work of Antonio Damasio. His work with brain-damaged people shows that the boundary between emotion and cognition is artificial, that one cannot function without the other (Damasio 2003). People without the capacity for emotion are incapable of making effective reasoned judgments; it is as though they have lost the gut feeling which tells them when they have arrived at the right answer. His work has been hailed as an essay in what it means to be truly human—and as an explanation of how all creativity is possible.

However, from the point of view of understanding emotional competence, Damasio's (2003) work tells us that there is more to it than getting in touch with one's feelings. To educate people to be fully human in this way, I would argue that as with the issue of ambiguity, we must first erode the fear and anxiety underpinning the conventional separation which fuels the cultural stories. Fear of ambiguity arises from the deep anxiety imbued in the child who is told to find the "right" answer and to avoid complexity. In some stories there is a fear that the power of emotion can sweep one out of control. In other stories the fear is that cognition is sterile, reductionist, and cold—and therefore not human(e) or wise. I argue that competence lies in recognizing the stories that culture offers and finding a way to integrate reason with affect, neither denying nor overprivileging either one.

Technological Competence

This competence refers to more than keyboard skills. The most important aspect of it, in my view, parallels Piaget's insights into *adaptation*—we first assimilate new information into our existing schemas, transforming it to fit them, and only over time do we accommodate those schemas to make better sense of the new information. The competence—and the creativity—lie in adaptively maximizing the implications of novel information. This is particularly true of our social practices. New technology initially allowed us to do better, or quicker, what we had always done, but did not at first change what we did. The electric typewriter was more efficient than the manual, and at first the word processor was used as an elaborated version of this. However, as the potential for the new tool becomes evident through our interaction with it, our technological and social practices change. The manual typewriter was the tool of women educated within a particular spectrum of skills and educational levels. The word processor, as part of the whole computer package, quickly became a gender- and status-neutral tool. Keyboard skills are now universal, and the secretary has become the personal assistant or administrator. And everyone from 6 to 96 years old who has the technology expects to have their own e-mail and Internet access.

Another example—which also touches on finding and sustaining community—is the mobile phone. It has transformed the social practices of telephoning; one's phone is now a personal prosthesis, not a machine located in one place, and it has enormous implications for how we construct our own and others' accessibility. We merely have to turn a machine off, not relocate ourselves, to prevent access. An unexpected new social practice is *texting*, which was not predicted by the manufacturers; it now dominates young people's communication in all areas of their social lives, including developing and ending romantic relationships (Haste 2005).

The competence here is the ability to adapt to the implications of technological change, to respond creatively to the new opportunities for social practices (and to ensure that valued practices are not lost). Furthermore, consideration of the ethical implications of all new technology is an increasing part of the public dialogue around science and society (Jackson, Barbagallo, and Haste 2005; Willis and Wilsdon 2004). No longer are the ethical issues and social consequences of technological and scientific developments regarded as a peripheral add-on, or as the domain of persons far removed from the day-to-day practice of science—a development which is consistent with the agenda laid out in Howard Gardner's target chapter.

EDUCATIONAL IMPLICATIONS

Competencies as I have described them share the commonalities that I identified in the pieces by Anna Craft, Howard Gardner, and Guy Claxton: flexibility, exploring the nonobvious options, taking multiple perspectives. Critical evaluation is also a necessary element of competence, but it is a particularly vital task for those who want to rethink their linear assumptions in order to equip young people for contemporary life. All these can be seen as components of the creative generative adaptation I referred to earlier.

What are the implications for education? I propose three, and they are not mere prescriptions for educational practice; they are challenges to the cultural framework within which education takes place—in this case, the Western cultural framework.

• We must explore the domains of anxiety which we currently, unwittingly or otherwise, foster in young people. These include fear of open-ended or multiple solutions, fear that there may not be a reassuring single "right" answer, but several possible options. This is particularly important in the area of science education, which often (though not always) seems to purvey the message that science is the pursuit of fact and that scientific progress depends purely on logic and the proper mathematics. For some children this is in itself reassuring because it removes worrying doubt. A more realistic account of how science progresses and greater exposure to the debates in the history of science, not only to the neatly factual outcomes, would help. But in the arts and humanities there are many ways to confront children with the experience of ambiguity in ways that do not permit them to slide into premature closure—the work of M. C. Escher is a good start; tolerating the discomfort of his drawings and discussing the implications of this discomfort, not just treating it as a weird excursion, could be both fun and valuable and can be done by even the youngest schoolchild.

• We must find ways to help young people use dialogue as a means of understanding multiple perspectives and positions, to manage parallel and dissonant points of view without seeking the hegemonic unitary solution. But at the same time we must teach them to interrogate the values and justifications that underpin each point of view so that they are not tempted to retreat into relativism, which is not the same as multiple perspective taking, but in fact an escape from it. It is important, educationally, to distinguish dialogue from the more traditional format of debate, in which one develops a persuasive argument. The skilled debater in fact implicitly uses his or her intuitive understanding of the perspective of the audience (and protagonist) to be an effective advocate. What dialogue requires is stepping back from that process, unpacking the assumptions that the parties in the discussion are making, and finding both common ground and areas of incommensurability as a basis for moving toward understanding (if not agreement). To unpack one's own assumptions is itself quite a task; few of us, even as adults, are fully aware of these. As an exercise in managing conflict, such unpacking has great value in itself, but as an exercise in managing perspective taking, it is even more useful because the skills developed have spin-offs in both cognitive and ethical areas.

• We must find a way to encourage a view of rationality that does not restrict students' resources for knowing to too narrow a cognitive perspective and does not define *objectivity* as the illusory separation of the self from the context—which is an impossible *god trick,* to use Haraway's (1991) words. We need to teach that objectivity involves recognizing one's inevitable subjectivity in a situation, and dealing with it in a synthesizing manner allows us to take a whole view of our perspectives, responses, and the resources we bring to the situation. Numerous examples from social science and natural science, as well as more obviously from literature and the humanities, demonstrate the embeddedness of the observer in the textuality. As with the process of unpacking the assumptions we bring to dialogue in order to make dialogue more effective, we can utilize the variety of perspectives in a classroom to explore how we implicitly value differently the different sources of knowing and how we might be more effective in using these processes. At the very least, the pursuit of the appropriate criteria for evidence falls into this style of thinking, but *evidence* can be narrowly defined as a certain kind of empiricism. To explore and make explicit what students intuitively deem to be a basis for valid judgments, whether in the social, ethical, aesthetic, or scientific domains, is surely the first step to their understanding how evidential reasoning is constructed.

Perhaps we can think of these as weapons of mass deconstruction?

REFERENCES

Clark, H. H., and S. E. Brennan. 1991. Grounding in communication. In *Perspectives on socially shared cognition,* ed. L. B. Resnick, J. M. Levine, and S. D. Teasley, 127–49. Washington, DC: American Psychological Association.

Damasio, A. 2003. *Looking for Spinoza: Joy, sorrow, and the feeling brain.* Orlando, FL: Harcourt.

Edwards, D. 1997. *Discourse and cognition.* Thousand Oaks, CA: SAGE.

Gosling, W. 1994. *Helmsmen and heroes.* London: Weidenfeld & Nicolson.

Haraway, D. J. 1991. *Simians, cyborgs, and women: The reinvention of Nature.* New York: Routledge.

Haste, H. 1994. *The sexual metaphor.* Cambridge, MA: Harvard University Press.

———. 2001. Ambiguity, autonomy and agency: Psychological challenges to new competence. In *Defining and selecting key competences,* ed. D. S. Rychen and L. H. Salganik, 93–120. Seattle: Hogrefe & Huber.

———. 2004. Constructing the citizen. *Political Psychology* 23:413–39.

———. 2005. *Joined-up texting: The role of mobile phones in young people's lives.* Nestlé Social Research Programme Report 3. Croydon, England: Nestlé Trust.

———. 2006. Beyond conventional civic participation, beyond the moral-political divide: Young people and contemporary debates about citizenship. *Journal of Moral Education* 35:473–93.

Jackson, R., F. Barbagallo, and H. Haste. 2005. Strengths of public dialogue on science-related issues. *Critical Review of International Social and Political Philosophy* 8:349–58.

Kahne, J., and J. Westheimer. 2003. Teaching democracy: What schools need to do. *Phi Delta Kappan* 85 (1): 34–40, 57–66.

Willis, J., and R. Wilsdon. 2004. *See-through science: Why public engagement needs to move upstream.* London: Demos.

Yates, M. 1999. Community service and political-moral discussions among adolescents: A study of a mandatory school-based program in the United States. In *Roots of civic identity: International perspectives on community service and activism in youth,* ed. M. Yates and J. Youniss, 16–31. Cambridge, UK: Cambridge University Press.

9

Creativity, Wisdom, and Trusteeship

Niches of Cultural Production

Patrick Dillon

An open brief is a rare luxury. So, too, is the opportunity to engage, unconstrained, with the ideas of some prominent thinkers in education. In my response to the chapters by Howard Gardner on trusteeship, Guy Claxton on wisdom, and Anna Craft on creativity, I have looked for connections: things that corroborate, things that contradict, things that unify. After an initial reading, I made a synopsis of each work, not a précis or a summary, but an account of the passages that struck me as saying something important or different. In doing this I first made connections, mapping them to the ideas that currently occupy my thinking about culture and education. From this emerged the theme of niches of cultural production.

In outline, my argument is that creativity, wisdom, and trusteeship are cultural patterns arising from mutually transformative transactions between individuals and their environments. Cultural patterns are essentially niches that may be explained through evolutionary, ecological, and market theories. They are manifestations of competition between beliefs, ideas, and forms of behavior and the arenas in which transactions take place between the people who hold or practice them. Education about and for creativity, wisdom, and trusteeship may be viewed as an intervention in this market of ideas and behaviors. Specific pedagogical or technological interventions will favor particular cultural patterns. Thus education may be seen as a means of producing cultural capital.

SYNOPSES

Gardner is concerned with the ethical responsibilities of professionals. He talks of good work that is excellent in quality and ethically orientated. He believes that professionals, especially scientists and technologists, cannot be indifferent to the social consequences of their work. They have a duty to listen carefully to critics, to ensure that their work is not misapplied, and, above all, to communicate to the public the essence of the work and its wider implications. Traditionally, the values of the community (especially religious values), the law, and the standards of professionals themselves have provided the benchmarks of ethical accountability. All of these, Gardner suggests, are in decline. He would like to see a new covenant between professionals and society.

Gardner asks whether there can be societal trustees in America today. His research throws some interesting light on changing views of trusteeship. The *pillar of society* model, popular in the early twentieth century, lost credibility in the 1960s. It was too hierarchical, too patronizing, not compatible with the wider responsibilities required of a democratic society. Globalization, the fragmentation of national identity, the impact of media, and the rise of the celebrity have all influenced contemporary thinking about trusteeship. Now the view is that organizations and foundations might be better placed to take on the role of trustees and that responsibilities are best discharged at a local rather than national level. Gardner is interested in the notion of trusteeship and its equivalents in other times and other places, the mental models that underlie these notions, the role of technology in trusteeship, and the training of future trustees.

Claxton is interested in the extent to which wisdom can be seen as advanced creativity. He asks about what conditions promote wise action and what sort of pedagogy should be associated with educating about wisdom. He sees wisdom as an overlapping rather than specific term; it may involve a great deal of intuition, it is often manifest in complicated human affairs, and it is not necessarily solely the prerogative of older people. His research suggests that, generally, the wise person has empathy for a situation but a degree of disinterest in it. Because the wise person has a deeper appreciation of dilemma, he or she is often able to subtly reframe his or her perception of a situation and thus take the heat out of it and find new possibilities. These deliberations lead Claxton to offer some putative dispositions for wisdom: an interest in and engagement with human affairs, tolerance of things that do not "fit," openness to and trust of intuition, a secure sense of self, tolerance of complexity and uncertainty, and a degree of courage. Many of these traits, he says, are also associated with creativity.

Claxton sees wisdom as not so much in quality of thinking, but more in the nature of motivational vectors. Cultivating motivational clarity and making choices that lead to optimal resolutions of motivational conflicts and complexities, he says, are key ingredients. In support of this argument, he draws on some long-standing ideas: the ability to look back at oneself and see one's own motivational perspectives (akin to Buddhist mindfulness?) and the way in which the classical Greeks divided wisdom into *sophia* (insight arising from philosophical, contemplative, or spiritual practice), *episteme* (insight arising from systematic study of the way things work), and *phronesis* (the qualities possessed by statesmen and lawmakers). Phronesis, with its prudent courses of action, he sees as particularly important, especially when applied in a localized and situated way.

Craft is concerned with creativity. She reviews the developing policy context for creativity in education and identifies two *blind spots*: the relationship of creativity with culture and with the marketplace. She explores the cultural *situatedness* of creativity by looking at its characteristics in different regional settings. She compares and contrasts Western and Asian traditions through individualistic and collectivist forms of socialization, different forms of thought, and different worldviews. While acknowledging the limitations of comparisons based on broad generalizations, she believes they do tell us something about the values that different cultures place on creativity and the products of innovation.

Craft's comparative approach includes the influence of macrolevel politics in cultural systems and how these impact the relationships between models of creativity, the environment, and ethics. The difficulty of reconciling these matters, she suggests, produces tensions and dilemmas at the level of education in schools. In particular, there is insufficient discrimination in distinguishing between human needs and wants, with the danger that creativity becomes overly associated with fashion and entertainment. For her, wisdom is to be found in a critical stance on, and the humane application of, creativity. Here, there are similarities with Claxton's view of wisdom as advanced creativity.

NICHE CONSTRUCTION

For me, the common theme that comes through in all three contributions, and is discussed in some detail by Craft, is the situatedness of creativity, wisdom, and trusteeship. This links with my work on education as a manifestation of both culture and environment, which in turn is part of a long-standing interest in *cultural ecology*.

Cultural ecology deals with the reciprocal relationship between people and their environments and thus offers a unifying frame for nature and culture. It is widely held that organisms adapt to their environments, but not that environments adapt to their organisms. This unidirectional view of adaptation, involving organisms' responses to environmentally shaped problems, has been a barrier to modeling human behavior on ecological principles. Human environments are palpably the outcomes of human activity as much as environments shape humans. Landscapes are as much a record of human enterprise as the genetic code is a record of human adaptation. One only has to look at the diversity of farming systems worldwide and the dynamic relationships they have with the lifestyles of the people who farm them.

A comprehensive evolutionary and ecological model of *niche construction*, in which organisms and environments are in mutually transformative relationships, has been developed by Odling-Smee, Laland, and Feldman (2003). By taking cultural practices as central to the relationship between people and their environments, this model is as appropriate to human systems as it is to the natural world. Indeed the authors include a chapter on human niche construction, dealing with the relationship between evolutionary change and cultural practices. My interest is in applying some of the ideas embodied in the notion of niche construction to culture in general and then education as a cultural phenomenon. This might be termed a *cultural-ecological approach*. In doing this, I hope to broaden some of the thinking associated with sociocultural theories to accommodate the notion of individuals shaping their worlds and being shaped by them.

There are two caveats to the application of niche construction to education via culture. First, niche construction is primarily a contribution to *new synthesis* evolutionary theory and is thus concerned with long-term change. The evolutionary focus has ecological ramifications, and it is these that interest me because they deal with shorter-term change in relations between people and their environments. There are difficulties in using ecological principles alone to explain the rapid change associated with globalization, so it is necessary to integrate with them some perspectives from economics. Here I draw heavily on the work of E. L. Jones (2006), notably his historical and economic critique of culture. Second, niche construction is concerned with populations, or more precisely the niches of species within ecosystems. I am more concerned with what happens at the individual level—the behavior of people within niches.

Ecosystems are now conceptualized as complex, adaptive systems rather than self-regulating systems. The structure and function of an ecosystem is regulated by the number and kind of constituent parts in the system, the number and kind of interactive links that connect these parts together, and the different kinds of "currency" (e.g., energy and nutrients; in human systems, information) needed to keep track of the state of the system's components when they interact (Odling-Smee, Laland, and Feldman 2003). These are simple but important characteristics that provide useful routes into cultural mechanisms in human systems.

The role of an organism within an ecosystem describes its niche. Odling-Smee, Laland, and Feldman (2003) adopt the definition of the pioneering early twentieth-century ecologist George Hutchinson: the niche is the sum of all the environmental influences acting on an organism. Following from Bock (1980), they describe an organism in terms of its subsystems (traits and characteristics), which they call *features,* and an organism's environment in terms of subsystems, which they call *factors*. Niche construction occurs when an organism modifies its feature-factor relationship. This can happen by physically perturbing factors at its current location or by relocating, thereby exposing itself to different factors.

This niche definition emphasizes the relationship between the traits and characteristics of an organism (i.e., the organism's place in the environment and behavior within it) and the environment itself. The feature-factor relationship stresses the importance of interactions and transactions between an organism and (the totality of) the environment. Social scientists have long recognized the importance of these relationships in human systems (see, e.g., Bronfenbrenner 1977). Niche construction provides a theoretical framework for understanding the mechanisms involved and their behavioral significance.

Odling-Smee, Laland, and Feldman (2003) discuss feature-factor relationship as a unified entity, meaning all the human traits and characteristics and all the components of the environment that make up the human niche. I am less concerned with the totality of the human niche, and more concerned with what is happening at the subsystems level, for example, within education or applied to a phenomenon like creativity. I use *feature-factor relationship* to mean the configuration of traits, characteristics, and environmental components—the cultural patterns that characterize these subsystems. This is a useful analytical device, but in practice all such subsystems can only be fully understood in terms of the niche as a whole.

Niche construction adds a further level of conceptualization to the sociocultural theories that are currently influential in education. Sociocultural theories emphasize individual and collective identities within sociocultural environments and the meanings people and groups create within those environments. Different formulations of sociocultural theory draw on Dewey's ideas about personally significant experience, the sense that someone has about a situation, and Leontev's ideas about the collective understanding captured in language and other social artifacts (Stevenson 2004). In both formulations the emphasis is on what the individual is doing, either with him- or herself or through his or her activities within the social system. Just as important is the nature of the exchanges that take place within the social group, the interactions and transactions through which identity and meaning emerge, and how these in turn relate to the situation itself (i.e., the environment). This picks up on the idea that knowledge is not constructed by the mind processing and selecting from the sensory data available to it, but is constituted in the interaction between the individual and his or her environment. This is the basis of Dewey's transactional theory of knowledge (Vanderstraeten 2002).

Because niche construction can be thought of in both ecological and evolutionary terms, the most fundamental way of exploring it is through the conditions (i.e., feature-factor relationship) that maintain life for a given organism. Boyden (1987) has proposed such a set of conditions for the human species. It includes conditions of the physical environment such as clean water, clean air, acceptable climatic conditions, and minimal contact with parasites and pathogens. There are also a number of dietary conditions concerning the quality of food, calorie intake, a balanced diet, and social norms governing the consumption of food. Most important for the arguments made here are Boyden's conditions of the personal and social environment:

- levels of sensory stimulation that are neither much less nor much greater than those of the natural habitat
- a pattern of physical work that involves short periods of vigorous muscular work and longer periods of lighter muscular work, but also frequent periods of rest
- a polyphasic sleeping pattern and the opportunity to rest or sleep in response to the urge to do so
- opportunities and incentives for the learning and practice of manual skills and for creative behavior in general
- opportunities and incentives for active involvement in recreational activities
- an environment that has high interest value and accommodates changes in the interests of individuals
- opportunities for considerable spontaneity in behavior
- opportunities for considerable variety in daily experience
- short goal-achievement cycles
- aspirations of a kind likely to be fulfilled
- an effective emotional support network providing a framework for eliciting, receiving, and giving care
- frequent interaction on a daily basis with members of an extended family as well as peer and friendship groups on matters of mutual interest and concern
- opportunities and incentives for small-group interaction on projects of mutual interest and concern
- a social environment that confers responsibilities and obligations on individuals toward their extended families as well as peer and friendship groups
- opportunities for individuals to move spontaneously and freely from one small group to another, and to and from a state of solitude
- an environment and a lifestyle that are conducive to a sense of personal involvement, purpose, belonging, responsibility, interest, excitement, challenge, satisfaction, comradeship, love, enjoyment, confidence, and security

This is a long list of largely self-evident, basic conditions for what might be considered a good life. But it is worth setting out because it provides a purchase on the rather abstract notion of *human niche* and an entry into the more specific cultural patterns that concern Craft, Gardner, and Claxton. Some general principles governing these conditions may be derived from niche construction: in the short term they are profitable and involve fitness-enhancing behaviors or processes, individuals actively select between alternative interactive outcomes in their environments, they are directed by cultural information whose structure and content are the result of prior selection, they work proactively—the constraints imposed by prior selection inform future choices (Odling-Smee, Laland, and Feldman 2003, 176).

Cultural information resides in artifacts, tools, practices (e.g., designing, cooking), modes of communication (e.g., symbols, language), lifestyles, and combinations of these (e.g., agriculture as a combination of tools, processes, and lifestyle). In evolutionary terms, cultural practices are shortcuts to acquiring adaptive information. Cultural information is transacted at different levels: "vertical (from parents), horizontal (from peers), oblique (from unrelated individuals), indirect (e.g., from key individuals), and *frequency-dependent* (e.g., from the majority [of individuals])" (Odling-Smee, Laland, and Feldman 2003, 258–259).

IMPLICATIONS

In terms of implications for creativity, wisdom, and trusteeship, several things follow from the perspectives on ecology and niche construction set out above. Creativity, wisdom, and trusteeship are cultural patterns. They are location specific and context dependent because they are manifestations of the environment *and* the individuals concerned *and* the interactions and transactions between them. They are temporally dependent because the feature-factor relationship that governs them is subject to constant selection. However, globalization increasingly mediates locational and temporal conditions or, more precisely, alters the scales and time frames of selection.

The local cultures of Southern Thailand, painstakingly documented by Pongpaiboon (2004), provide an example. The cultural phenomenon of *tahna* in southern Thai corresponds to local Malay *tanda* and to the original Pali-Sanskrit form *suntan,* or *subdan* in general Thai. It is "the functional cultural capital of each person and expands in a close-knit way into community culture, varying with the forces of nature and of power base in a correlation of circumstance, place and time" (p. 10).

Tahna is an integrated worldview involving belief, faith, legend, ritual, and locally adapted language (dialect) related to systems of production and consumption. Production and consumption not just of material goods, but of "a body of knowledge . . . inculcation of ideas about how to consume rights and duties (knowing rightful power and duty) and social standards, and the production and consumption of systems of values, esthetics, and art, all at the same time with several dimensions involved, in concrete as well as spiritual form" (Pongpaiboon 2004, 96). *Tahna* is functional through "action, management, exercise of wisdom . . . expressed in behavior, thought, and procedure either in concrete or in abstract form. These functions, when repeated or retested by groups of people . . . for a certain period, would be selected for common practice so that they become formalized and serve as commonly shared ways or behaviors, as systems and conventions and patterns of livelihood of a group of people. These make up the culture or the mode of behavior of that group" (p. 63). Wisdom, in the sense that it is used here, corresponds closely with "belief that has truth and is used constructively" and "mastery born of accumulated experience" (pp. 68, 86). Belief that is lacking in truth is a misguided thought, a wrong belief.

This example illustrates the point made by Craft about the situatedness of culture and cultural processes. It helps locate not just creativity but also wisdom and trusteeship. Wisdom is a core construct in *tahna,* and the way in which wise action is integral to decision-making processes fits well with Claxton's notion of optimal resolution of motivational conflicts. One can also see how some of the qualities that Gardner associates with trusteeship might provide the social expression of wisdom in such a culture.

Odling-Smee, Laland, and Feldman (2003), drawing on the work of Durham (1991), see behavioral predispositions and motivational biases as both evolved (primary values) and affected by socially transmitted cultural values (secondary values). The secondary values arise through collective experience and social history—what educationalists call *prior learning* and *prior experience.* Some of these values, such as rules of thumb, proverbs, conventions, and moral or ethical principles, are determined by what Boyd and Richerson (1985) call *positive-frequency dependency,* better known as conformity. When individuals conform, they bias their adoption of cultural information toward that expressed by the majority and may be particularly prone to adopting cultural variants exhibited by authoritative or charismatic individuals (Boyd and Richerson call this *indirect bias*). Indirect bias can be interpreted in two ways: (1) benevolently, arising from the sort of qualities that Gardner would like to see associated with trusteeship and that Claxton would see as a means of optimally resolving motivational conflicts through localized and situated phronesis, or (2) as a form of internal protectionism, maintaining the interests of those who hold power over the population's freedom to choose. Both may be adaptive, and it is here that a finer explanatory resolution is required than that offered by evolutionary approaches alone.

E. L. Jones (2006) argues that the addition of some economic constructs to the theoretical mix improves its resolution and that an understanding of the market is essential to an understanding of culture. He claims that because economics is the analysis of an abstract category of human behavior—choice—its techniques are by definition culturally neutral and universal. He defines the market as "not just places where goods and services are sold or exchanged, [but] any state of competition between beliefs and ideas and forms of behavior, or the arena in which interaction takes place between the peoples who hold or practice them" (p. 49). This is essentially an ecological definition: the emphasis is on *transactions* as they occur in the relationship between the traits and characteristics of an organism and its environment. In other words, it provides another take on the feature-factor relationship in the definition of *niche* adopted earlier.

E. L. Jones (2006) makes a number of related points about market processes that are relevant to the analysis presented here:

- They depend on and are affected by custom. Whereas custom probably adapts to economic change, psychological rigidities can restrict the scope of economic activities.
- Young people find it easier to change than older people who have had longer to internalize some prior set of values. On the other hand, there may be an imprinting period, and young people influenced by

propaganda may find themselves trapped by allegiance to norms inculcated even earlier in their lives.

- Cultural values adapt to opportunity. Behaviors once unthinkable may subsequently, and surprisingly rapidly, become new norms.
- The cultures of no two generations have ever been identical, if only because history serves up different traumatic imprinting events to each cohort.
- Every fixed assumption about society alters, at least if one takes a long enough perspective.
- Whatever forces prompt cultural change, not all the values of society respond simultaneously.

The fluidity implied here creates a number of tensions, not least in the relationship between old and new. Pongpaiboon's (2004) documentation of Southern Thai *tahna* is motivated by a desire to preserve at least some elements of what he sees as a worthwhile cultural system. But he acknowledges that it is fast being overtaken by globalization, a process that E. L. Jones (2006, 48) describes as cultural fusion resulting from markets coalescing and the advent of competition between behaviors and symbols that formerly seldom came into contact. Jones's prognosis is not good: ancient cultural features may survive as relicts when there is no special reason to dispense with them. He cites dialects as an example that illustrates the persistence of sluggishly changing forms when markets for modes of speech remain isolated. With increased mobility of people and mass communication, dialects vanish quickly. In the 1980s, I carried out field work on dialect in a region of central southern England better known as the northern part of Hardy's Wessex. With linguistic historian Malcolm Jones, I set out to show how the survival of some dialect words could be attributed to their association with ecological and landscape features. The words had utility as long as people continued to use them in their local environment. Not only were we able to trace continuity of use back through the twentieth and into the nineteenth century and earlier, through the literature of Thomas Hardy, Richard Jefferies, and others, we were also able to record middle-aged and elderly people speaking in north Wessex dialect (M. Jones and Dillon 1987). Now this dialect is all but extinct; the children and grandchildren of the people we interviewed sound much the same as any other 20- or 30-year-olds in southern England and use a similar nonlocalized vocabulary.

Similar processes of globalization have contributed to the demise, or more precisely reconfiguration within the niche, of the form of trusteeship that Gardner identifies with early and middle twentieth-century America. Ecologically we are dealing with *mutualistic interactions*—investing in others so as to enhance the benefits that eventually return to us. The extended family is a manifestation of this, as is patronage in its many forms. The counterinfluence in recent decades has been that incidental benefits that normally accrue to individuals through forms of patronage (e.g., longer-term benefits to parents from their children in the extended family) have become devalued as the same benefits are provided by society (Odling-Smee, Laland, and Feldman 2003, 359–363). Just as society has assumed responsibility for some parts of the feature-factor relationship that used to be associated with the family, so has the locus of trusteeship transferred from the individual to organizations, as Gardner has observed.

In each generation, people persistently construct and reconstruct significant components of their environments. As time passes, they "drag part of their environment with them" (Odling-Smee, Laland, and Feldman 2003, 367) and leave other parts behind, thereby transforming their own adaptive landscapes. Like many dialects and minority languages, pillar-of-society trusteeship (Gardner) and wisdom as an integral part of worldview (Claxton) have been compromised by changed feature-factor relationships.

All forms of formalized education—institutions, curricula, pedagogies, and the policies and practices that shape them—are interventions in the market of ideas and behaviors. As such, they are integral to niche construction and contribute to complex mixes of cultural patterns. "Education for life" and "education for change" are old clichés. But, as with many simple assertions, they hide some profound concerns. It is the same with creativity, wisdom, and trusteeship. It is easy to educate *about* them, but very difficult to educate *for* them because of the difficulty of finding meaningful contexts, notwithstanding the real progress made with teaching life skills and cross-curricular concerns such as citizenship. Educating for them means addressing what it is to construct a niche wisely or creatively, indeed what constitutes a wise or creative niche and what it is to act as a niche trustee. It follows from the principles set out above that the form of the educational environment is a manifestation of the experiences, presences, and practices of the people within it. It also follows that all educational environments are adaptive in that they accommodate changing relationships between people and resources. By modeling the processes through which educational environments are maintained and developed (i.e., particular facets of the feature-factor relationship), it is possible to design interventions that favor certain outcomes.

Niche construction is derived from evolutionary and ecological theories, both of which model relationships as systems. Some important principles follow from this. First, systems can be scaled from macro to micro with successive subsystems nesting inside the larger systems. Second, change in a subsystem will have implications for the larger system of which it is a part and vice versa. Third, with certain caveats, niches may be considered as small, localized systems relative to the larger systems of which they are a part. Questions of scale, of generality and specificity, of what constitutes locality, and of interventions appropriate to that locality are important. For example, the history of curriculum development in Europe and the United States is replete with examples of initiatives that have been resoundingly successful at the local level but have not scaled up so well. In terms of niche construction, this is because they are manifestations of local particularities: "fitness" comes through location-specific and context-dependent behaviors. The mistake is to think that there is a generalizable set of conditions that can be applied elsewhere to generate similar behaviors; adaptation comes from the internal dynamic. Here the argument is for decentralization so that interventions for the qualities that Claxton associates with wisdom, or Gardner with trusteeship, may be developed at the local level. Of course there are generalizable things that can be said about wisdom and trusteeship, but niches are wisely created when generalizations are adapted to local conditions rather than being imposed on them.

Another characteristic of systems is their connectedness. Again, this throws up questions of generality and specificity. My recent work in higher education, adult education, and continuing professional development has been concerned with interventions that favor working across disciplines (Dillon 2006). Cross-disciplinarity as a creative enterprise is particularly challenging. On the one hand, the major issues of the day (e.g., climate change, fundamentalism, globalization) are complex and multifaceted. They cannot be addressed adequately from the perspective of any single discipline, nor can they be treated in the abstract as things to be studied in isolation from their real world or, one could say, *realized-niche* contexts. On the other hand, curricula are structured around disciplines that are remarkably resilient and whose gatekeepers staunchly defend their niches. One can make an educational case for working across disciplines, for example, that it utilizes all three of the intellectual abilities that Sternberg and Lubart (1999) identify with creativity: the analytic ability to recognize which of one's ideas are worth pursuing and which are not, the synthetic ability to see problems in new ways and escape the bounds of conventional thinking, and the practical-contextual ability to realize new ideas and persuade others of their value. However, facilitating cross-disciplinary work requires interventions not just with tutor-student transactions, but also at higher organizational levels in the educational system. Here the argument in for recentralization.

The Reggio Emilia system provides an insight into what an educational system might look like if it were recentralized around cultural-ecological principles. Reggio Emilia is a town in northern Italy where an ecological approach to early education was pioneered in the 1960s and has since been developed and refined into a system of international renown. In this approach, the reciprocal relationship between people and their environment takes the form of *relational architectures* and *relational pedagogies*. The focus is on the different ways that spaces may be used, the connections between things, and the experiences offered by the spaces and connections. Space is given shape and identity by the relationships created within it. Children inhabit the space by continuously constructing places, imaginary and real. Within these spaces, children's relationships and transactions with others, and with the environment itself, determine the possibilities and qualities of learning. Learning is situated, adapted, localized, and connected through a continual dialogue between the children and their environment (Ceppi and Zini 1998).

Extending these principles more widely, one might see educational niches formulated around all the learning resources (human and physical, institutional and virtual) in current educational sectors, homes, libraries, workplaces, community and adult learning centers, science and art museums, television and public services, and so on—anywhere learning takes place. The image here is of individuals coconstructing learning journeys with families, communities, networks, and educational professionals. In a recent think tank involving a number of educational agencies in the United Kingdom, we explored some of the organizational implications of education based on cultural-ecological principles and envisaged a shift from managed to coconstructed learning and reintegration of learning with lifestyle and community concerns (Green et al. 2005)—fertile ground for new formulations of creativity, wisdom, and trusteeship.

CONCLUSION

In this response to the contributions of Craft, Gardner, and Claxton, I have used a cultural-ecological approach to frame certain characteristics of human systems, and from this derive some generalizations about education and pedagogy. I have stopped short of adopting a full biological theory of culture (although a convincing and sophisticated case is made for it by Plotkin [2003]), because adaptationalist explanations alone do not focus a fine-enough lens on the vagaries of human practice. Therefore, I have integrated some market theory into my ecological account. This enables judgments to be made about the loci of agents of change within the cultural system and some anticipation of their educational consequences.

Sensitivity to local conditions at the point of intervention in a system emerges as a major concern; it is important to reconcile the distinctive needs of local communities with the generalities of living in a globalized world where control of major social systems such as health and education is centralized. And because education cannot be considered in isolation, many of the local concerns will also surface in other parts of the human system. For example, in the European Union, where transnational policies have lead to greater freedom of movement of people, goods, and services, there is still a need to recognize and celebrate what is distinctive and special about not just the member states, but also the many and diverse regions within those states. People travel not simply to work or use their holiday time, but increasingly to experience the distinctiveness of place; to appreciate local forms of building, the vernacular, traditional food and produce; and to learn about heritage and the lifestyles associated with it. Cultural heritage makes a significant contribution to the economy in these regions. These are not fossilized niches. They are finely adapted to nuances and variations in the character of the places concerned, the people within them, and the people who visit them.

Creativity, wisdom, and trusteeship may be similarly viewed as niches of cultural production. They reflect the particularity, subtlety, idiosyncrasy, and patina of locality at scales, at time frames, and through modes of organization appropriate to those places and the enterprises within them. Educational niches for creativity, wisdom, and trusteeship should give rise to outcomes that are of consequence within these local configurations. An outcome is of consequence when learners transform their understandings of themselves in relation to their environments by connecting personal sense and other kinds of meaning. Beach (1999) calls such outcomes *consequential transitions:* constructs, ideas, and beliefs that have been consciously reflected on and often struggled with. When internalized, they become part of the individual's repertoire of psychological tools (Kozulin 1998). Consequential transitions typically involve challenging existing continuities and regularities and forging new connections. Interventions can lead to consequential transitions only if the learning environment is conducive to them, that is, if the feature-factor relationship *affords* these actions and outcomes. Thus the notion of affordance (Gibson 1979) links interventions and the use of tools with the contexts and niches in which they are situated. It is in this way that creativity, wisdom, and trusteeship might become manifestations of local conditions, of the reciprocal relationship between people and their environments. As adapted cultural patterns, they have the potential to make important contributions to both the knowledge economy and social cohesion.

REFERENCES

Beach, K. 1999. Consequential transitions: A sociocultural expedition beyond transfer in education. *Review of Research in Education* 24:101–39.

Bock, W. J. 1980. The definition and recognition of biological adaptation. *American Zoologist* 20:217–27.

Boyd, R., and P. J. Richerson. 1985. *Culture and the evolutionary process.* Chicago: University of Chicago Press.

Boyden, S. 1987. *Western civilization in biological perspective: Patterns in biohistory.* Oxford, UK: Clarendon Press.

Bronfenbrenner, U. 1977. The ecology of human development in retrospect and prospect. In *Ecological factors in human development,* ed. H. McGurk, 277–86. Amsterdam: North-Holland.

Ceppi, G., and M. Zini. 1998. *Children, spaces, relations: Metaproject for an environment for young children.* Reggio Emilia, Italy: Commune di Reggio Emilia and Ministero della Pubblica Istruzion.

Dillon, P. 2006. Creativity, integrativism and a pedagogy of connection. *Thinking Skills and Creativity* 1:69–83.

Durham, W. H. 1991. *Coevolution: Genes, culture, and human diversity.* Stanford, CA: Stanford University Press.

Gibson, J. J. 1979. *The ecological approach to visual perception.* Hillsdale, NJ: Lawrence Erlbaum.

Green, H., K. Facer, T. Rudd, P. Dillon, and P. Humphreys. 2005. *Personalisation and digital technologies.* http://www.futurelab.org.uk/resources/documents/opening_education/Personalisation_report.pdf.

Jones, E. L. 2006. *Cultures merging: A historical and economic critique of culture.* Princeton, NJ: Princeton University Press.

Jones, M., and P. Dillon. 1987. *Dialect in Wiltshire and its historical, topographical and natural science contexts.* Trowbridge, England: Wiltshire County Council.

Kozulin, A. 1998. *Psychological tools: A sociocultural approach to education.* Cambridge, MA: Harvard University Press.

Odling-Smee, F. J., K. Laland, and M. W. Feldman. 2003. *Niche construction: The neglected process in evolution.* Princeton, NJ: Princeton University Press.

Plotkin, H. 2003. *The imagined world made real: Towards a natural science of culture.* New Brunswick, NJ: Rutgers University Press.

Pongpaiboon, S. 2004. *Southern Thai cultural structures and dynamics vis-à-vis development.* Bangkok: Thailand Research Fund.

Sternberg, R. J., and T. I. Lubart. 1999. The concept of creativity: Prospects and paradigms. In *Handbook of creativity,* ed. R. J. Sternberg, 3–15. Cambridge, UK: Cambridge University Press.

Stevenson, J. 2004. Developing technological knowledge. *International Journal of Technology and Design Education* 14:5–19.

Vanderstraeten, R. 2002. Dewey's transactional constructivism. *Journal of Philosophy of Education* 36:233–46.

10

Wise Creativity and Creative Wisdom

Hans Henrik Knoop

The target chapters by Anna Craft, Guy Claxton, and Howard Gardner take issue with what they call "a particular model of engagement—Western individualism, fed by market economy—which colors ambient values." (p. 6). Among other problems, this model imposes *threats to cultural diversity* (Craft), *threats to wisdom/sociality* (Claxton), and *threats to trust in social and cultural authorities* (Gardner). Agreeing with the authors that it may be helpful, even necessary, to regard these problems as strongly interrelated, I offer some comments, ideas, and perspectives.

First, I view the problems above as not only strongly interrelated but also in part emanating from the same source. Indeed, to some extent I even regard them as being the same problem in differing dressing, namely, insufficiency as regards necessary balancing of (differentiating) diversity and (integrating) unity in biological, psychological, cultural, and social systems. This general failure seems to lie at the root of such diverse problems as ailing ecology, stress, depression, and flawed educational control systems breeding distrust, cheating, and inefficiency, all more or less directly touched upon by Craft, Claxton, and Gardner.

Second, I believe it is important to keep a sharp eye on the context in which virtues of creativity, wisdom, and trust unfold in order to understand whether and how this state of affairs may come about, especially facing the current global turmoil. For instance, at the societal level it has become particularly clear that—after a couple of rather successful centuries—"free" competitive forces within both market economies and democratic politics now threaten to degenerate into their own "un-free" opposites as concentrations of power tighten and accumulate. Thus, the socially polarizing effects of the so-called winner-take-all economies have very little to do with ideal (real) markets in which citizens can buy and sell based on substantial freedom of choice and insight. Equally, extreme concentrations of political power have very little to do with real democracy in which citizens feel that they do have political influence. Moreover, as chief economic and political forces often converge, a substantial civic challenge materializes. It seems appropriate to regard these societal challenges within a broader scientific context by taking into consideration how accelerating tendencies of growth have been identified in both biology and culture. For these very tendencies go a long way in explaining the breathtaking frequencies of scientific breakthroughs and technological advances—not to mention the severe difficulties of governing societies and professions by the rather slow-paced, steady democratic means in our hands (Chaisson 2001; Knoop 2004, 2005; Kurzweil 1999, 2005).

Given such insight, democratic citizens will be looking anxiously to their leaders for reassurance, knowing that the last thing needed is a corrupt leader. However, as corruption in high offices is now reported on an almost daily basis, it should come as no surprise if many tend to lose trust in authorities, including the trustees of these authorities (relating to Gardner). Alarmingly, in 2002 the World Economic Forum declared that in its *Global Survey on Trust,* no less than two thirds of 36,000 respondents from 47 countries, statistically representing the views of 1.4 billion individuals on six continents, lacked trust in democratic institutions. Follow-up surveys have been conducted biannually, with the latest summarizing how "trust in governments, corporations and global institutions continues to decline" (GlobeScan 2005, n.p.). Likewise, I think it is important to understand the issue of cultural diversity (relating to Craft). There is a need for *supracultural* ethical unity and the political ideal of using socially integrating power positively as a basis for diverse creativity, rather than an obstruction of it—though I agree that the latter is often regrettably the case. And for the sake of completeness, the question of wisdom (relating to Claxton) obviously relates to both the need to trust others as a precondition for acting responsibly toward them and the need for balancing cultural diversity (individualism being at the extreme end of cultural diversity) with the increasing integration of our multipolarized social world.

To sum up, it seems to me we have little chance of moving forward on the diversity, wisdom, and trust issues discussed in this book without taking into consideration the unprecedented global forces of which economies and politics are now part. In this chapter I offer some reflections that might guide trusteeship and education. I start with three examples of how individuals may interact so as to unite in mutual benefit on a daily basis.

The first example regards playing music in a band. When doing so, it is obvious to the individual players that now and then they are individually in that completely immersed state of consciousness, which Csikszentmihalyi (1990) calls *flow*. It is also clear that individual players' actions have direct consequences on the other players, so there needs to be an investment (refrain) of degrees of freedom in order to function collectively when performing music in a band. Yet, when a band is good, something else may happen, namely the emergence of a symphonic "whole"—the Music (big-M) of the band—to which attention can now be primarily directed. By definition, this Music will occur at a level above the individual players' focused attention on the scores and their own playing. If this happens, there may be a sense of *collective flow* (though, of course, individually experienced), and the rather small investment in this whole may hold existential and aesthetic rewards of a very high order (Lyhne 2005).

Another example regards littering. Some people may find choosing not to litter to be rather costly compared to just throwing things on the ground once they are done with them. Yet, by thinking just slightly ahead, the investment of using a garbage can is obviously miniscule compared to the reward of having a liveable and clean world. However, in contrast to musicians instantly being able to appreciate the potential of playing for the greater symphony, the greater society that people care for by not littering may be far more elusive. This is quite ironic because while the musical whole is physically and phenomenologically "gone" the moment the musicians stop playing, society remains more or less intuitively present at all times. Of course, the point is that for many people, society—the greater social and existential field of meaning—is far from an intuitively recognizable whole to identify with. Moreover, whereas music has clear goals, as well as rules for playing that support the goals and allow for immediate gratification (all of which provides for flow), society does not provide these qualities so readily. The (in)famous words of former British Prime Minister Margaret Thatcher, that "there is no such thing as society, only individuals and families," seem to come closer to the intuitive perception of many than at least I would like to think.

The third example, which is actually almost a generalization of the first and second, regards the human need for order. As summarized within the field of *positive psychology* (Csikszentmihalyi 1993; Knoop 2006; Seligman 2002), human beings are in basic need of three types of order, three types of complex harmony. First, the body (including the mind), shaped by all that it has learned, needs to be in order: healthy, in good condition, and with sufficient positive emotions. Second, consciousness needs to be sufficiently ordered as to allow for focused attention and thus the deep joy of engagement and flow. Third, as the self appears to be an unfortunate place to look for higher meaning in life, individuals need to experience existential order by being part of meaningful social communities and meaningful projects aimed at desirable futures. When combining these three human needs, it is clear that though they all serve the individual's self-interest, their combined effect should easily be set to serve others as well.

Obviously, these examples are interrelated in that they all concern the intimate relation between individuals and their surroundings. However, they also clearly indicate how a person must be able to recognize larger "wholes" and be able to observe the effects of his or her own actions on these larger wholes in order to identify with the latter realms. Against this background I wish to share some thoughts on creativity, wisdom, and education in response to the target chapters by Craft, Claxton, and Gardner.

THOUGHTS ON CREATIVITY

By approximation, the main topics in the diverse literature on (human) creativity can be grouped in studies focusing on *processes, products, persons* (especially traits, strengths, and characteristics of very creative individuals), *pressures* (promoting and inhibiting), and combinations of these (Knoop 2006; Murray 1938; Runco 2004). There seems to be a fair amount of consensus that creativity entails the ability to create new ideas or behaviors that are adaptive, that is, something new that functions in the relevant contexts and/or that is acknowledged by others (Peterson and Seligman 2004, 110), including the ability to identify and solve/handle/cope with problems (Runco 2004). Also, there appears to be agreement that it is often useful to differentiate between *little-c* creativity that does not change culture in any significant way and *big-C* Creativity that does (big-C and little-c are sometimes found as extremes in finer graduated taxonomies), though the exact relation between these types of creativity is still not well understood (see Feldman 1980). Moreover, it seems consensual that we do not know enough about the role of genetic factors underlying creativity and that we do not know enough about how creativity relates to other personal virtues such as courage, integrity, fairness, optimism, generosity, leadership, and spirituality (Peterson and Seligman 2004, 123). These insights underline the urgency and difficulty of the complex issues discussed by Craft, Claxton, and Gardner, but, as the authors show, it has been no easy task to gain more than vague understandings of creativity and wisdom.

I think it can be constructive to employ broader and more abstract definitions. Therefore, in what follows I briefly present framings of creativity and wisdom, which I believe may aid in furthering the cultural diversity as proposed by Craft, the psychosocial ideal of an *allocentric motivational field* forwarded by Claxton, and the need for some form of strengthened basic trust in authorities as argued by Gardner. The definition of *creativity* that I propose joins the process, product, person, and pressure perspectives on creativity in a coherent view. Furthermore, it can be brought to bear on any content without (as far as I can see) any negative reductionist effects:

> Creativity can be defined as processes and products brought into the world by the work of autonomous agents, in settings that continuously promote and inhibit creativity. (Adapted from Knoop 2006)

Of course, by using a definition this broad, more specific aspects and distinctions of creativity may get lost. Yet, in my view this need not happen. My wish is not to replace the more distinct aspects of creativity described above, but rather to strengthen these by anchoring them at a deeper conceptual level. The definition is modelled graphically in Figure 10.1.

Figure 10.1   Basic Elements of Creativity

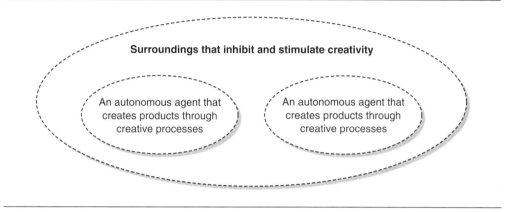

SOURCE Knoop 2006.

The concept of an *autonomous agent* covers any system that has inner drive and aims, and that can react to its surroundings. Autonomous agents can be found at any level, from the molecular (Kauffman 1996) to the universal (the universe apparently "creates" itself through cosmic expansion with local growth of complexity; Chaisson 2001). With humans, their Culture (big-C) resides about midway between these extremes (the human body being about as many times bigger than a quantum as the universe is bigger than the human body). According to Kauffman (2000), an autonomous agent can refer to any "self-reproducing system able to perform at least one thermodynamic work cycle" (p. 4), from the molecular level to the biosphere, one that is "profoundly generative—somehow fundamentally always creative" (p. 135).

Turning to human creativity, my definition covers the identification of problems (creative observation), problem solving (reactive, creative processes), and innovation (proactive, creative processes)—relating equally to little-c and big-C endeavors. In addition, any physical, phenomenological, and social emergence can be captured by it, if only one is allowed to take due account of wholes of interacting agents' contributions as being more than their sum. Elaborating even further, there seem to be a few universal criteria for creativity anchored in two fundamental types of processes: growth processes (something simple becoming more complex) and balancing processes (regulation according to preferred directions or states; Knoop 2005; Senge 1990). These two processes interrelate in that harmonious growth generally seems to entail that (1) a given system is differentiated through new and diverse elements to be united by integrating forces (Csikszentmihalyi 1993, 1996; Knoop 2005), (2) living organisms adapt creatively to optimize their own life chances in surroundings of continuous livability, and (3) the surroundings stimulate and endure this growth by means of selective pressure. Following up on my definition above, we may thus formulate a second, narrower definition of creativity:

> Human creativity unites diverse elements while ensuring efficient regulation to be performed in order to avoid disharmony, within the agent and between the agent and its surroundings. (Adapted from Knoop 2006)

Though this definition may seem tautological in that creativity in any long-term sense is an epitome of growth and balance in human life, many current problems, from stress to climate change, are clear signs of unbalanced, even dangerous, growth that shows how much of what is called *human creativity* would be better named *human destructiveness*. Of course, by definition, creativity always implies destruction of some existing order, but still I speculate whether we ought to consider definitions of what counts for benign and malignant types of creativity in order to wisely guard against the latter. To be sure, censorship is most often in direct contrast to a free society, but not always as Popper (1971) argues: "Less well known is the paradox of tolerance: Unlimited tolerance must lead to the disappearance of tolerance. If we extend unlimited tolerance even to those who are intolerant, if we are not prepared to defend a tolerant society against the onslaught of the intolerant, then the tolerant will be destroyed, and tolerance with them" (p. 265). Maybe Popper's contention applies not only to social tolerance but also to cultural tolerance, and thus creativity. Should the latter be the case, the question then becomes what kind of creativity to tolerate or, even more to the point of this book, what kind of creativity it is wise *not* to tolerate. I shall not attempt to elaborate any answers here, but I do think they are worth considering.

Using such a general approach to creativity obviously does not in itself guarantee more social responsibility or less cynicism. Still, I believe it may contribute a framework for better understanding of how the interests of the individual and the larger whole are in fact rather inseparable—echoing the famous problem with the environmental movement using the concept of *environment* to indicate misleadingly that individuals are separated from their environment, when indeed they are completely part of it. Indeed, a main obstacle in combining creativity and wisdom may be the very conceptualization of them as fundamentally separate human virtues. Rather, I suggest viewing them as complementary, thus regarding *creativity as advanced wisdom* and *wisdom as advanced creativity*, which Craft and Claxton also consider, as I understand their texts. I shall briefly expand this approach in the following section.

THOUGHTS ON WISDOM

As in the case of creativity, the complexity of wisdom challenges our ability to define it. Claxton clearly illustrates the scope of the task and I shall not pretend to be able to simplify it here. Yet, while Claxton's inclination is toward the more concrete, even anecdotal, I tend to once more lean the other way toward a more general conception. This is not done for the abstract per se but because I often find the abstract more practical, if sufficiently well understood, due to its broad applicability of general principles. I allude specifically to Gardner's (1999) concept of *deep understanding* in education, in which the deep (including more abstract) understanding makes for better use of knowledge and skills, and to Kahneman's (2003) distinction between cognitive systems of intuition versus reason. But I should mention that many other examples point to the practical benefit of abstraction: William of Occam's famous *razor principle* (in Albert Einstein's spirit, implying that theories should be made as simple as possible, but not simpler), Darwin's simple evolutionary principles in biology, the simple binary codes guiding the primary domains of society suggested by Niklas Luhmann, and the simple guiding principles of human interaction in everyday life. In all these cases it seems to be precisely the high transferability of general/abstract principles that make them so practical.

Staying with my two definitions above, we are all born small-c creators. But the definitions also imply that we are all born *small-w* wise, if wisdom is defined by at least some degree of consideration for the continuation of the surroundings. First, human adaptation by means of learning and creativity happens through not only manipulation and selection *of* the larger world but also obviously through hormonal and cognitive accommodation, thereby "wisely" submitting *to* it. Second, we inherently depend on our surroundings being liveable, which prompts us to preserve it and prevent damage to it—or to put it in evolutionary terms, it would not make much sense to replicate genes (by having children) or memes (by upbringing, teaching, instilling tradition) while disregarding the surroundings, for this would imply higher risk of both genes and memes being unfit in the future.

Hence, the small-w concept of wisdom may be as broadly applicable as that of small-c creativity. Specifically, it would cover (1) biologically determined moral inclinations toward genetic relatives and others with whom to share *reciprocal altruism*, (2) the universal human drive to optimize life conditions (including all aspects of a healthy environment), and (3) the inherent joy of learning (potentially leading to ever greater wisdom)—before even beginning to consider (4) the inculcation of cultural norms of morality in the individual. Figure 10.2 illustrates this broad potential for social responsibility and wisdom.

This concept of wisdom does not compromise the needs of the individual. Quite to the contrary, it supports the individual by potentially being highly economical in the sense that a person in many cases may get a huge reward for a rather small investment, as we saw in the three examples earlier in this chapter. However, two crucial preconditions for this wisdom to flourish for the benefit of the larger whole are that *the larger whole can be recognized* and that *the effects of individual actions are convincingly clear to the individual*. The examples in the beginning of this chapter show how experiences with music, littering, and happiness all indicate the preference for, and indeed the presence of, a greater whole for individuals to identify with. Moreover, in all three cases the greater wholes (musical symphony, ecology, and higher social-existential order) were both recognizable and possible to influence.

Figure 10.2   Basic Elements of Wise Creativity and Creative Wisdom

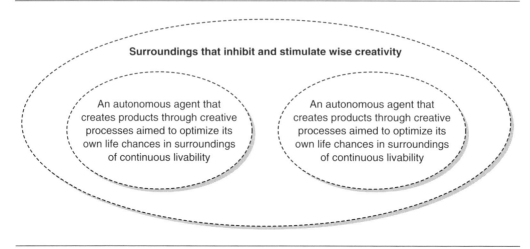

SOURCE Knoop 2006.

Yet, in human interaction the greater biological, social, or cultural wholes have hitherto remained rather "partial." In nature, through millennia the meat of one group was the poison of another; in culture, the success of particular ideas have probably always suppressed others; and in society, as in nature, the struggle to make a living continues to play out in win-lose relations much too often. In other words, despite seemingly numerous examples of win-win games in evolution (Wright 2000), human history also has a long and marked record of zero-sum gaming, often implying extreme evil and social exclusion. In my view, humanity's two most urgent questions may indeed be the following: How can we create a wise set of shared basic assumptions about the universe, life, and humankind that unites humanity against the all-overriding external enemy: the extinction of human life on Earth? How can we create shared global visions for the future that enable and encourage rich human diversity and creativity?

The recent uproar over the Danish cartoons depicting the prophet Muhammad was but one example of how seriously we lack a necessary minimum of shared basic wisdom and vision about the world and our place in it. Thus, I may not entirely share Craft's fear of the universal concept of creativity because, though unilateral strategies for global dominance make desperation and war more likely, a multicultural world without common frames of reference and vision seems to guarantee them. Indeed, I am somewhat optimistic in this respect because we are all biologically and culturally well programmed to fight threats based on shared assumptions and ideals—yet it should not be forgotten that hitherto the far greater part of human fighting has been directed toward harming other human beings.

Maybe there is new hope in the proclaimed wisdom of the crowds that is especially enabled by electronic technologies. An example of how such decentralized wisdom may be gathered is the Yahoo! Answers Web site, where anybody can pose a question and get answers from others. The physicist Stephen

Hawking (2006) recently asked the following question at this site after pondering the fate of humans: "In a world that is in chaos politically, socially and environmentally, how can the human race sustain another 100 years?" (n.p.).

In a subsequent speech in Hong Kong, Hawking said that the survival of the human race depends on its ability to find new homes elsewhere in the universe because there is an increasing risk that a disaster will destroy Earth. So if humans can avoid killing themselves in the next 100 years, he suggested, they should have space settlements that will be able to continue without support from Earth (Jesdanun 2006). Later, the *China Daily* asked Hawking about the environment, and he responded through his computerized voice synthesizer that he was "very worried about global warming" and that he was afraid that Earth "might end up like Venus, at 250 degrees centigrade and raining sulphuric acid" ("Hawking: I Like Chinese Culture" 2006, ¶ 4). At the time of writing this chapter, the counter at Yahoo! Answers registered 23,681 responses to Hawking's question, all of which he apparently plans to analyze in collaboration with Yahoo! staff to highlight the best responses.

Such sites as Wikipedia, Amazon, Google, MSN, and various news services around the world offer still more services aiming to tap the collective intelligence—based on the assumption that humans in groups sometimes can do a better job of finding information than individuals or machines can. In any case, if Earth turns out to be the only place in the universe where life has evolved, destruction of this life, according to cosmologist Martin Rees (2003), may mean no less than whether the future of the universe will be green or gray. One can hardly imagine a finer, more engaging, and more meaningful collective perspective.

CREATIVITY AND WISDOM IN EDUCATION

The mathematician Bertrand Russell is said to have stated that the whole problem with the world is that fools and fanatics are always so certain of themselves, but wiser people so full of doubts. Assuming Russell actually said this, I doubt he would ultimately have phrased his conviction exactly so, had he had more time. For though few would fail to understand the sentiment, on second thought doubtfulness is clearly an equally valid sign of ignorance as of wisdom. Yet I do think that the present culture of black-and-white debate grants some merit to Russell's content—obviously very few things in life are completely black or white, and a debating culture favoring the cocksure therefore seems bound to stupefy. Indeed, many of the very best, most joyful, most adventurous moments in life are fueled by, and filled with, doubt and other forms of uncertainty. Few would care to play a soccer game if there were no doubt at all about which team would win. The same can be said of any other game. If someone was guaranteed not to encounter any surprise for a day, chances are that it would be the most boring day in that person's life. The world is thoroughly based on uncertainty. What humans do when learning and creating is more than anything else to be regarded as attempts to use uncertainty as chaotic raw material for new discoveries and inventions, thereby adapting so as to assume optimal (though never complete) control over their own situation and destiny. And like other mammals, humans even experience joy when doing so. Specifically in education, the inability to live with uncertainties would be crippling to both the quality of teaching and the quality of life more broadly. For example, when teaching, the most important outcome—the knowledge and skills of the learner—cannot be predicted to anything approaching exactness. Likewise, success of any curriculum will depend on trillions of simultaneous neurological processes almost completely outside of our grasp. These examples alone suffice to make the case for honoring joyful and creative uncertainty. Yet the counter pole of wise foresight and action is equally important, as no living organism or ecology can sustain without some stabilities. Consequently, when considering how to bring about creativity and wisdom by educational means, it seems more than appropriate to choose an approach that respects the intimate relatedness of these two virtues.

In this vein I offer two brief proposals of relevance to educators. The first is a specific framing, illustrated in Table 10.1, showing how certain virtues may comfortably serve as enablers of the target-virtues: creativity and wisdom.

Table 10.1   Enabling Virtues That Promote Creative Wisdom and Wise Creativity

		Target Virtue: Wisdom (w-W)	
		Little-w wisdom, relating to more predictable and directed development	Big-W Wisdom, relating to more unpredictable and undirected evolution
Target Virtue: Creativity (c-C)	More short-term, process-oriented, formative, intrinsic, and intuition-based (little-c) creativity	Examples of enabling virtues: curiosity, engagement	Examples of enabling virtues: sensitivity, awareness, kindness
	More long-term, result-oriented, summative, extrinsic, and reflection-based (big-C) creativity	Examples of enabling virtues: higher purpose, social commitment	Examples of enabling virtues: courage, resilience, social responsibility

Each enabling virtue may also fit in other quadrants, but it is important to note that there are enablers for each quadrant. The main point of this framing is that fundamental psychological qualities of good teaching—students who are sensitive, aware, resilient, engaged, concentrated in meaningful activities of which they share some level of responsibility—may easily induce both creativity in the short and long terms and wisdom regarding predictable and less predicable events. I find the latter distinction particularly appropriate as science has shown the world to be utterly uncertain and in this sense *undirected,* and as our attempts to survive and thrive as biological species, cultures and societies are basically *directed* to counter uncertainty. Even more to the point: ironically, we may realize that while we are certainly capable of destroying future life on Earth, it is quite uncertain whether we will be able to sustain it. Let's hope Murphy's Law (broadly stating that things will go wrong in any given situation, if you give them a chance) doesn't apply universally.

Of course, all the enabling virtues in Table 10.1 are also full virtues in their own right, as convincingly laid out in positive psychology (Peterson and Seligman 2004). Indeed, they could all be said to relate somewhat to all four quadrants. Still, I think it may be helpful to frame them as I have done in order to show how much of what drives humans at the basic daily level may actually indirectly contribute to both creativity and wisdom. In other words, by creating good pedagogy based on students living by the enabling virtues, essentially promoting a joyful and meaningful life (Csikszentmihalyi 1993; Seligman 2002), one may expect both more creativity and more wisdom as well. And the mere contiguity of creativity and wisdom should strengthen the association between these virtues, thereby making both wise creativity and creative wisdom more likely. To my knowledge this hypothesis has not yet been extensively tested, but along with a group of Danish colleagues I have recently devised a Web-based instrument (Danish University of Education n.d.) for assessing happiness and well-being in schools, and we plan to use it for this specific purpose also.

As my second proposal, I invite teachers to investigate intriguing concepts such as the universal drive to optimize life chances and the interdependency of creativity and wisdom through the minicurriculum suggested below or some other combination of disciplined study and open-ended activity. And I recommend considering doing so in an atmosphere that includes the following:

- *biological, social, and cultural inclusiveness* whereby teachers and students, however counterintuitive to some, are understood and taught as individuals *in* the environment rather than individuals acting *upon* the environment
- *positive expectations of students' skillful contributions,* indirectly signaling acknowledgment of each student's talent and significance (since without student talent nothing could be expected, and without significance nothing should be expected)
- *exceptional intergenerational mutuality* whereby the urgency and gravity of creativity and wisdom, and the obvious failures of previous generations to avoid human tragedy, are channeled into a sincere invitation for students to immediately engage in some sort of wise creativity

The main content of the minicurriculum could be laid out as follows:

1. Plenary lectures, individual readings, and group discussions investigating the universal tendency to optimize life chances (including human creativity) by looking at direct or indirect evidence of
   - *altruism experienced by the students themselves,* such as feeling good by helping, and being helped by, others; caring for weaker individuals; the benefits of taxation on welfare; true love; and so on
   - *altruism found in biology,* including kin-selection, reciprocal altruism, the handicap principle, the reputation-principle, and social trends toward non-zero-sumness in evolution
   - *altruism found in psychology,* showing that people feel better when they are acknowledged by others rather that just by themselves, when they are somewhat creative rather than just repetitive, when they have long-term goals rather than just short-term goals, when they feel that they are a significant part of something much bigger than themselves, and so on
   - *altruism found in social and cultural sciences,* showing how people all over the world engage in unselfish behavior under certain conditions (e.g., voluntary work, philanthropy)

2. Student-projects and plenary discussions based on insights gained from the above lectures, readings, and discussions aimed at generating deep, informed, and personalized answers to questions such as the following:
   - What qualifies as creative wisdom and wise creativity—as opposed to alternatives such as conformist wisdom, unwise creativity, and unwise conformity? And what are the difficulties involved in determining, not to mention agreeing upon, which is which?
   - What can be done to bring about wise creativity and creative wisdom in school, at home, in the workplace, in the local community, and globally?
   - How can one choose, and act upon, a personal standing on these issues in ways that allows oneself ongoing creativity and growing wisdom? Since many social forces inhibit/prohibit important changes in personal conviction, what can be done to better allow people to openly change their convictions without losing their status, friends, and so on?
   - Which kinds of societies and cultures support wise creativity and creative wisdom, and which do not? Based on this, which kinds of societies and cultures could be considered tolerant and intolerant from, for instance, Popper's (1971) perspective?

Of course, these are demanding topics that should not be introduced prematurely. Indeed, the last thing needed in education is learned helplessness, often leading not only to despair but also to irresponsibility resulting from the felt lack of influence. Like everyone else, students should be protected from what they cannot handle. That said, however, it is plain to see how much many small children are actually witnessing through the media today, and how they may often feel a need to talk seriously and sincerely about these issues rather than just be protected from them. Obviously, which it will be is for the teachers and parents to decide in each situation, but ultimately very few of us will escape challenging information about strengths and weaknesses regarding human creativity and human wisdom. And no one escapes the choice of whether to engage with and act on this information, once it is received.

Thus, applauding the spirit and thought of Anna Craft, Guy Claxton, and Howard Gardner and their attempts to better understand creativity and wisdom in education, I remain convinced that a creative and wise future will be best brought about by conceptualizing creativity and wisdom as mutually dependant virtues. While wisdom without creativity appears to predict a rather dull future, creativity without wisdom doesn't predict much of a future at all. We need both, and I trust we can have them.

REFERENCES

Chaisson, E. 2001. *Cosmic evolution: The rise of complexity in nature.* Cambridge, MA: Harvard University Press.

Csikszentmihalyi, M. 1990. *Flow: The psychology of optimal experience.* New York: Harper & Row.

———. 1993. *The evolving self.* New York: HarperCollins.

———. 1996. *Creativity: Flow and the psychology of discovery and invention.* New York: HarperCollins.

Danish University of Education. n.d. *GodSkole* [GoodSchool]. https://www.god skole.dk/.

Feldman, D. 1980. *Beyond universals in cognitive development.* Norwood, NJ: Ablex.

Gardner, H. 1999. *The disciplined mind: What all students should understand.* New York: Simon & Schuster.

GlobeScan. 2005. *Trust in governments, corporations and global institutions continues to decline.* http://www.globescan.com/news_archives/WEF_trust2005.html.

Hawking, S. 2006. *How can the human race survive the next hundred years?* http://answers.yahoo.com/question/index;_ylt=AlvNa7eHedXIZsScobHvQJ0jzK IX?qid=20060704195516AAnrdOD.

Hawking: I like Chinese culture, women. 2006. *China Daily,* June 21. http://www.chi nadaily.com.cn/china/2006-06/21/content_622829.htm.

Jesdanun, A. 2006. Seeking answers from the cosmic consciousness. *Boston Globe,* July 8. http://www.boston.com/ae/media/articles/2006/07/08/seeking_answers_from _the_cosmic_consciousness/.

Kahneman, D. 2003. A perspective on judgment and choice: Mapping bounded ratio-nality. *American Psychologist* 58:697–720.

Kauffman, S. A. 1996. Self replication: Even peptides do it. *Nature* 382:496–97.

———. 2000. *Investigations.* Oxford, UK: Oxford University Press.

Knoop, H. H. 2004. På tærsklen til det virtuelle liv—psykologiske og pædagogiske aspekter af den digitale teknologi [On the threshold of virtual life—psychological and pedagogical aspects of digital technology]. *Pædagogisk Psykologisk Rådgivning* 41:280–308.

———. 2005. Kompleksitet: Voksende orden ingen helt forstår [Complexity: Growing order nobody quite understands]. *Kognition & Pædagogik* 15:6–24.

————. 2006. Kreativitet [Creativity]. *Dansk Pædagogisk Tidsskrift* 1:1–10.

Kurzweil, R. 1999. *The age of spiritual machines.* London: Orion Business Books.

————. 2005. *The singularity is near: When humans transcend biology.* New York: Viking.

Lyhne, J. 2005. Kollektivt flow: Et interview med musikeren Peter Bastian [Collective flow: An interview with the musician Peter Bastian]. In *Et nyt læringslandskab: Flow, intelligens og det gode læringsmiljø* [A new landscape of learning: Flow, intelligence and the good learning environment], H. H. Knoop and J. Lyhne, 165–87. Copenhagen: Dansk Psykologisk Forlag.

Murray, H. A. 1938. *Explorations in personality.* New York: Oxford University Press.

Peterson, C., and M. E. P. Seligman. 2004. *Character strengths and virtues: A handbook and classification.* Washington, DC: American Psychological Association and Oxford University Press.

Popper, K. R. 1971. *The open society and its enemies.* Princeton, NJ: Princeton University Press.

Rees, M. 2003. *Our final hour: How terror, error, and environmental disaster threaten humankind's future in this century—on Earth and beyond.* New York: Basic Books.

Runco, M. A. 2004. Creativity. *Annual Review of Psychology* 55:657–87.

Seligman, M. E. P. 2002. *Authentic happiness.* New York: Free Press.

Senge, P. M. 1990. *The fifth discipline: The art and practice of the learning organization.* London: Century Business.

World Economic Forum. 2002. *Global survey on trust.* Geneva, Switzerland: World Economic Forum.

Wright, R. 2000. *Nonzero: The logic of human destiny.* New York: Pantheon Books.

11

Creativity and Wisdom

Christopher Bannerman

This response centers on tensions which have been provoked by the three target chapters by Anna Craft, Guy Claxton, and Howard Gardner. I use the word *tensions* to denote the richness of the questions raised in their chapters and to acknowledge their location within a dynamic field that is subject to movement and change. The tensions arise for me largely as a result of my work with six artists from the performing arts at the Centre for Research into Creation in the Performing Arts (ResCen) at Middlesex University, in the United Kingdom.[1] The work of ResCen recognizes the artist as a knowledge holder and expert practitioner and so privileges the voice of the artist in its work, which has drawn us into debates focused on creativity in education and, perhaps less explicitly, into discussions of wisdom as a facet of artistic practice. The interest in wisdom may stem from the fact that each of the artists has accumulated decades of experience, and they have all reached a point at which they feel able to reflect on their current artistic practice and how it has evolved and developed. Their works have continued to be in demand from professional venues and producers, and they are often supported by funding bodies such as the Arts Council England. The artists were not selected at random; they each felt motivated to apply to be part of a center which would involve them in discussing artistic practice and reflecting, individually and collectively, on that practice. The research findings should be seen as contingent and situated, particularly as the involvement of the artists came about through the process of self-selection. Recently the artists have been involved in writing a book, *Navigating the Unknown* (Bannerman, Sofaer, and Watt 2006), and some of the observations in this chapter draw on material gathered for that publication.

ResCen's work is also grounded in the practicalities of artistic practice as it exists and operates in what might be called the real world. *Real world* can be seen as a deeply problematic term, but as Robson (2002) notes, it is useful nonetheless and indicates clearly that we are considering applied settings and dynamic social situations. I welcome the fact that the three target chapters share the groundedness of the real world and that each relates its themes to the often messy realities of teaching, doing business, running a school, or making decisions in a complex, diverse, and globalized world. My experiences as witness to grounded and dynamic ResCen debates form a lens through which I examine the tensions provoked by Craft, Claxton, and Gardner.

CREATIVITY: AN ABSTRACT NOUN

The first tension is prompted by the term *creativity* itself, and although Claxton points out that this is an abstract noun, it appears to me that much current educational debate ignores this fact and promotes a view of creativity as spontaneous, intuitive insight—a quality allegedly shared by children and artists. The ResCen experience suggests that it is true that intuitive insight is a key feature of artistic work but reveals that this is matched by a skilful, expert engagement, which draws on a storeroom of accumulated knowledge. In spite of the fact that this is clearly evident in artists' work, those extolling the virtues of creativity often privilege mysterious, romanticized aspects and neglect craft, skill, knowledge, and expertise. An example of this can be found in Philip Pullman's (2003b) Isis Speech, in which he promotes the idea of writing as *fishing at night*. He describes this as an activity without rationality, which may be why he includes only one brief reference to knowledge and skills. The lecture was reproduced in *The Guardian* in an article presented as an open letter to the British Secretary of State at the Department for Education and Skills (Pullman 2003a). Perhaps his message was tailored to present aspects of the creative endeavor that he felt were missing from schools today, but as an account of artistic practice it is incomplete.

If we can generalize from the findings from the six artists associated with ResCen, we will see that such debates often appear to negate the fact that the practice of artists takes place in relation to a disciplinary framework, even when their work challenges its boundaries or even its existence. Too often the promotion of creativity appears to be devoid of a meaningful context in which it can be manifested. My observation suggests that the relationship to a disciplinary framework offers both greater scope and greater significance to the creative, intuitive insight which is activated and mediated by the knowledge and experience that the artist has accumulated, allowing the achievement of a meaningful form.[2]

This situatedness of intuition within a field of knowledge appears to produce a dancing interplay between the unconscious and conscious processes of expert practice. This does not diminish the significance of the intuitive insight in the work of the ResCen artists, and they have all spoken about its power. But it is only part of a palette of strategies; the conscious mind, with its knowledge craft and skills, must be consciously engaged while simultaneously holding an awareness of the unconscious, leaving space for the intuitive to arise. This militates against seeing creativity only as idealized, abstract spontaneity because it clearly exists at an intersection of a spontaneous unconscious and an expert, conscious agency. Creativity achieves meaning when it is manifested in the work of the expert artist who has responded to the intuitive moment. As noted previously, this view stems from work at the ResCen with six artists and therefore represents a *situated understanding* which may or may not be applicable in other contexts. But all the evidence indicates that creativity in the work of artists results from an interplay between the intuitive and the conscious. This focus on knowledge and skills coupled with spontaneous insight may not be fashionable, but it might provide a more stable basis for sharing creative insights and processes.

THE INDIVIDUAL AND CREATIVITY

This notion of sharing brings me to the second tension; it arises from the discourse of individualism which Craft points out is founded on Western values which promote innovation as means of achieving economic development. Individualism is also a key feature of creative practice in the performing arts, as can be seen by the fact that the name of a creative artist is a kind of trademark which accrues value in the arts marketplace. But the work with the ResCen artists reveals that this received "fact" of arts practice might not be the whole picture because the artists are almost always engaged with others in the making of their work. This is true even for artists such as the composer Errollyn Wallen and the performance artist Richard Layzell, who do a large proportion of their work alone. Wallen cannot finish a composition until she can visualize the performers playing the piece, and Layzell combines individual investigation with hours of discussion with commissioners, assorted collaborators, and often communities in the creation of a work.

In fact, most creative work in the performing arts is dependent on performers. It is they who realize the performance—in a very real sense the performers own the work or, at the very least, share ownership with the creator. Engagement with others is central to creative practice in the performing arts, a fact that is at odds with the view of the artist as a singular, misunderstood, idiosyncratic genius alone in a garret, a view which appears to have influenced much of the discourse on creativity. This stereotype may be viewed as an anachronism, but it remains, in my view, a potent influence on discussions of creativity, in spite of those artists who openly acknowledge the importance of collaborative contributions. Not only are the ResCen artists deeply engaged with others, in many cases they are trying to initiate a sense of group creativity in order to make the work. The degree of collective creative engagement usually shifts during the process, with greater group engagement in the initial development of ideas, but the creative involvement of everyone in the work is vital to its success. The shifting level of creative participation also implies a shift of role, which means that everyone must be sensitive and empathetic, both to each other and to the creative process.

The ResCen artists are highly skilled at these interactions, and their success as creators depends on their ability to communicate with, inspire, respond to, and lead a group. This team-based approach seems to be almost entirely absent from many current discussions of creativity, and yet, creative work in groups might present a model that could be of use in education and the workplace. A focus on collaborative creative processes might alter the rationale for creativity in education because currently it is promoted in large part as a means of achieving economic development. This was made clear in a speech by Lord Sainsbury of Turville, Parliamentary Under Secretary of State for Science and Innovation, speaking at the Creative Economy Conference in October 2005: "The Creative Economy is one of the fastest growing parts of the European economy. In the face of growing global economic challenges, we in Europe need to look to our strengths. Increasingly they will lie in the talent of our people, our capacity to innovate, and our ability to turn that creativity into products and services that people around the world want to buy" (Sainsbury 2005, ¶ 4). This view of creativity is part of a movement toward a world of ever-increasing consumer choice and increasingly individualized identity. The momentum seems irresistible, although we are simultaneously reminded frequently of the need for social cohesion and the requirement of the workplace for those with highly developed interpersonal skills.

Squaring the circle of the highly individualistic innovator and the collectively minded group may seem impossible, but this apparent contradiction lies at the heart of artistic practice in the performing arts. The world of the professional performing arts could do more to acknowledge this, but an education system that privileges individual creativity and achievement will not encourage such a development. And arguably it is interaction with others that is central to the activation and development of the artists' wisdom. The aphorism "How do I know what I think until I hear what I say?" sometimes credited to the organizational theorist Karl Weick (1995) often seems apposite, as the artists frequently identify key developments that have been stimulated through working with others. The empathy required when they engage with collaborators to create their artistic work may also be pivotal in their ability to communicate successfully with audiences—and their ability to reflect and challenge the concerns of contemporary society. The artist's insight into others is important both in devising the work with performers and in terms of being relevant to audiences, and it is arguably this empathy which allows the development of their work and is responsible for their success over decades. Empathy and insight alone are not enough, as artists must have the knowledge and skill to make use of them and the collaborative relationship between creator and performer can be rich and complex. An example of the centrality of this exchange, and the significance of empathetic insight, can be seen in *The Suchness of Heni and Eddie*, a documentary about the making of a performance work by the choreographer Rosemary Lee.

CREATIVITY AND PROXIMITY

The six ResCen artists appear to have developed these interpersonal skills through working in close proximity to others, which may be critical to the development of insight and the ability to deploy wise action. It is noticeable that the examples of wisdom in the three target chapters focus on exchanges that feature direct human contact, and it seems likely that human beings have been conditioned to be sensitive to social interactions that are dependent on close proximity. Mechanization, urbanization, and digitization now offer remote communication as well as anonymity unrestrained by direct encounter, but interestingly the principle of proximity, especially as it relates to eye contact, now informs the layout of urban centers. A philosophy pioneered in the Netherlands by the traffic engineer Hans Monderman is known as *shared space* (see *Shared Space: Room for Everyone* 2005). Reducing the use of signage, paint, dedicated routes for cars, and other traditional methods of traffic control forces the establishment of eye contact between pedestrians, cyclists, and drivers which alters human behavior and leads to more responsible and responsive road use and fewer accidents. This may seem a fanciful tangent from creativity and wisdom, but these are all matters of human exchange, as the target chapters point out, and it appears that proximity is key. Exactly what this means in a world ever more dependent on e-mail and text messages is not clear, but the potential for increasingly dysfunctional human interaction should not be discounted. The driver who feels able to speed through streets with no barriers or restraints to his or her progress may be a metaphor for the individual, alone at a computer, who speeds down a broadband highway oblivious to the well-being of others.

One strategy to mitigate such potential effects might be for education to focus more on the development of group, as well as individual, creativity in order to provide a cornerstone which will inform communication and the use of more remote communications. The ResCen experience suggests that artists in the performing arts have refined and developed their ability to communicate over the course of their careers. These communication skills are intrinsic to their expert practice and are coupled with knowledge and craft to enable the development of creative work and its presentation to an audience—an act on which their livelihoods depend. Acknowledging the knowledge and craft of artists is important not only because it accurately reflects their practice, but also because it recognizes their status as skilled professionals. This acknowledgment rescues them from being relegated to the realm of the otherworldly amateur or even the infantile, a tendency reinforced by the romanticized view of creativity noted earlier.

THE VALUE OF THE UNCOUNTABLE

Of course, as Gardner points out, it is not only artists whose professional status is undervalued today, and this brings us to the third tension: the tension between accountability and evaluation. This discussion is relevant because it is central to determining the worth of things, especially things such as creativity and wisdom which are difficult to quantify. The terms *accountability* and *evaluation* represent processes which are often confused, even though a distinction is evident in the derivation of the two words. Accountability is not only a calling to account; it implies an attempt to establish worth by measurement, or literally by counting. This may be part of a commendable desire to achieve transparency in public life, or at least in public expenditure, and to make sound, evidence-based decisions, but the process should be distinct from evaluation, which involves qualitative judgment, as the root term *value* implies. The attempt to understand the worth of something simply through calculation often displaces any meaningful discussion of the collective values which inform evaluation. Too often our only attempt to deal with value is represented by the phrase *value for money*, which simply returns us to the counting/accounting model. Our reluctance to link values with evaluation may stem from the difficulty of discussing whose values are being represented, but avoiding the issue of identifying shared or collective values disempowers professional judgment, inhibits the identification of Gardner's societal trustees, and undermines the development of creativity and wisdom.

The recognition that values inform evaluation may be problematic, but it would be better to acknowledge this problem explicitly in order to understand that determining the worth of something inevitably involves a discussion of values. Proposing that everything can be accounted for in monetary or statistical terms only avoids the issue. This ought to be a key debate in increasingly diverse societies, and the ResCen experience suggests that artistic practice which couples creativity with wisdom can be an effective means of identifying, debating, and developing a meaningful collective sense.

CREATIVITY AND WISDOM

The last tension is the one at the center of the target chapters: the tension between creativity and wisdom. In some ways this replicates the earlier theme of the individual and the collective because we can see the individualism of creativity tempered by the skillful human exchange that wisdom represents. Arguably the tempering effect of wisdom is critical in a time in which excessive individualism appears to be the order of the day. An example of this is the development of what might be termed *gratuitous fame* through vehicles such as so-called reality television, which has resulted in a heightened cult of the personality, enabling people to be famous for being themselves or, perhaps more accurately, for performing a caricature of themselves. The excessive individualism promoted in this way may simply be unsustainable on a densely populated planet. The model of ecology that Craft references has demonstrated that we and our environment are interdependent, and recognizing this fact may be the first step in restoring a sense of community and shared values. Doing so may lead to a different way of understanding ourselves and our world so that we see interrelationships and interconnectedness, rather than fixed, reified entities that stand in isolation.

Seeing interconnectedness rather than isolation might also instigate the conditions that encourage the development of wisdom, or at least the conditions to recognize, acknowledge, and value it. As I argued previously, a group focus might offer opportunities to foster creativity and wisdom. And within the group roles may not be fixed; someone who is creative or wise in one context may not be creative or wise when confronted with another. This may be a model which combines the freedom of individual thought and expression associated with the west, with the collective sense that has been attributed to the east. James Surowiecki, author of *The Wisdom of Crowds* (2004), proposes that crowd or group decisions are most accurate when individuals do not feel constrained by the need to conform and yet are part of a collective process. Perhaps this principal can be extended and we could see the group as a vehicle for enabling and containing dynamic interconnections between individuals, stimulating creativity and wisdom, as well as strengthening a collective sense and negotiating social frameworks.

I do not wish to suggest, however, that the recognition of the merits of the collective creative process negates either the importance of the individual within the group or the importance of individual creative work. Pullman, too, makes this point and it is valid, despite the concerns voiced earlier about his tendency to over-romanticize the individual artist. In a *Guardian* newspaper article he recounts his involvement in an event which celebrated the place of the arts in education, and he notes that "all the art that was talked about and displayed at the conference was performance art, collaborative, interpretive art. It stressed the value of teamwork, and it culminated in public performance and immediate understanding and approval. It was very good; but there are other kinds of art as well, which are private, secret, personal and which take time to reveal their effects. These forms of art are shadowed by mystery; their outcomes are unpredictable; they carry with them the continual possibility of failure" (Pullman 2003a, ¶ 3).

Once again I fear the overindividualized approach, but it is important to acknowledge the multiple ways in which creativity is manifested—the ResCen artists remind me of this continually—and to note that for some people the individual and private process is the way. However, Pullman (2003a) is in danger of adding to the confusion by presenting the dichotomy of "performance art, collaborative, interpretive art" versus the "private, secret, personal" (¶ 3). In short, he is comparing performing with creating (probably in the realm of writing), rather than comparing the creating of performance work with the creating of the written work of art. This undermines his point about the nature of creative work and indicates that he is simply not familiar with group creative processes. The ResCen artists have all spoken about the private, secret, and personal in the making of their work, and the tensions that arise in the social context of making art which require them, above all, to convince performers that they are fully in command of the process, even when they feel insecure, uncertain, or uninspired.

Pullman's (2003a) potentially confusing comparison unfortunately chimes with another tendency in education, which is to conflate self-expression with creativity. In this sense the clarity of the distinction he makes between creative and interpretive engagements in art is useful. The distinction is important, especially because creative contributions in the performing arts can come often from those who seem shy or retiring, and for whom the overt self-expression of performing is alien. Pullman, who has been a teacher as well as a writer, is right to remind us that those whose work involves the recognition, activation, encouragement, and development of creativity in schools, colleges, universities, and the workplace must be able to identify it in a variety of forms—vibrant and overt, or secret and personal. Doing so requires insight and wisdom on the part of the teacher, tutor, or leader, and it may be that we do not sufficiently acknowledge the importance of those who foster creativity. They must develop a "barometer" that is sensitive to creative engagements that are manifested in numerous ways and sometimes occur suddenly without explanation. Pullman also reminds us that mystery is often intrinsic to creative processes. The ResCen artists have worked with a wide variety of groups in education and community settings and have noted the phenomenon of individuals experiencing a sudden unleashing of creative energies, which appeared to be entirely hidden previously, through contact with a new context or discipline.

Fostering creative engagement is also complicated by the fact that it can take a variety of forms which are often activated at different stages of a creative process and can involve almost opposing inclinations: a divergent phase might require reaching out to gather references and associations, whereas a convergent phase requires selection and distillation as things "come together" and the work takes its final form. The creative abilities required in each phase can present challenges to one individual, whereas they might match another's creative abilities more easily. The barometer must be sensitive to both kinds of engagement, especially in relation to the scale of the creative contribution. It may be that many artists in the West had formative experiences in the 1960s when "radical" solutions were sought for societal imbalances. In any case, I detect a tendency today to seek the radical artistic statement which redefines a discipline or even a generation's perspective. This is at odds with the previous generation's use of the term *progressive*, implying that a foundation was in place which could support future development. I note the term *progressive* creeping back into our vocabulary, and in an artistic context, I think that this is useful.

We all acknowledge the groundbreaking contributions of certain great artists, and there is a parallel syndrome in science, identified by Kuhn (1962): the notion of the revolutionary *paradigm shift* when the "normal" science of an older paradigm is swept away. However, I would like to make a case for the small, perhaps incremental creative contribution and take issue with the term *normal* in this context. It is easy today to dismiss the incremental as less valuable, but the example of J. S. Bach illustrates the benefit of a perspective informed by the passage of time. Many contemporaries saw him as a competent craftsman working within a well-known paradigm, but we now recognize the genius of someone who achieved the supreme pinnacle of a form. This seems to me to be beyond the "normal" and leads me to wonder if today we often overlook those whose creativity refines the work of others. To acknowledge or achieve a creative refinement we need to be aware of the work of others, whether this occurs because of group creative work or because the individual has been guided toward, or found, the relevant context to ignite the creative spark. And we need to acknowledge a disciplinary framework in which meaningful creativity takes place.

These multiple ways, individual and collective, in which creativity manifests itself, and the various forms it takes, can challenge the most sensitive barometer and make demands upon a key part of the equation—the person who recognizes and nourishes creativity, often in an embryonic form. Recognition of the potential for creative action and engagement can be as important as the thing itself. Doors need to be opened with insight so that creative engagement is activated, fostered, and guided. The mystery of this process eludes reductionism and formulaic strategies and challenges schools, colleges, universities, and the workplace to allow and contain the play of creativity and wisdom.

The three target chapters have provoked these responses from me by raising questions about our capacity to be creative and wise, and to recognize and value those things. This is a timely debate which should be conducted widely. We need new insights and a collective will to address current social changes and environmental concerns, we need creativity to imagine new paradigms and solutions, and we need wisdom in order to take effective action. Time will tell if we are successful in achieving this, but thanks are due to Craft, Claxton, and Gardner for raising these pressing issues.

NOTES

1. See www.resecen.net for further information.
2. See ResCen (2003) and Bannerman, Sofaer, and Watt (2006) for fuller discussions of this.

REFERENCES

Bannerman, C., J. Sofaer, and J. Watt. 2006. *Navigating the unknown: The creative process in contemporary performing arts.* London: Middlesex University Press and ResCen.

Kuhn, T. E. 1962. *The structure of scientific revolutions.* Chicago: University of Chicago Press.

Pullman, P. 2003a. All around you is silence. *The Guardian,* June 5. http://books .guardian.co.uk/news/articles/0,970760,00.html.

————. 2003b. *Isis speech.* http://www.philip-pullman.com/pages/content/index .asp?PageID=66.

ResCen. 2003. *Seminar: Intuition and the artist.* http://www.mdx.ac.uk/rescen/archive/ intuition03.html.

Robson, C. 2002. *Real world research: A resource for social scientists and practitioner-researchers,* 2nd ed. Oxford, UK: Blackwell.

Sainsbury, D. (Lord Sainsbury of Turville). 2005. *Creative economy conference.* http://www.dti.gov.uk/ministers/speeches/sainsbury071005.html.

Shared space: Room for everyone: A new vision for public spaces. 2005. Groningen, Netherlands: Keuning Instituut. http://www.shared-space.org/files/18445/SharedSpace_ Eng.pdf.

Surowiecki, J. 2004. *The wisdom of crowds: Why the many are smarter than the few and how collective wisdom shapes business, economies, societies and nations.* London: Little, Brown.

Weick, K. 1995. *Sensemaking in organizations.* Thousand Oaks, CA: SAGE.

12

Leadership as a Basis for the Education of Our Children

Robert J. Sternberg

Question: What is much worse than being lost? Answer: Being lost and not knowing it. The current obsession with educational tests in the United States is based on the serious misconception that the goal of education is knowledge and rather trivial processing of it. The problem with this view is that the knowledge most students acquire is largely inert. They stuff their heads with facts that they cannot use and that are poorly integrated with each other. Consider three examples from everyday life: First, think about a written driver's test. What does it mean to obtain a score of 100%? Obtaining a score of 100% is no guarantee that one can drive well, or truly, drive at all. Second, think about speaking. One could get 100% on a test of vocabulary, grammar, spelling, and even reading comprehension, and be unable to speak one word. Third, think about education courses. Anyone who has taken courses in education knows that the fact that someone is a professor of education in no way guarantees that he or she is an excellent or even good teacher.

As Pink (2005) has pointed out, we are no longer living in an information age, if we ever did live in one. What matters now is broad conceptual understanding that people can use to make decisions. In this chapter, I argue that what students need to learn in schooling is almost orthogonal to what many schools and teachers teach. The problem is that teachers think that if they "teach," students learn. Oftentimes, the students either do not learn or do not learn what they need to know. For example, I have been in the field of psychology for 30 years, and never once have I taken a multiple-choice test of the kind that I had to take in my introductory psychology course.

So what do we need to teach for? I would argue that we need to teach for leadership. Many of us, when we think of leadership, think of presidents, CEOs, governors, mayors, and superstars in creative endeavors. This kind of macroleadership is important to society, of course. But it is not the principal kind of leadership that occurs in our society. The principal kind of leadership is microleadership—the teacher as the leader in a classroom, the parent as the leader in the home, the head of a task force or committee at work, the person who serves in a community or church leadership role. How can we develop the kinds of skills that will lead people to exercise good judgments in such situations? Leadership is essential to the successful functioning of virtually any organization; therefore, scholars of leadership attempt to understand what leads to success in leadership.

In this chapter, I discuss a model of leadership called WICS, which stands for *wisdom, intelligence, and creativity, synthesized*. WICS synthesizes many aspects of previous models, thus drawing on much that is old, including trait, situational, behavioral, contingency, and transformational models.

THE NATURE OF WICS

WICS attempts to show how successful leadership involves the synthesis of three qualities: wisdom, intelligence, and creativity. Schooling, done right, develops these three attributes working together. It does not just teach "facts."

When I took Introductory Psychology in 1968, the course was taught in a way that emphasized almost exclusively memorization of facts. But was the memorization of facts really what was most crucial to learning about psychology? Today, in the early years of the twenty-first century, there is little overlap between the content of an introductory psychology book now and then. Whatever is "core" to psychology must transcend those facts—it is about how psychologists think. And what they need to do, like people in all disciplines, is to create ideas, analyze them, put them into practice, and ask whether they will help people achieve a common good—whether they are for the good or the detriment of humankind. These skills are important, but they are not the skills measured on conventional standardized tests. Infamous dictators may have done or may do well on standardized tests of factual content, but they are never wise. Now consider the WICS model in brief.

According to the model, successful intelligence is one's ability to attain one's goals in life (given one's sociocultural context) by adapting to, shaping, and selecting environments through a balance of analytical, creative, and practical skills (Sternberg 1997). Underlying this ability are fundamental executive processes, or *metacomponents* (Sternberg 1985): recognizing the existence of a problem, defining and redefining the problem, allocating resources to the solution of the problem, representing the problem mentally, formulating a strategy for solving the problem, monitoring the solution of the problem while problem solving is ongoing, and evaluating the solution to the problem after it has been solved. Analytical intelligence is involved when one applies these processes to fairly abstract problems that nevertheless take a relatively familiar form (e.g., intelligence-test items). Creative intelligence is involved when one applies the processes to relatively novel tasks and situations. Practical intelligence is involved when one applies the processes to everyday problems for purposes of adaptation to, shaping, and selection of environments. As a leader, one needs creative intelligence to generate new ideas, analytical intelligence to ascertain whether they are good ideas, and practical intelligence to implement one's ideas and convince others to listen to them.

Creativity is the ability to formulate and solve problems so as to produce solutions that are relatively novel and high in quality (Sternberg and Lubart 1995). Creativity involves creative intelligence in the generation of ideas, but it also involves more—in particular, knowledge; a desire to think in novel ways; personality attributes such as tolerance of ambiguity, propensity toward sensible risk taking, and willingness to surmount obstacles; intrinsic, task-focused motivation; and an environment that supports creativity (Sternberg and Lubart 1995). At the base of creativity, again, are the metacomponents. Crucial to creativity are one's creative-intellectual skills in recognizing and finding good problems to solve and then defining and redefining the problems until they are understood in a way that allows a novel solution. Creative individuals are good problem finders who devote their resources to solving problems that are worth solving in the first place. Good leaders recognize and tackle the problems that are important for them to solve and delegate or even ignore the rest. Intelligent individuals are good problem solvers, but they do not necessarily devote their resources to solving problems that are important to solve. Analytical and practical intelligence, not just creative intelligence, are also important to creativity. Analytical intelligence is used to determine whether one's creative solutions to a problem are good solutions, and practical intelligence is used to implement the solutions and to convince others that one's solutions are, indeed, good ones that they should heed. In the end, true creativity in leadership requires solving not just any problems, but the important ones.

Wisdom is the ability to apply one's successful intelligence, creativity, and knowledge toward a common good by balancing one's own (intrapersonal) interests, other people's (interpersonal) interests, and larger (extrapersonal) interests over the short and long terms, through the infusion of values, in order to adapt to, shape, and select environments (Sternberg 1998a). Thus, wisdom involves both intelligence and creativity, as they are applied to serve not just one's own ends, but also the ends of other people and of larger interests. At the base of wisdom, as with intelligence and creativity, are the metacomponents. One needs to recognize when problems, such as injustice, exist and to define them in a way that is respectful of multiple points of view (dialogical thinking). One then needs to solve them in ways that take into account the needs of all stakeholders as well as the resources at hand.

Intelligence, wisdom, and creativity build on each other. One can be intelligent without being creative or wise. Civilization is, in a way, cursed by those who have the intelligence to generate and implement policies that are unwise and that often are uncreative as well. To be creative, one must be intelligent at some level, but one need not be wise. To be wise, one must be both intelligent and creative because wisdom draws upon intelligence and creativity in the formulation of solutions to problems. WICS holds that the best leaders exhibit all three qualities of intelligence, creativity, and wisdom. It also holds that these skills can be developed.

The theory proposed here views leadership as, in large part, a matter of how one formulates, makes, and acts upon decisions (Sternberg 2003, 2004; Sternberg and Vroom 2002). According to this model, leadership consists of a synthesis of wisdom, intelligence, and creativity. The basic idea is that one needs these three components working together (synthesized) in order to be a highly effective leader.

One is not "born" a leader. In the framework of WICS, one can speak of *traits* of leadership (Zaccaro, Kemp, and Bader 2004), but properly, they should be viewed as flexible and dynamic rather than as rigid and static. Wisdom, intelligence, and creativity are, to some extent, modifiable forms of developing expertise (Sternberg 1998b, 1999b), which one can decide to utilize or not in leadership decisions. The environment strongly influences the extent to which people are able to utilize and develop whatever genetic potential they have (Grigorenko and Sternberg 2001; Sternberg and Grigorenko 1997, 2001). But poor leadership depends less on failed genetic potential than on poor decisions. People with substantial innate potential may fail to take much advantage of it. Others with less potential may decide to take more advantage of it.

Leadership involves both skills and dispositions (i.e., attitudes). *Skills* refers to developing expertise based on how well you can execute certain functions of leadership. *Dispositions* refers to developing expertise based on how you think about these functions. The dispositions are at least as important as the skills. One needs creative skills and dispositions to generate fresh and good ideas for leadership, intellectual skills and dispositions to decide whether they are good ideas and to implement the ideas and convince others of the value of the ideas, and wisdom-related skills and dispositions to assess the short- and long-term impacts of these ideas on other individuals and institutions as well as oneself. The following discussion considers the elements of creativity, intelligence, and wisdom in that order because, usually, generation of ideas comes first, then analysis of whether they are good ideas, and then, ideally, application of the ideas in a way to achieve a common good.

CREATIVITY

Creativity refers to the skills and dispositions needed for generating ideas and products that are (a) relatively novel, (b) high in quality, and (c) appropriate to the task at hand. Creativity is important for leadership because it is the component whereby one generates the ideas that others will follow. A leader who lacks creativity may get others to go along with his or her ideas, but they may be inferior or stale ideas.

Leadership as a Confluence of Skills and Dispositions

A confluence model of creativity (Sternberg and Lubart 1995, 1996) suggests that creative people show the following variety of characteristics, which represent not innate abilities, but rather, largely, decisions and ways of making these decisions (Sternberg 2000a). In other words, to a large extent, people decide to be creative; they exhibit a creative attitude toward leadership.

• *Problem redefinition.* Creative leaders do not define a problem the way everyone else does simply because everyone else defines the problem that way. They decide on the exact nature of the problem using their own judgment. Most important, they are willing to defy the crowd in defining a problem differently from the way others do (Sternberg 2002a; Sternberg and Lubart 1995).

• *Problem analysis.* They are willing to analyze whether their solution to the problem is the best one possible.

• *Willingness to sell solutions.* They realize that creative ideas do not sell themselves; rather, creators have to decide to sell their ideas and then decide to make the effort to do so.

• *Ability to recognize how knowledge can both help and hinder creative thinking.* They realize that knowledge can hinder as well as facilitate creative thinking (see Frensch and Sternberg 1989; Sternberg 1985). Without this knowledge, leaders sometimes become entrenched and susceptible to tunnel vision, letting their expertise hinder rather than facilitate their exercise of leadership.

• *Willingness to take sensible risks.* Creative leaders recognize that they must decide to take sensible risks, which can lead to success but also can lead, from time to time, to failure (Lubart and Sternberg 1995).

• *Willingness to surmount obstacles.* They are willing to surmount the obstacles that confront anyone who decides to defy the crowd. Such obstacles arise when those who accept paradigms confront those who do not (Kuhn 1970; Sternberg and Lubart 1995).

• *Belief in one's ability to accomplish the task at hand.* This belief is sometimes referred to as *self-efficacy* (Bandura 1996). Creative leaders believe that they are able to do the job at hand.

• *Willingness to tolerate ambiguity.* They recognize that there may be long periods of uncertainty during which they cannot know for sure that they are doing the right thing or that what they are doing will have the desired outcome.

• *Ability to find extrinsic rewards for the things one is intrinsically motivated to do.* Creative leaders almost always are intrinsically motivated about the work they do (Amabile 1983, 1996). They find environments in which they receive extrinsic rewards for the things they like to do anyway.

• *Desire to continually grow intellectually rather than to stagnate.* Creative leaders do not get stuck in their patterns of leadership. Their leadership evolves as they accumulate expertise. They learn from experience rather than simply letting its lessons pass them by.

Types of Creative Leadership

Creative leadership can take various forms (Sternberg 1999a; Sternberg, Kaufman, and Pretz 2003). Some accept current ways of doing things, while others do not; some attempt to integrate different current practices. Which of the following types are more acceptable depends on the interaction of the leader with the situation.

• *Replication.* The leader attempts to show that a field or an organization is in the right place at the right time. The view of the leader is that the organization is where it needs to be. The leader therefore attempts to keep the organization where it is rather than move it.

• *Redefinition.* The leader attempts to show that a field or an organization is in the right place, but not for the reason(s) that others, including previous leaders, think it is. Redefiners often end up taking credit for the ideas of others because they find a better reason to implement the others' ideas, or say they do.

• *Forward incrementation.* The leader attempts to lead a field or an organization forward in the direction it is already going. Most leadership is probably forward incrementation. In such leadership, one takes the helm with the idea of advancing the leadership program of whomever one has succeeded. The promise is of progress through continuity. Creativity through forward incrementation is probably the kind that is most easily recognized and appreciated as creativity. Because it extends existing notions, it is seen as creative. Because it does not threaten the assumptions of such notions, it is not rejected as useless or even harmful.

• *Advance forward incrementation.* The leader attempts to move a field or an organization forward in the direction it is already going, but by moving beyond where others are ready for it to go. The leader moves followers in an accelerated way beyond the expected rate of forward progression. Advance forward incrementations usually are not successful at the time they are attempted because followers are not ready to go where the leader wants to lead. Or a significant number of them may not wish to go to that point, in which case they form an organized and sometimes successful source of resistance.

• *Redirection.* The leader attempts to redirect an organization, a field, or a product line from where it is headed toward a different direction. Redirective leaders need to match their leadership style and efforts to environmental circumstances to succeed (Sternberg and Vroom 2002); otherwise their best intentions may go awry.

- *Reconstruction/redirection.* The leader attempts to move a field, an organization, or a product line back to where it once was (a reconstruction of the past) so that it may move onward from that point, but in a direction different from the one it took before.

- *Reinitiation.* The leader attempts to move a field, an organization, or a product line to a different, as yet unreached starting point and then move from that point. The leader takes followers from a new starting point in a direction that is different from the one they previously pursued.

- *Synthesis.* The leader integrates two ideas that previously were seen as unrelated or opposed to each other. What formerly were viewed as distinct ideas now are viewed as related and capable of being unified. Integration is a key means by which progress is attained in the sciences. It represents neither acceptance nor rejection of existing paradigms, but rather, a merger of them.

(SUCCESSFUL) INTELLIGENCE

Intelligence seems to be important to leadership, but how important? Indeed, if a leader's conventional intelligence is too much higher than that of the people he or she leads, the leader may not connect with them and may become ineffective (Williams and Sternberg 1988). Intelligence, as conceived of here, is not just intelligence in its conventional, narrow sense—as some kind of general factor (*g*; Demetriou 2002; Jensen 1998, 2002; Spearman 1927; see essays in Sternberg 2000b; Sternberg and Grigorenko 2002) or as IQ (Binet and Simon 1905; Kaufman 2000; Wechsler 1939)—but rather, in terms of the theory of successful intelligence (Sternberg 1997, 1999c, 2002b). *Successful intelligence* is defined in part as the skills and dispositions needed to succeed in life, given one's own conception of success, within one's sociocultural environment (Sternberg 1997). Two particular aspects of the theory are especially relevant: academic and practical intelligence (see Neisser 1979).

It is clear how intelligence would have aspects of skill. But how would it have aspects of a disposition? The main way is through the decision to apply it. Many leaders know better, but do anyway. Their minds tell them what they should be doing, but their motives—for power, fame, money, sex, or whatever—lead them in a different direction. Leaders often fail not because they are not smart enough, but because they choose not to use the intelligence they have.

Academic Intelligence

Academic intelligence refers to the memory and analytical skills and dispositions that, in combination, largely constitute the conventional notion of intelligence—the skills and dispositions needed to recall and recognize but also to analyze, evaluate, and judge information.

These skills and dispositions matter for leadership because leaders need to be able to retrieve information that is relevant to leadership decisions (memory) and to analyze and evaluate different courses of action, whether proposed by themselves or by others (analysis). But a good analyst is not necessarily a good leader.

Schools in the United States, and in much of the world, overwhelmingly emphasize the measurement and development of academic intelligence. The problem with this strategy is that the value of academic intelligence is probably at a greatest premium when children are in school. When they mature, and are called into positions of leadership, academic intelligence will continue to matter, but not as much. Even in academia, academic intelligence is most important in the pursuits most similar to those of school, such as reviewing articles or grant proposals. More important are the creative skills used to generate excellent ideas, the practical skills used to implement those ideas, and the wisdom to be able to discern how to make a positive difference in the world.

The long-time primary emphasis on academic intelligence (IQ) in the literature relating intelligence to leadership perhaps also has been unfortunate. Indeed, as mentioned above, recent theorists emphasize other aspects of intelligence, such as emotional intelligence (e.g., Caruso, Mayer, and Salovey 2002; Goleman 1998a, 1998b) or multiple intelligences (Gardner 1995). In this chapter the emphasis is on practical intelligence (Hedlund et al. 2003; Sternberg et al. 2000; Sternberg and Hedlund 2002), which has a somewhat different focus from emotional intelligence. Practical intelligence overlaps with emotional intelligence, in that practical intelligence involves understanding and managing one's self, others, and tasks. It is a part of successful intelligence. Practical intelligence is a core component of leadership and thus receives special attention here.

Practical Intelligence

Practical intelligence refers to the set of skills and dispositions needed to solve everyday problems by utilizing knowledge gained from experience in order to purposefully adapt to, shape, and select environments. It thus involves changing oneself to suit the environment (adaptation), changing the environment to suit oneself (shaping), or finding a new environment within which to work (selection). One uses these skills to manage oneself, others, and tasks.

Different combinations of intellectual skills engender different types of leadership. Leaders vary in their memory skills, analytical skills, and practical skills. A leader who is particularly strong in memory skills but not in the other skills may have vast amounts of knowledge at his or her disposal, but be unable to use it effectively. A leader who is particularly strong in analytical skills as well as memory skills may be able to retrieve information and analyze it effectively, but may be unable to convince others that his or her analysis is correct. A leader who is strong in memory, analytical, and practical skills is most likely to be effective in influencing others. But, of course, there are leaders who are strong in practical skills but not in memory and analytical skills (Sternberg 1997; Sternberg et al. 2000); in conventional terms, they are shrewd but not smart. They may be effective in getting others to go along with them, but they may end up leading these others down garden paths.

An important part of practical intelligence is *tacit knowledge,* or having the procedural knowledge to handle everyday life situations, which typically is not formally taught in schools or other institutions. In one study of three levels of military leadership, tacit knowledge scores were not found to correlate with the number of months leaders had served in their current positions (Hedlund et al. 2003), presumably because successful leaders spent less time in a job before being promoted than did less successful leaders. Subsequent research, however, found that tacit knowledge scores did correlate with leadership rank, such that leaders at higher levels of command exhibited greater tacit knowledge than did those at lower ranks (Hedlund et al. 2003).

WISDOM

A leader can have all of the above skills and dispositions and still lack an additional quality that, arguably, is the most important quality a leader can have, but perhaps also the rarest: wisdom. It is viewed here according to a proposed balance theory of wisdom (Sternberg 1998a, 2003), according to which an individual is wise to the extent that he or she uses successful intelligence, creativity, and knowledge as moderated by values (a) to seek to reach a common good, (b) by balancing intrapersonal (one's own), interpersonal (others'), and extrapersonal (organizational/institutional/spiritual) interests, (c) over the short and long term, (d) to adapt to, shape, and select environments. Wisdom is in large part a decision to use one's intelligence, creativity, and experience for a common good.

Wise leaders do not look out just for their own interests, nor do they ignore these interests. Rather, they skillfully balance various interests, including their own, those of their followers, and those of the organization for which they are responsible. They also recognize that they need to align the interests of their group or organization with those of others groups or organizations because no group operates within a vacuum. Wise leaders realize that what may appear to be a prudent course of action over the short term does not necessarily appear so over the long term.

Leaders who have been less than fully successful often have been so because they have ignored one or another set of interests. For example, Richard Nixon and Bill Clinton, in their respective cover-ups, not only failed to fulfill the interests of the country they led, but also failed to fulfill their own interests. Because their cover-ups ended up bogging down their administrations in scandals, they were unable to make the positive accomplishments they had hoped to make. Freud was a great leader in the fields of psychiatry and psychology, but his insistence that his followers (disciples) conform quite exactly to his own system of psychoanalysis led him to lose those disciples and the support they might have continued to lend to his efforts. He was an expert in interpersonal interests, but not as applied to his own life. Napoleon lost sight of the extrapersonal interests that would have been best for his own country. His disastrous invasion of Russia, which appears to have been motivated more by hubris than by France's need to have Russia in its empire, partially destroyed his reputation as a successful military leader and paved the way for his later downfall.

Leaders can be intelligent and creative in various ways, but it does not guarantee that they are wise. Indeed, probably relatively few leaders at any level are particularly wise. Yet the few leaders who are notably so—perhaps Nelson Mandela, Martin Luther King Jr., Gandhi, Winston Churchill, Mother Teresa—leave an indelible mark on the people they lead and, potentially, on history. It is important to note that wise leaders are usually charismatic, but charismatic leaders are not necessarily wise, as Hitler, Stalin, and many other charismatic leaders have demonstrated throughout history.

Unsuccessful leaders often show certain stereotyped fallacies in their thinking. Consider five such flaws (Sternberg 2002a, 2002b). The first, *unrealistic-optimism fallacy*, occurs when they think they are so smart and effective that they can do whatever they want. The second, *egocentrism fallacy*, occurs when successful leaders start to think that they are the only ones who matter, not the people who rely on them for leadership. The third, *omniscience fallacy*, occurs when leaders think that they know everything and then lose sight of the limitations of their own knowledge. The fourth, *omnipotence fallacy*, occurs when leaders think they are all-powerful and can do whatever they want. And the fifth, *invulnerability fallacy*, occurs when leaders think they can get away with anything because they are too clever to be caught; even if they are caught, they figure that they can get away with what they have done because of who they imagine themselves to be.

RELATED APPROACHES

The view described here fits in well with related views of other behavioral scientists. Perhaps most notable is its fit with the GoodWork Project of Gardner, Csikszentmihalyi, and Damon (2002). These researchers asked, in a different way, about the intersection of wisdom, intelligence, and creativity. In particular, they studied very creative individuals of high intelligence and asked what leads them to do good works—that is, to exercise wisdom in their work. The researchers studied two occupations in particular, genetics and journalism. In their own ways, both fields exert great pressure to cut corners. In the case of genetics, the field is moving extremely fast, and its leadership positions are difficult to maintain. As the recent case of Woo Suk Hwang of South Korea showed, the temptations are enormous. Scientists in the field of genetics have the potential of reaching the kind of fame enjoyed by rock stars, and Hwang succumbed to the pressure. He and his colleagues falsified not only data, but experiments, in order to achieve fame, glory, and financial return. Whatever creativity and intelligence they had was channeled unwisely so as to give the appearance of doing good work when in fact they were doing anything but. Similarly, as the cases of Jayson Blair and Judith Miller showed at *The New York Times*, journalists operate under enormous pressures and sometimes find themselves cutting corners to get scoops. Blair invented stories; Miller apparently only misreported on them. Gardner, Csikszentmihalyi, and Damon point out five ways in which bright people in any profession can keep their focus on good work: creating new institutions, expanding functions of existing institutions, reconfiguring existing institutions' membership, reaffirming their values, and taking personal stands.

One way to achieve good work is through the existence of *societal trustees,* described by Gardner in his target chapter. Companies, foundations, and universities have boards of trustees to oversee their operations and to deal with issues of social responsibility. Who are the trustees of society? Politicians, to the extent that they have been placed in such a position, have for the most part failed miserably. The 98% reelection rate of members of Congress suggests that the veneer of democracy in U.S. society has become very thin indeed—redistricting takes place in order to ensure not the perpetuation of democracy, but rather the privileges enjoyed by the ruling class. At present, the situation is compounded by an executive branch that has arrogated more power to itself than has any other executive branch in history. Meanwhile, sycophants in Congress, for the most part, sit idly by, more concerned with the perpetuation of their own power than with the restoration of democratic traditions. The research of Gardner and Benjamin, described by Gardner in this volume, has suggested that trusteeship has become more local over time. This may well be due to the fact that people have largely given up on those in central positions of power.

Another related view is that of Claxton, who asks in his target chapter whether wisdom can be conceptualized as a form of *advanced creativity.* Claxton sensibly points out that wisdom inheres in real and specific actions in everyday situations, not in some kind of abstract trait that people possess in some degree. He further correctly points out that wisdom always involves interaction with others—one cannot be wise in solving an abstract problem that has nothing to do with human affairs. And he notes perceptively that wisdom involves conflicts and impasses. When a problem is easily solved, we do not refer to it as something that challenges our wisdom.

Claxton further accurately notes that the mere study of wisdom does not in any way assure that one will act wisely. People can know the wise thing to do, and then do something else. Bill Clinton, as an attorney, had the knowledge and sense to know that lying in court about his relationship with Monica Lewinsky was unwise; he did it anyway. Andrew Fastow, Kenneth Lay, and Jeffrey Skilling were all extremely intelligent and creative. They certainly knew what they were doing at Enron was wrong, but they, too, did it anyway. George W. Bush and his team ran a campaign through a combination of deception, smoke, and mirrors, focusing on issues largely irrelevant to people's lives (e.g., gay marriage, flag burning), while hiding important issues such as the impoverishment of already poor people and huge giveaways to corporate cronies; they did it anyway. Claxton's approach shows that wisdom must be studied in its own right because intelligent, well-educated, and knowledgeable people often use their skills not for a common good, but rather for their own selfish and often blatantly cynical ends.

Claxton identifies some key aspects of wise thinking, namely, its moral quality, the disinterest of the judge, and the ability to empathize. This last quality shows that some kind of emotional intelligence is key to wisdom. But as people such as Karl Rove show, emotional intelligence can be used to bad ends—not to help people, but rather to manipulate them. So once again, the question regarding wisdom is not just what qualities one possesses, but how one uses them in one's daily life. For Claxton, creativity is a necessary but insufficient condition for wisdom. Rove is one of many examples of people who are creative but not wise. We need to develop in people creativity that will be used for wise purposes—for Gardner, Csikszentmihalyi, and Damon's "good work."

Claxton and Gardner share an interest in how wisdom in action can be cultivated. Cultivation is the main focus of Craft's target chapter. She views wisdom as making appropriate, thoughtful, and well-informed judgments that lead to sound courses of action. Wise people always take into account the potential consequences of their actions and let such consequences guide what they decide both to do and not to do.

Craft points out that we often neglect the role of culture in creativity. As Lubart (1999) points out, cultures may differ both in conceptions and in levels of creativity. Moreover, expressions of creativity may vary cross-culturally. Craft notes, for example, that Eastern values place more emphasis on the group, Western values on the individual (see also Nisbett 2003). People who are socialized more to conform to group norms and expectations may not show the same kinds or levels of individual creativity that would be manifest in people less attentive to, or restricted by, group norms.

Another factor Craft (2002, this volume) identifies as affecting creativity is socioeconomic status. She points out that some children may be more socialized into the importance of resilience, self-reliance, persistence, and control over the environment than are others. Political context also affects creativity. As she points out, in some political contexts creativity is so suppressed that its expression is barely possible; if it is possible, it is often a great risk. Craft also agrees with Gardner (2004) that certain religious values may interfere with creativity, such as a value whereby someone decides that his or her mind is simply not open to change in any significant way. In effect, someone who adopts the unwise position of having a closed mind closes off any possibility of his or her own to be truly creative.

If there is a common theme in all of our work, it is that learning to be wise, intelligent, and creative is a lifelong pursuit, not one that ends when schooling is over (see Claxton 1999). Moreover, the greatest challenge is neither learning declarative knowledge (knowing what) nor even learning procedural knowledge (knowing how), but rather implementing what one has learned to make a positive difference in the world.

CONCLUSION

There probably is no model of leadership that will totally capture all of the many facts—both internal and external to the individual—that make for a successful leader. The WICS model may come closer to some models, however, in capturing dimensions that are important. It is based on the notion that a successful leader decides to synthesize wisdom, intelligence, and creativity. The work of Gardner, Claxton, and Craft comes to much the same conclusion, perhaps using different language.

An effective leader needs creative skills and dispositions to come up with ideas, academic skills and dispositions to decide whether they are good ideas, practical skills and dispositions to make the ideas work and convince others of the value of the ideas, and wisdom-based skills and dispositions to ensure that the ideas are in the service of the common good rather than just the good of the leader or perhaps some clique of family members or followers. A leader lacking in creativity will be unable to deal with novel and difficult situations, such as a new and unexpected source of hostility. A leader lacking in academic intelligence will not be able to decide whether his or her ideas are viable. A leader lacking in practical intelligence will be unable to implement his or her ideas effectively. And an unwise leader may succeed in implementing ideas, but may end up implementing ideas that are contrary to the best interests of the people he or she leads.

Schooling should develop the new leaders of tomorrow. But the mindless emphasis U.S. schools place on the model of producing "walking encyclopedias" leads students away from rather than toward leadership roles. Arguably, this emphasis is a failure of our own generation of leaders and of those generations that have come before us. The expression "Knowledge is power" is incorrect. Knowledge without wisdom, intelligence, and creativity is blind and deaf. Unfortunately, it is not also mute.

Author Notes

Preparation of this chapter was supported by Contract MDA 903–92-K-0125 from the U.S. Army Research Institute and by Grant Award # 31–1992–701 from the United States Department of Education, Institute for Educational Sciences, as administered by the Temple University Laboratory for Student Success. Grantees undertaking such projects are encouraged to express freely their professional judgment. This chapter, therefore, does not necessarily represent the position or policies of the U.S. government, and no official endorsement should be inferred.

Correspondence regarding the chapter should be sent to Robert J. Sternberg, Dean of Arts and Sciences, Ballou Hall, 3rd Floor, Tufts University, Medford, MA 02155. E-mail: Robert.Sternberg@tufts.edu. In my work on intelligence, I have collaborated with many people over the years. My work on practical intelligence has particularly relied on the contributions of Anna Cianciolo, Elena Grigorenko, Jennifer Hedlund, Joseph Horvath, Cynthia Matthew, Richard Wagner, and Wendy Williams. My work on creativity has also depended on the contributions of many people, especially Elena Grigorenko, James Kaufman, Todd Lubart, and Jean Pretz. My work on stories of leadership is being done in collaboration with Christopher Rate.

REFERENCES

Amabile, T. M. 1983. *The social psychology of creativity*. New York: Springer.
———. 1996. *Creativity in context*. Boulder, CO: Westview.
Bandura, A. 1996. *Self-efficacy: The exercise of control*. New York: Freeman.
Binet, A., and T. Simon. 1905. Méthodes nouvelles pour le diagnostic du niveau intellectuel des anormaux [New methods for diagnosing the intellectual level of non normals]. *L'Année psychologique* 11:191–336.
Caruso, D. R., J. D. Mayer, and P. Salovey. 2002. Emotional intelligence and emotional leadership. In *Multiple intelligences and leadership*, ed. R. Riggio, 55–74. Mahwah, NJ: Lawrence Erlbaum.
Claxton, G. L. 1999. *Wise up: The challenge of lifelong learning*. London: Bloomsbury.
Craft, A. 2002. *Creativity in the early years: A lifewide foundation*. London: Continuum.
Demetriou, A. 2002. Tracing psychology's invisible giant and its visible guards. In *The general factor of intelligence: How general is it?*, ed. R. J. Sternberg and E. L. Grigorenko, 3–18. Mahwah, NJ: Lawrence Erlbaum.
Frensch, P. A., and R. J. Sternberg. 1989. Expertise and intelligent thinking: When is it worse to know better? In *Advances in the psychology of human intelligence*, vol. 5, ed. R. J. Sternberg, 157–88. Hillsdale, NJ: Lawrence Erlbaum.
Gardner, H. 1995. *Leading minds*. New York: Basic Books.
———. 2004. *Changing minds: The art and science of changing our own and other people's minds*. Cambridge, MA: Harvard Business School Press.
Gardner, H., M. Csikszentmihalyi, and W. Damon. 2002. *Good work: When excellence and ethics meet*. New York: Basic Books.
Goleman, D. 1998a. What makes a good leader? *Harvard Business Review* November–December: 93–102.
———. 1998b. *Working with emotional intelligence*. New York: Bantam.
Grigorenko, E. L., and R. J. Sternberg, eds. 2001. *Family environment and intellectual functioning: A life-span perspective*. Mahwah, NJ: Lawrence Erlbaum.
Hedlund, J., G. B. Forsythe, J. A. Horvath, W. M. Williams, S. Snook, and R. J. Sternberg. 2003. Identifying and assessing tacit knowledge: Understanding the practical intelligence of military leaders. *Leadership Quarterly* 14:117–40.
Jensen, A. R. 1998. *The g factor: The science of mental ability*. Westport, CT: Praeger/Greenwood.
———. 2002. Psychometric g: Definition and substantiation. In *General factor of intelligence: How general is it?*, ed. R. J. Sternberg and E. L. Grigorenko, 39–54. Mahwah, NJ: Lawrence Erlbaum.
Kaufman, A. S. 2000. Tests of intelligence. In *Handbook of intelligence*, ed. R. J. Sternberg, 445–76. New York: Cambridge University Press.
Kuhn, T. S. 1970. *The structure of scientific revolutions*, 2nd ed. Chicago: University of Chicago Press.
Lubart, T. I. 1999. Creativity across cultures. In *Handbook of creativity*, ed. R. J. Sternberg, 339–50. Cambridge, UK: Cambridge University Press.
Lubart, T. I., and R. J. Sternberg. 1995. An investment approach to creativity: Theory and data. In *The creative cognition approach*, ed. S. M. Smith, T. B. Ward, and R. A. Finke, 269–302. Cambridge, MA: MIT Press.
Neisser, U. 1979. The concept of intelligence. *Intelligence* 3:217–27.
Nisbett, R. E. 2003. *The geography of thought*. New York: Free Press.

Pink, D. H. 2005. *A whole new mind: Moving from the information age to the conceptual age.* New York: Riverhead Books.

Spearman, C. 1927. *The abilities of man.* London: Macmillan.

Sternberg, R. J. 1985. *Beyond IQ: A triarchic theory of human intelligence.* New York: Cambridge University Press.

———. 1997. *Successful intelligence.* New York: Plume.

———. 1998a. A balance theory of wisdom. *Review of General Psychology* 2:347–65.

———. 1998b. Abilities are forms of developing expertise. *Educational Researcher* 27:11–20.

———. 1999a. A propulsion model of types of creative contributions. *Review of General Psychology* 3:83–100.

———. 1999b. Intelligence as developing expertise. *Contemporary Educational Psychology* 24:359–75.

———. 1999c. The theory of successful intelligence. *Review of General Psychology* 3:292–316.

———. 2000a. Creativity is a decision. In *Teaching for intelligence II,* ed. A. L. Costa, 85–106. Arlington Heights, IL: Skylight Training and Publishing.

———, ed. 2000b. *Handbook of intelligence.* New York: Cambridge University Press.

———. 2002a. Creativity as a decision. *American Psychologist* 57:376.

———. 2002b. Smart people are not stupid, but they sure can be foolish: The imbalance theory of foolishness. In *Why smart people can be so stupid,* ed. R. J. Sternberg, 232–42. New Haven, CT: Yale University Press.

———. 2003. WICS: A model for leadership in organizations. *Academy of Management Learning & Education* 2:386–401.

———. 2004. WICS: A model of educational leadership. *Educational Forum* 68(2): 108–14.

Sternberg, R. J., G. B. Forsythe, J. Hedlund, J. Horvath, S. Snook, W. M. Williams, R. K. Wagner, and E. L. Grigorenko. 2000. *Practical intelligence in everyday life.* New York: Cambridge University Press.

Sternberg, R. J., and E. L. Grigorenko, eds. 1997. *Intelligence, heredity, and environment.* New York: Cambridge University Press.

———. 2001. *Environmental effects on cognitive abilities.* Mahwah, NJ: Lawrence Erlbaum.

———. 2002. *The general factor of intelligence: How general is it?* Mahwah, NJ: Lawrence Erlbaum.

Sternberg, R. J., and J. Hedlund. 2002. Practical intelligence, g, and work psychology. *Human Performance* 15:143–60.

Sternberg, R. J., J. C. Kaufman, and J. E. Pretz. 2003. A propulsion model of creative leadership. *Leadership Quarterly* 14:455–73.

Sternberg, R. J., and T. I. Lubart. 1995. *Defying the crowd: Cultivating creativity in a culture of conformity.* New York: Free Press.

———. 1996. Investing in creativity. *American Psychologist* 51:677–88.

Sternberg, R. J., and V. H. Vroom. 2002. The person versus the situation in leadership. *Leadership Quarterly* 13:301–23.

Wechsler, D. 1939. *The measurement of adult intelligence.* Baltimore: Williams & Wilkins.

Williams, W. M., and R. J. Sternberg. 1988. Group intelligence: Why some groups are better than others. *Intelligence* 12:351–77.

Zaccaro, S. J., C. Kemp, and P. Bader. 2004. Leader traits and attributes. In *The nature of leadership,* ed. J. Antonakis, A. T. Cianciolo, and R. J. Sternberg, 101–24. Thousand Oaks, CA: SAGE.

13

Liberating the Wise Educator

Cultivating Professional Judgment in Educational Practice

Dave Trotman

How can we tell if a teacher is nurturing students' creativity in the class-room? What sort of things should we look for? What experiences might we point to? As a lecturer in education and professional studies, with research interests in imagination and creativity, these are questions that I invariably end up asking student teachers during the course of their professional training. For the most part, the answers tend to be short with long silences; more experienced teachers fare only marginally better. Enabling pupil creativity in schools, contrary to the party line, is of course a complex business; fostering it wisely, even more so. Indeed, what we understand by *educational practice* and what we mean by *creativity* both have long, contentious, and well-documented histories. This in itself would make any seminar devoted to creativity and wisdom of important educational worth. But it assumes even greater importance in an educational policy context in which imperatives around globalization, environmental sustainability, social justice, and cultural and religious expression remain curiously subordinate to approved versions of pupil learning and centrally determined standards.

In the target chapters, Claxton, Craft, and Gardner offer a critical starting point for a necessary reassessment of our understanding of creativity in educational practice, calling upon us to re-examine many of the implicit values and assumptions that have now largely come to be taken for granted. In questioning both the conventional wisdom and dominant orthodoxies, their individual perspectives, taken collectively, represent an important step in restoring to the professional consciousness the mystery and emotional heart of what it is to learn, teach, educate, and be truly creative. Not surprisingly, *professional educational judgment* emerges as a pivotal concept and, by inference, the necessary conditions in which it can be properly exercised by teachers, educators, and practitioners in the settings and contexts in which they work. In response to some of these issues, and for the purpose of this short chapter, I have chosen to focus on four aspects of professional educational judgment which I consider to be significant to the idea of wisdom in creative education:

1. The centrality of *intuition* and *indeterminacy* in professional judgment of creativity

2. *Empathy* as a cornerstone of wise professional practice

3. The ability to suspend predispositions and prejudgments in encounters with creative processes and outcomes

4. The relationship between curriculum, educational practice, and professional judgment in the creative development of young people

INTUITION AND INDETERMINACY IN PROFESSIONAL JUDGMENT

Creativity in all sorts of educational settings involves (as the authors in this book have sought to demonstrate) a complex weave of cognitive processes and orientations: affective, aesthetic, sociocultural, ethical, and spiritual, and so on. And it is in this mix that educators are required to make any number of judgment calls throughout the participant-learner experience. The capacity to distill such complexity into informed professional judgment is, of necessity, a core professional characteristic, and it requires a degree of practice and subtlety of critical reflection that can be neither mandated nor codified in routine forms of performance training. Like Claxton, I am of the view that acting wisely, particularly in regard to the complexity of the creative activities of young people, involves the capacity for *intuition* as a professional practice. Moustakas (1990, 23) describes the intuitive as a kind of bridge between tacit and explicit knowledge in which we draw on clues, a sense of pattern, or underlying conditions that enable us to imagine and then characterize the reality, state of mind, or condition. Moustakas argues that the more we exercise and test our intuition, the more likely we are to develop an advanced perceptiveness and sensitivity to what is essential in the discovery of knowledge. In educational practice this perceptiveness and sensitivity becomes central to our day-to-day judgment calls. Tripp (1993) reminds us that these are effectively "expert guesses" that have "more to do with reflection, interpretation, opinion and wisdom, than with the mere acquisition of facts and prescribed 'right answers'" (p. 124). In the province of creative education (where educators necessarily have to come to an individual and collective interpretation of the participant's creative *lifeworld*) this becomes increasingly important in developing a sense of "it is happening" rather than the "what is happening." Then we can begin to apply imaginative experimentation and variation to our interpretations of creative events in the explicit absence of blunt or reductive criteria—this is the province of what Lyotard calls *indeterminate judgment* (quoted in Readings 1991, 106). In our interpretation and promotion of young people's creativity and imagination, it seems to me that this sort of intuition is pretty much essential. Wise judgment calls in the arena of creative education also invariably involve a moral quality that Claxton refers to, in which we are required to deal with problematic notions of the greater good, common good, and lasting values, all of which are terribly tricky to pin down. A possible key to this, though, is through Claxton's identification of empathy.

EMPATHY

Empathy, like creativity, is one of those slippery concepts that has been adopted and variously applied in the policy language of education (see, e.g., Department for Education and Skills 2004). In the field of healthcare, its use is applied with a greater degree of precision. In Rogers's (1961, 1980; Rogers and Freiburg 1994) well-known work in this area, empathy is framed in terms of sensitivity to changing, felt meanings, and experiences which flow in the other person without recourse to judgment. To pursue Claxton's thinking further, however, the orientations that emerge in the literature on empathy offer something important in the development of professional wisdom. Gould (1990), for example, considers the defining feature of empathy to be a person's ability to appreciate the feelings of people who are unlike him or her. Holden (1990, 72) views empathy as a form of "emotional knowing" in which one projects oneself into the physical being of the other (in this case the patient) while simultaneously retaining detached objectivity. Others suggest that empathy is characterized by "self-abandonment and openness to others," enabling "a type of freedom or neutrality from intense emotions that are not one's own" (Zderad 1969, quoted in Yegdich 1999, 85). Verducci (2000; drawing on Noddings's [1984] widely recognized work in this field) argues that empathy entails the indispensable function of "cognitive understanding of the other's situation and emotional resonance with the other. . . . [N]ot only must the one caring emotionally resonate with the other, she must *move* to do so. She must shift herself into the other's perspective and affective life" (p. 89). To contextualize empathy as an attribute of professional wisdom, however, Kunyk and Olson's (2001, 318) five dominant conceptualizations of empathy offer a useful starting point for the development of wisdom in action:

- a human trait
- a professional state
- a communication process
- caring
- a special relationship

While it is not possible in the scope of this chapter to discuss the detail of each of these, my intention is to draw the reader's attention to a concept of empathy as professional practice that transcends often vague or naïve notions of it simply being a good trait to possess. In the pursuit of wise creative education, I would argue that empathy is the single most important aspect of professional practice to attend to—what Claxton refers to as the cultivation of a *component disposition.*

THE WISE PROFESSIONAL

In any discussion around matters of wisdom in education, we might expect to see the emergence of the Greek concept of *phronesis*: practical wisdom based on the disposition to act truly and rightly. As Carr (1987) argues, this is an essential element of practical wisdom, situated and context bound, which cannot be subject to the impartial application of codified rules: "It is that form of wise and prudent judgment which takes account of what would be morally appropriate and fitting in a particular situation" (p. 172). This is the province of Gardner's concern, in which the thoughtful professional wrestles with competing interests but is mindful that "personal responsibility cannot be delegated to someone else" (p. 57). *Mindfulness* is an important idea because, while it is relatively easy to talk about matters of professional responsibility, practical wisdom requires the development and practice of professional techniques that constitute a form of mindfulness. On this point Claxton refers readers to Buddhist meditative practices and the phenomenological method of *bracketing.* I, too, agree that such approaches offer useful ways in which teachers might be able to develop their powers of interpretation and evaluation of complex educational experiences in the areas of creativity and imagination (Trotman 2006). While I have drawn upon such methods as part of my own research tool kit, more important, I have been privileged to witness hard-pressed classroom teachers apply similar strategies in their own search for the meaning of pupils' creative and imaginative experiences. These are teachers who have developed the skill of setting aside, or bracketing, their often deeply ingrained predispositions to pupils' creative processes and outcomes in order to enter into a more mindful, reflexive, and reflective connection with pupils' creative experiences. As Moustakas

(1990) points out, this form of practice involves self-search, self-dialogue, and self-discovery—professional attributes that teacher education programs in the United Kingdom have only the most limited opportunities to promote. The following extracts, taken from discussions and diary accounts of experienced primary-phase practitioners, intimate something of the personal self-search and professional moral imperatives that lie at the center of prudent judgment in the interpretation of creative imaginative form:

> Creativity involves risk. I think we've been taught as profession if the lesson has this shape then it's terribly safe . . . it isn't going to go wrong . . . a lesson that is imaginative looks different, it sounds different and it probably feels different, teachers may worry that they're not fully in control . . . and if anyone comes in they might not immediately identify learning that is happening in that environment. . . . [A]s a profession we need to understand that there are rich learning environments that have a different look from the Ofsted [inspection] model. (Barry)

> It was really emotional. . . . [W]e had a show-and-tell session—where the children get the opportunity to talk about themselves or something that's close to them—and she brought in her mom's old jewelery box and handbag. . . . [T]he other children just experience what she's thinking at the moment. And she stood there, she felt as proud as anything at the front of the class just getting that opportunity to talk about her mom . . . [S]he did a drawing . . . just a fantastic time, it really was, just talking to the class, you know. . . . [I]t was emotional for the other children but it's what we need, that raw emotion, you know. She got the opportunity just to talk about something that related to her as a child. . . . I didn't feel uncomfortable because I was quite aware that this was an ideal opportunity for her to talk about something like that. (Terry, following Davina's recent loss of her mother; Trotman 2006, 253–56)

The combination of empathic practice, the suspension of prejudgments, and sensitivity to intuitive felt awareness are the hallmarks of the wise professional. In my research on the evaluation of pupil imagination, I have been fortunate to work with teachers who continue to reveal these aspects as a conscious and practiced ability. Such teachers are able to mediate complex external macro sociopolitical forces (manifest in the often deprived urban communities in which they work) with the interior imaginative lifeworlds of their pupils, adopting a position of enthused naïveté in the presence of pupils' original ideas, impulses, and projects, while maintaining an attuned "with-it-ness" of the context in which these experiences are situated. Hence, and despite the continued erosion of professional values in the model of the "remodernized" professional, I remain optimistic that there are communities of teachers who have undertaken what Woods (1995) calls *strategic redefinition* (p. 11), in which they find ways to redefine their work in line with their own professionally informed values. There can be little doubt that professional strategic redefinition has become increasingly necessary in enabling and safeguarding the wise promotion of creativity and imagination in young people in schools, despite the fact that this has become ever more difficult to sustain both in the United Kingdom and elsewhere.

PROFESSIONAL JUDGMENT AND THE CURRICULUM-PRACTICE RELATIONSHIP

As a victim of the misappropriation of his own work, Gardner is one of many eminent academics whose studies have been subject to a deliberate or unwitting distortion through a selective and/or reckless application of scientific research to educational practice. While I agree with Gardner that the scientific community has a moral responsibility for how its work is applied, the ease with which evolving aspects of contemporary neuroscience have been enthusiastically and uncritically pursued in educational settings in the United Kingdom (under various banners, e.g., *accelerated learning, VAK, neurolinguistic programming, brain gym, emotional competencies*) is also attributable to a wave of educational policy imperatives that have progressively blunted and devalued the profession's capacity for practiced critical professional judgment. This, too, has resulted in unquestioned credence being given to particular fields of cognitive and behavioral science that now occupy a privileged position in Western theories of learning—largely at the expense of the empathic, emotional, and imaginative dimensions of the learner experience.

It is in this regard that educators face a significant challenge in the wise promotion of creativity, as the bonds between educational practice, curriculum, and the participant experience become increasingly fractured. In the United Kingdom this has been typified by state-mandated versions of creativity (Office for Standards in Education [Ofsted] 2003) and a discourse of state-approved professional practices (Ball 1990). While it can be argued that the curriculum is inevitably part of a particular tradition of what constitutes legitimate knowledge, studies of creativity consistently point to the common traits of an acceptance of risk, ambiguity, complexity, and uncertainty (e.g., Craft 2005; Cropley 2001), which implies a quite different set of relationships between curriculum, participants, and educational practice than those that continue to be promoted in mainstream education in the United Kingdom. Pinar (1998) reminds us that the Latin root word for curriculum, *currere* (to run the racecourse), reveals curriculum not as static, prespecified, or mandated, but motivated by "the unanticipated, the ambiguous, the complex, the strange, the queer, the incomprehensible" (p. 84). This idea of currere necessarily embraces the promotion of individual cultural identity over fixed, minority, and elite notions of culture and calls instead for the creation of a "personalised cultural map" (Willis 1990, 53). This, I would argue, *is* curriculum and, as such, corresponds directly with common creative traits and the need for intuitive, indeterminate judgment in wise educational practice.

IN THE SERVICE OF EDUCATION

While I regard the restoration of the curriculum-practice relationship as essential for the development of wise creative practice, my research in primary schools leads me to the view that there is a cadre of teachers whom we might come to regard as *trustees* of creative education (in Gardner's use of the term). These are teachers who are able to function with a high degree of technical dexterity in the manualization of their work (the implementation of national strategies and the routine management of external inspection) but, in tandem, have also created space (literally, in some instances) to enable the development of personalized professional imperatives governed by strong moral and ethical motivations. These motivations are powerfully shaped by an empathic connection to their pupils, the contexts and communities in which they live and learn, and an outward global consciousness for social justice. In this regard these teachers are, as Claxton suggests, skillful in the conduct of human affairs and the resolution of complex human predicaments; moreover, they are committed to an overriding imperative of educational service. The idea of educational service does not, however, imply an austere, slavish, or humorless subscription to the traditions, rituals, and routines of schooling, nor should it entail an unquestioning adherence to externally "authorized" practice. It is, in fact, something quite different. It is service that celebrates the symbolic creation and expression of ideas, feelings, and aspirations. Per Claxton's reference to Tagore, it is a joy of service. In *Lifelong Education*, Yeaxlee (1929) also puts it rather well:

> Life, to be vivid, strong, and creative, demands constant reflection upon experience, so that action may be guided by wisdom, and service be the other aspect of self-expression. (p. 28)

CONCLUSION

The increasing corpus of research around creativity in schools reveals a broad, multidimensional, and, at times, complex phenomenon. However, common themes do emerge. In addition to the necessary acceptance of risk, ambiguity, complexity, and uncertainty, studies typically identify increased ownership and the control of learners over their learning, contemplation and incubation of ideas, celebration of alternative ways of being and doing, and provision of learning environments that encourage exploring and transcending conventional boundaries (Craft 2005). The implications for professional educational practice might simply be construed as *letting go*. Indeed, Ofsted (2003, 18), in its own report into creativity, has argued this. Yet to do this with any level of wisdom, in the terms I have described, requires skilled educational judgment in the intuitive, indeterminate, and empathic that few in the profession are seriously encouraged to exercise as part of their training and continuing professional development.

To undertake the wise promotion of creativity in school settings is to recognize and be able to suspend our predispositions and prejudgments; to be conscious of, and account for, our cultural baggage and predilections that we bring into the creative educational sphere; and to position the pupils' imaginative and creative lifeworld as the central agency of the creative enterprise—in short, to know what we are letting go of, and a conscious willingness to *enter into*. In wise creative education the corollary of letting go is the elevation of intuition, indeterminacy, and empathy in our interpretative educational judgments of the creative encounters of young people. This requires a level of personal confidence that enables us to develop trust in our intuition (and being trusted by others to do so) as a meaningful professional endeavor. Developing empathy in conjunction with intuition makes possible wise educational judgment as a collaborative enterprise in which all participants (e.g., teachers, educators, practitioners, pupils, students, parents) can begin to reflect upon, share, and articulate their interpretations of creative phenomena in the service of individual and collective creative expression—what Eisner (1985) calls "the artful use of critical disclosure" (p. 93). Educators might then be able to change the locus of their practice to embrace, with confidence, the unanticipated, the ambiguous, the complex, and the risky. If a genuine political will to promote meaningful creativity in schools exists in the United Kingdom, then it necessarily demands a significant shift in thinking in educational policy, in which serious commitment is made to the development and practice of professional judgment over preoccupations with performance, prescription, and regimes of training. To restore professional judgment of this sort is, in my view, a significant step toward the liberation of the wise creative educator.

REFERENCES

Ball, S. J. 1990. *Politics and policy making in education*. London: Routledge.

Carr, W. 1987. What is an educational practice? *Journal of Philosophy of Education* 21:163–75.

Craft, A. 2005. *Creativity in schools: Tensions and dilemmas*. Abingdon, England: Routledge.

Cropley, A. 2001. *Creativity in education and learning: A guide for teachers and educators*. London: Kogan Page.

Department for Education and Skills. 2004. *Primary national strategy. Excellence and enjoyment: Learning and teaching in the primary years (Creating a learning culture: Conditions for learning, professional development materials)*. London: Department for Education and Skills.

Eisner, E. W. 1985. *The art of educational evaluation: A personal view*. Lewes: Falmer Press.

Gould, D. 1990. Empathy: A review of the literature with suggestions for an alternative research strategy. *Journal of Advanced Nursing* 15:1167–74.

Holden, R. J. 1990. Empathy: The art of emotional knowing in holistic nursing care. *Holistic Nursing Practice* 5(1): 70–79.

Kunyk, D., and J. K. Olson. 2001. Clarification of concepts of empathy. *Journal of Advanced Nursing* 35:317–25.

Moustakas, C. 1990. *Heuristic research: Design, methodology and applications*. London: SAGE.

Noddings, N. 1984. *Caring: A feminine approach to ethics and moral education*. Berkeley: University of California Press.

Office for Standards in Education (Ofsted). 2003. *Expecting the unexpected: Developing creativity in primary and secondary schools*. London: HMI.

Pinar, W. E. 1998. *Curriculum: Toward new identities*. New York: Garland.

Readings, B. 1991. *Introducing Lyotard: Art and politics*. London: Routledge.

Rogers, C. R. 1961. *On becoming a person: A therapist's view of psychotherapy*. London: Constable.

———. 1980. *A way of being*. Boston: Houghton Mifflin.

Rogers, C., and H. J. Freiburg. 1994. *Freedom to learn,* 3rd ed. Upper Saddle River, NJ: Prentice Hall.

Tripp, D. 1993. *Critical incidents in teaching: Developing professional judgement*. London: Routledge.

Trotman, D. 2006. Interpreting imaginative lifeworlds: Phenomenological approaches in imagination and the evaluation of educational practice. *Qualitative Research* 6:245–65.

Verducci, S. 2000. A moral method? Thoughts on cultivating empathy through method acting. *Journal of Moral Education* 29:87–99.

Willis, P. 1990. *Moving culture*. London: Calouste Gulbenkian Foundation.

Woods, P. 1995. *Creative teachers in primary schools*. Buckingham, England: Open University Press.

Yeaxlee, B. A. 1929. *Lifelong education: A sketch of the range and significance of the adult education movement*. London: Cassell.

Yegdich, T. 1999. On the phenomenology of empathy in nursing: Empathy or sympathy. *Journal of Advanced Nursing* 30:83–93.

Zderad, L. 1969. Empathic nursing: Realization of a human capacity. *Nursing Clinics of North America* 4:655–62.

PART THREE

Synthesizing Creativity, Wisdom, and Trusteeship

14

Concluding Thoughts

Good Thinking—Education for Wise Creativity

Guy Claxton, Anna Craft, and Howard Gardner

If our goal was to promote debate about the relationship among our four key concepts of creativity, wisdom, trusteeship, and education, we have surely succeeded. The responses to our stimulus chapters have proven thoughtful and challenging, and have widened and deepened our thinking in ways that we had not foreseen. In this concluding reflection, we seek not to rebut or argue with our respondents in detail, but rather to pick out some of the recurrent themes in their responses and focus on those which seem to us to be the most promising to pursue. We hope these reflections, in turn, will provoke yet further thoughts and conversations with the readers of this book.

Most basically, our primary concern with the way in which creativity has often been interpreted and handled within education is shared by our respondents. They help home in on this more precisely in a number of ways. First, creativity is wasted if it simply translates into occasional bursts of "light relief," leaving a dull and unimaginative curriculum in place. Creativity is debased if it serves only as the spoonful of sugar that helps the medicine go down. Enjoyable though such activities may be, there is little evidence that, without any stronger rationale, they make a lasting impact on children's development. Virtually all the chapters are agreed on that.

Second, we misrepresent creativity if we show students only the side of it that is fun and easy. Several of the chapters, such as Bannerman's, stress that real-life creativity often requires disciplined hard work, fraught with passages of frustration or indecision. Anything certainly does not go. Bannerman also demonstrates that adult creativity relies crucially on a mass of experience in the chosen domain, and therefore we again misrepresent it if we lead children to assume that creativity is a generic faculty they already possess that can be instantly brought to bear on any given topic or project.

Third, many of the authors, including Knoop, remind us that creativity is not merely—perhaps not even principally—a solitary activity. The lone artist in the garret, struggling with her manuscript, is a misrepresentation. Creativity, whether in the arts, in science, in product design, or indeed in school, is as much a collective process as it is an individual one. Innovation springs from groups and teams that contain diverse perspectives, share common goals and ideals, and are capable of monitoring and adjusting their own collective process. Fostering creativity in young people, therefore, requires not just communal cutting out and composing, but a more sustained development of the attitudes and capabilities that enable groups to run well.

Fourth, it has strongly emerged that creativity is not a culturally universal or neutral idea. Dillon, Feldman, and Knoop, for example, all pick up on this theme, discussed in Craft's chapter. Their chapters remind us, in different ways, that creativity reflects a combination of biological, social, and cultural influences. Creative products and performances are imbued with the distinctive values and beliefs of their time, place, history, and society. Nurturing creativity in education therefore requires an awareness of and sensitivity to its locally unique context.

The fifth facet of our concern about creativity begins to bring us closer to wisdom. It is clear from several of the contributions to this book that creativity, as a valuable human quality, is not restricted to the set-piece activities of a painting, a scientific experiment, or the design of a new piece of technology. It has much wider currency than that, and we both find and need considerable creativity especially in the conduct of human affairs. Maybe the products do not last as long, and maybe there is no well-defined field of experienced practitioners to evaluate and arbitrate on creative contributions. But the imaginative conduct of family life—the discovery of skillful ways to negotiate teenage moods and needs, for example—is arguably as valuable as the creation of a new kind of breakfast cereal. Most of the authors agree that wisdom is primarily found in the conduct of complex human affairs and that such wisdom frequently involves the discovery of innovative possibilities that resolve conflicts and reduce tensions.

Seeing creativity as an essential aspect of everyday life brings us to a sixth concern: the need for creativity to be exercised responsibly, to have some moral underpinning. Many of the authors are worried by forms of creativity that are self-indulgent, egotistical, driven by materialism, and wasteful of both mental and material resources. Simonton, for example, points out that many current forms of creativity, in school and out, are very far from anything that we would associate with wisdom. Creativity that is unbridled by any concern for its moral responsibilities or social or ecological consequences is, we seem to agree, potentially dangerous. Unprincipled creativity can lead to the testing of dubious drugs on unsuspecting poor Africans or the invention of new forms of human degradation that leave no marks and manage to comply, but only technically, with the Geneva Convention. As educators we are therefore faced with the question of how we encourage responsible forms of creativity.

We seem to live in a time of what the social commentator Christopher Booker (1992) called *neophilia*, whereby new is by default assumed to be good—new technology, new lifestyle choices, New Labour—and conventional and traditional are by the same token automatically stigmatized as fuddy-duddy and risk averse. The business world is awash with dire warnings for those who cannot or will not live in a constant state of creativity and change. Yet conservatism can be wise as well as reactionary, and creativity can be gratuitous and ill-considered, as well as smart and appropriate. There is a widespread feeling in these pages, articulated as well by Haste as anyone, that we may not have gotten the delicate balance between conservatism (with a very small c) and creativity quite right. (The great social theorist Neil Postman cowrote a book in 1971 called *Teaching as a Subversive Activity*—and then felt the need, 15 years later, to write another to balance it, which was called, inevitably, *Teaching as a Conserving Activity*.)

The idea of wisdom has struck a chord with our respondents, as they try to help us articulate these worries and to see a way beyond them. Although we are far from an accepted definition of *wisdom*, or a common approach to its investigation, the concept does seem to offer a rallying point for those who share our concerns. It invites us to look for depth in how we think of creativity and to explore its moral and ethical dimensions. As Gardner's lead chapter helps unravel the concept of *good work,* so the study of wisdom leads us to ask "What is good creativity?" and, by implication, "How do we educate for good creativity?" Although we don't yet have clear answers, we think the ruminations in this book help us make progress.

Let us take as a starting point Dillon's use of systems theory. We might speculate that one of the reasons why Western creativity has become somewhat egotistical and individualistic is because it reflects the Cartesian view of human identity. The Enlightenment sense of self roots itself in the conscious, personal world of desires and deliberations and downplays the aspects of identity that are both subpersonal (the silent, intelligent workings of the embodied brain) and suprapersonal (the social and cultural world which we not only inhabit, but by which we are profoundly constituted).

Systems theory reminds us that human psychology reflects all three of these layers. An eye, for example, can't be understood without knowing about how its components work and how those components are modified and integrated by their relationships. Nor will it continue to be a functioning eye if it is deprived of the complex conversations which it constantly carries on with the larger bodily system of which it is a part. Thus, says the theory of complex adaptive systems, is a person constituted by a subpersonal world of neuronal and biochemical networks, *and* the ecological and sociocultural body politic in which it is embedded. Our phenomenal world of thoughts, feelings, and actions is suspended between these larger and smaller worlds and constantly resonates with and is influenced by them. We are midi-systems in constant reverberation with the hierarchy of megasystems and minisystems that surround them. If we forget that our identity reflects this trinity of layers, and inheres not just in the conscious personal layer in the middle, we misconstrue ourselves.

Several contributions to this book stress the importance, in trying to get a handle on wise creativity, of looking upward at these larger systems in which we are embedded. Most visible is the immediate flux of people, objects, and events of which we ourselves are resonating parts (or, perhaps more accurately, aspects). Knoop and Dillon both emphasize the importance of seeing wisdom and creativity in terms of their participation in this intricate dance. Good creativity and wise action emerge out of an acceptance of this resounding contingency. They are appropriate, custom-made responses to the momentary big picture, not interventions based on either a solipsistic pursuit of individual goals or an attempt to apply the predetermined rule book of what Schon (1984) calls *technical rationality*. Wise action is creative because it is subtle and nuanced, respecting and responding to the unprecedented array of hopes, fears, and opportunities that are latent, or evident, in the present moment.

To be capable of such subtle, contingent, creative interaction, people have to feel themselves to be a resonant part of the situation, not an individual collection of needs and projects looking for any opportunity to be pursued. They have to operate with a systemic awareness and a systemic psychology. Perhaps emerging from the various contributions to this volume are the beginnings of a description of what such a psychology might look like. It must involve, for example, an accurate, honest, detailed perception of the situation. If perception is too top-down, driven by personal needs and beliefs, then much of that detail may well be missed. Perceptions will run the risk of being neatened up and skewed to fit with preexisting categories and agendas. This perspicacity in turn seems to require a degree of patience: a temperament that is able to wait while impressions form, without rushing to impose order or convention on them. To see a three-dimensional "magic eye" image emerge from a two-dimensional page, the trick is to gaze and wait, letting the brain conduct its own hunt for a binocular pattern, not to peer and think. And so it may be with wisdom.

Wise creativity would also seem to need the disposition to look below the surface, to detect a wider range of affordances and constraints within a situation than other people might see. And a vital aspect of this, as Trotman and others argue, is empathy: the inclination, and the ability, to look beyond other people's appearances to deeper aspects of their psychologies. As Rowson points out, the old man in Claxton's story of the Tokyo subway is able to see beyond the drunk's aggression to his distress and beyond the young American's brash heroism to his deeper desire to be more skillfully compassionate. The old man's harmless babbling allows both of these deeper states to surface: the drunk lets himself relax and be comforted, while the young hero is left in rueful but productive contemplation of the master class in kindness he has just been privileged to witness and of how much learning he has yet to do before he achieves that high degree of systemic sensibility.

Another cognitive disposition that seems to be associated with wise creativity is intuition.[1] There is experimental evidence that experienced intuition can work better than deliberation when solving problems and making decisions in highly complex environments (Dijksterhuis 2004). Indeed, the very job of teaching—as well as the process of professional development—involves intuitive practitioner judgment based on complex and often deep experience (Dadds 1993, 1995; Nias 1996; Woods 1990).

Conscious reason can only handle a rather restricted number of separate considerations at once, so when the complexity exceeds theses limitations, a preconscious selection of what seem to be the most salient variables has to be made—and thus potentially relevant information has to be preemptively discarded. Informed intuition seems able to keep a running total of greater complexity. As wisdom prototypically operates in complex predicaments, in which the optimal course of action is not clear (at least to ordinary mortals), it is here that we might expect intuition to come into its own.

To extrapolate, we might posit a wise cognitive mode in which a clear, detailed, and deep perception of the situation, with all its apparent complexities and contradictions, is allowed to resonate internally with a deep repository of experience in human affairs. As this resonance is not a conscious or deliberate process, we cannot account for it in midi-level language. Instead, as creativity theorists like Martindale (1999) have done, we may need to resort to the microlevel language of cell assemblies and neural networks to capture something of this subpersonal level of cognition. Martindale suggests that, where a coarse, rule-bound, and impatient cognitive mode might force the neural network into finding a local minimum solution that satisfies some but not all of the situational constraints, the slower, intuitive mode might allow a more delicate and patient settling into a solution that is more subtle, more inclusive, and more creative.

For wisdom to temper creativity, people also seem to need to be in touch with a deeper set of values which reflect that systemic sensibility. Feeling oneself to be part of a wider whole is, as Feldman notes, traditionally a matter for religion and spirituality, but the systemic view may offer a secular way of approaching the same territory. Knoop draws our attention not just to the sociocultural milieu discussed earlier, but to the wider ecological fields in which we inevitably find ourselves. He suggests that a greater feeling of connection to the natural and material worlds—and therefore a naturally arising desire to "take good care of our living room"—is an essential aspect of wisdom, one that is much needed to counter the wasteful attitude toward resources that characterizes the short-term egotistical forms of creativity. Einstein (1954), in a contemplative moment, summed up this widening sense of responsibility thus:

> A human being is a part of the whole called by us "Universe," a part limited in space and time. We experience ourselves, our thoughts and

feelings, as something separated from the rest—a kind of optical delusion of our consciousness. This delusion is a kind of prison for us, restricting us to our personal desires and to affection for a few persons nearest to us. . . . Our task must be to free ourselves from this prison by widening our circle of compassion to embrace all living creatures, and the whole of nature in its beauty. (p. 86)

In cognitive terms, then, as Simonton and others stress, wisdom seems to require us to think in terms of rebalancing modes and broadening identities, rather than developing a whole new faculty. Wise creativity may well require patience as well as purposefulness; intuition as well as deliberation; soft, detailed, bottom-up perception as well as focused analysis; gentle dialogue as well as hard-nosed deliberation. To an extent, as Einstein suggests, this rebalancing may follow from a relaxation and broadening of the sense of self, so that it can include both wider ecological and cultural forces and less-controlled, less-rational forms of thinking that seem to "bubble up" from the brain, rather than being figured out by the conscious mind. Certainly, many of the apocryphal stories of wise action appear to involve a kind of creative and trustworthy spontaneity—a rather enviable clarity and immediacy—as much as they do the implementation of well-worked-out plans.

CREATIVITY, WISDOM, AND TRUSTEESHIP: IMPLICATIONS FOR EDUCATION

As we begin to think about what all this might mean for education, we need to remember the use that several authors make of the notion of *dispositions* or, as Haste calls them, *competencies*. If our educational aim is the ambitious one of helping young people develop some of the putative rudiments of wisdom we have been discussing, then we have to look beyond models of schooling that focus on the transmission of knowledge and skill. Clearly, teaching young people *about* wisdom is only a very small step toward helping them become wiser—and no step at all if all they are able to do as a result is regurgitate a few phrases. But developing the component skills or abilities of wisdom is also insufficient, for the ability to think wisely by no means guarantees the disposition to do so. We are all capable of thinking and behaving in better ways than we habitually do.

Rowson's story of Gandhi's second sandal illustrates the difference between abilities and dispositions. Most of us can recognize the compassionate motive in the story. And, as Rowson points out, in a similar situation many of us could perhaps have worked our way around to realizing that throwing out the second sandal would have been a good idea—but by the time we had gotten there, the train would have been several miles down the track, and the gesture would have become pointless. Gandhi is so often held up as a paragon of wisdom not just because of his creativity, but also because his commitment to his core wise values was so immediate and so unwavering. He walked the talk and often, apparently, without even having to think.

We might say that the motivation to be compassionate and generous was so engrained in his mind, in his thinking, that they sat right at the top of his mental stack of priorities. Semiconsciously perhaps, he was always, naturally, on the lookout for opportunities to put them into practice. So he saw the affordance to be kind in the sandal situation long before we would have. It might, though, be more accurate to say that these motives and responses came more naturally to him not because they had become automated through practice, but because he had achieved the broader shift of identity advocated by Einstein. He was spontaneously generous to an unknown stranger because they were as much kin to him as a child is to its mother. And he was so "minded" to respond this way that he did not often need re-minding.

Several of the chapters present ideas about what it would mean to educate for wise creativity. Simonton argues that the effort to develop creativity will not of itself lead to wisdom; as he wryly suggests, "the cognitive skills necessary to generate numerous and varied uses for a toothpick or a paper clip are only weakly connected with the intellect required for true wisdom" (p. 73). The focus of concern, if creativity is to become wise, has to be people, not gadgets. And educational practice has to concern itself as much with the functionality and appropriateness of the solution as with its mere originality. Students must develop the habit of thinking about broad human and ecological consequences, as well as the gratification, or creation.

Rowson rightly stresses that dispositions cannot be simply taught; they have to be encouraged and exemplified. The job of the teacher becomes, in his view, to provide suitable affordance (engagement with which will strengthen the component dispositions of wise creativity) and to be a role model of those dispositions in his or her own teaching life. Rowson also argues that students should be encouraged progressively to take on the responsibility of seeking and creating increasingly demanding opportunities for wise creativity for themselves. Likewise, both Haste and Knoop suggest that students should be helped to become more familiar with, and therefore less anxious about, the kinds of complex human predicaments in which wise creativity is of use. They emphasize the importance of practicing the kinds of dialogue that can explore complexity and ambiguity, and also interrogate presuppositions.

Bannerman's experience with performance artists leads him to stress the social and communicative side of wise creativity as well. Creativity in schools should mirror the social and collaborative process that it so often is in "real life." He also highlights the balance of craft, experience, intuition, and hard thinking in bringing a creative project to fruition, and he implies that education should give students opportunities to develop their fluid facility with this delicate balance. Trotman, too, sees educational opportunities to develop such component dispositions as intuition and empathy. And Sternberg's WICS model offers a portmanteau theory that embraces many of these educational suggestions, and much more besides. He argues that education's core purpose in the twenty-first century must be to develop young people who can be leaders wherever they go, capable of good judgment. And he offers comprehensive lists of the kinds of dispositions that schools should be cultivating.

Sternberg's emphasis on leadership brings us to the final theme that emerges from these chapters, and the one which Gardner highlighted in his target chapter: the role of the elders, the trustees, in promoting wisdom in human affairs and protecting deep values that might get swept away in the widespread enthusiasm for personal advancement and amoral creativity. Trustees, whether they be teachers in the classroom or public figures, need, like Gandhi, to walk the talk. They are role models of wise creativity. They hold back from impulsive or one-sided judgment. They show balance in the way they think. They see the big picture. And they are trustworthy. Shakespeare said true love "does not alter when it alteration finds," and neither does true wisdom.

The discussion throughout this book has broadened the sense of *trustee*, as originally put forth by Gardner. While trustees are individuals possessed of certain virtues, they are better thought of as part of a larger system. To begin with, individuals do not just become trustees; they typically have been raised with certain values and often have been picked out at an early age because of their wider perspective. Indeed, within many cultures, there are honorary societies, awards, fellowships, certain firms, or organizations from which the future trustees are likely to be drawn. Very often these promising individuals are in touch with one another and discuss the issues of the day; recalling a famous phrase of Margaret Mead's, no cultural progress occurs unless a small group of persons has begun by talking about it. Nascent trustees are able to take the perspectives of others across space and time, are never certain that they are right, and are vigilant about new trends, while still adhering to the core values of the culture. Trustees succeed because, in a sense, they reflect the best—the highest possibilities in the society, perhaps even on the planet. But without the support, respect, and allegiance of others, they cannot succeed. And so, the times make the trustee possible, even as the trustee helps move the times in a positive direction.

We live in cynical times. We have been let down by our public figures so often and so badly that we are constantly on the lookout for the feet of clay. Like the foster parent of an abused child, they have to prove themselves over and over, showing, through their consistency, that they are worthy of our moral trust. In traditional societies, there were the elders, those with what Polynesian culture calls *mana*, who had earned the respect of the community, and whose words were taken as wise and heeded. Their moral courage, not their physical bravery, had made them heroes. As Gardner (and David Bowie) says, there are no more heroes anymore—or precious few—only fat cats and celebrities. And though that may be sadly true in public life, maybe nearer at hand we have instead what Sternberg calls *micro heroes*: parents, community leaders, and teachers. Perhaps one of the most urgent educational issues is not the endless reorganizing of curricula and examinations, but the encouragement of teachers (as well as others concerned with learning in related, informal contexts) to take on more of that leadership role, mixing good work which faces out with good work that faces in to home and family (Craft 2006). Education shied away from taking moral stands over the last few decades, preferring to busy itself with knowledge. If it is not too late, it may be time for education to overcome its reticence and be more willing to stand up for the Good.

NOTE

1. We are distinguishing here between naïve or impulsive gut feeling and informed or developed intuition, which is underpinned by a rich accumulated database of experience.

REFERENCES

Booker, C. 1992. *The neophiliacs.* London: Pimlico.

Craft, A. 2006. Changing minds about GoodWork? In *Howard Gardner under fire: The rebel psychologist faces his critics,* ed. J. A. Schaler, 217–29. Chicago: Open Court.

Dadds, M. 1993. The feeling of thinking in professional self-study. *Educational Action Research* 1:287–303.

———. 1995. *Passionate enquiry and school development: A story about teacher action research.* London: Falmer Press.

Dijksterhuis, A. 2004. Think different: The merits of unconscious thought in preference development and decision making. *Journal of Personality and Social Psychology* 87:586–98.

Einstein, A. 1954. *Ideas and opinions.* London: Souvenir Press.

Martindale, C. 1999. Biological bases of creativity. In *Handbook of creativity,* ed. R. J. Sternberg, 137–51. Cambridge, UK: Cambridge University Press.

Nias, J. 1996. Thinking about feeling. *Cambridge Journal of Education* 26:293–306.

Postman, N. 1986. *Teaching as a conserving activity.* New York: Delacorte.

Postman, N., and C. Weingartner. 1971. *Teaching as a subversive activity.* New York: Delta.

Schon, D. 1984. *The reflective practitioner: How professionals think in action.* New York: Basic Books.

Woods, P. 1990. *Teacher skills and strategies.* Basingstoke, England: Falmer Press.

Index

CORWIN PRESS

The Corwin Press logo—a raven striding across an open book—represents the union of courage and learning. Corwin Press is committed to improving education for all learners by publishing books and other professional development resources for those serving the field of PreK–12 education. By providing practical, hands-on materials, Corwin Press continues to carry out the promise of its motto: **"Helping Educators Do Their Work Better."**